Pastor's Birthday, 1960

From Lois Nelson

EMBLEMS OF THE HOLY SPIRIT

EMBLEMS OF THE HOLY SPIRIT

BY
F. E. MARSH

KREGEL PUBLICATIONS
Grand Rapids 6, Michigan

LIBRARY OF CONGRESS CATALOG CARD NUMBER 63-11465

FIRST AMERICAN REPRINT EDITION 1957
SECOND PRINTING. 1959
THIRD PRINTING. 1963
FOURTH PRINTING. 1967

PRINTED IN THE UNITED STATES OF AMERICA

CONTENTS

CHAP.		PAGE
I.	The Dove	2
II.	The Seal	26
III.	The Holy Anointing Oil	38
IV.	The Anointing	69
V.	The Oil	92
VI.	The Fire	113
VII.	The Rain	135
VIII.	The Atmosphere	147
IX.	The Wind	160
X.	Rivers	178
XI.	The Dew	191
XII.	The Water	208
XIII.	Clothing	229
XIV.	The Earnest	242

"O blessed Paraclete,
    Assert Thine inward sway;
My body make Thy temple meet,
    For Thy perpetual stay.

"Too long this house of Thine,
    By alien loves possessed,
Has shut from Thee its inner shrine,
    Kept Thee a slighted guest.

"Now rend, O Spirit blest,
    The veil of my poor heart;
Enter Thy long forbidden rest,
    And nevermore depart."

"Oh, to be filled with Thee!
    I ask not aught beside;
For all unholy guests must flee,
    If Thou in me abide."

                        A. J. Gordon

INTRODUCTION

THE Bible is a Book of Metaphors, Similes, Symbols, Types, Parables, Allegories, and Emblems. " I have used similitudes by the hand of the prophets " (Hosea xii. 10), declares the Lord, but we must never forget, behind every figure of speech there is a reality of truth. The word "*similitudes*" in the above Scriptures is rendered "*like*" and "*compared.*" The Psalmist says, " I am *like* a pelican in the wilderness " (Psalm cii. 6), in comparing himself to that bird in its isolation and solitariness ; and the Beloved in the Song of Solomon says to the Bride, " I have *compared* thee, O My love, to a company of horses in Pharaoh's chariots " (Canticles i. 9), in denoting her costliness and preciousness, for horses were brought from India to Egypt at great cost, and only the rich could afford to have them.

Technically there is a slight difference between a metaphor simile, symbol, type, parable, allegory, and emblem. A *metaphor* is a figure of speech, in which one object is made to stand for another. When we say Christ is led as a lamb to the slaughter, it is a simile ; but when He is called " The Lamb of God," it is a metaphor. A *simile* is figurative language descriptive of one object in its likeness to another : " As cold water to a thirsty soul, so is good news from a far country " (Proverbs xxv. 25), is a simile. A *symbol* is something which stands for something else, thus in Christendom the cross is a symbol of Christ's suffering, the hand a symbol of God's power, and the Dove the symbol of the Holy Spirit. A *type* is an object which is used to prefigure another object, thus the lifting up of the brazen servent in the wilderness was a type of Christ's death on the Cross (John iii. 14). A *parable* is a truth illustrated by fact, as the little girl said, " It is an earthly story with an heavenly meaning," like the seven parables of Matthew xiii. An *allegory* is a story which represents a fact, or illustrates a thing in parabolical language, as Jotham's story of the trees did the action of Abimelech (Judges ix. 1-21) ; and an *emblem* is a figurative representation of anything, such as the sceptre is an emblem of sovereign power.

There are many figurative representations which are used to set forth the work and the ways of the Spirit, and with each emblem there is some one phase of His grace and love.

The *Dove* speaks of the beauty and gentleness of the Spirit's character (Matthew iii. 16 ; x. 16).

The *Seal* indicates the security of the Spirit's grace and the proprietorship of His love (Song of Songs iv. 12 ; John vi. 27 ; II. Corinthians i. 22 ; Ephesians i. 13 ; iv. 30 ; II. Timothy ii. 19 ; Revelation vii. 3-8).

The Holy Anointing Oil is emblematic of the Holy Spirit's character and claims as the Holy One (Exodus xxx. 25-38 ; Leviticus xxi. 10).

The *Act of Anointing* is suggestive of the Spirit's consecrating grace and guidance in qualifying and ministering in Divine things (Leviticus xxi. 10 ; II. Corinthians i. 21 ; Heb. i. 9).

The *Oil* is typical of the Spirit's grace and the illumination of His teaching (Luke iv. 18 ; Acts x. 38 ; II. Corinthians i. 21 ; I. John ii. 27).

The *Fire* is an emblem of the purification and penetration of the Spirit's operations (Exodus iii. 2 ; xix. 18 ; Malachi iii. 2 ; Matthew iii. 11 ; Acts ii. 3 ; Hebrews xii. 29 ; Rev. iv. 5).

The *Rain* designates the abundance and grace of the Spirit's supply (Deuteronomy xxxii. 2 ; Psalm lxxii. 6 ; lxxxiv. 6 ; Hosea vi. 3 ; Jeremiah v. 24 ; Zechariah x. 1).

INTRODUCTION ix.

The *Atmosphere* portrays the element and use of the Spirit's exclusiveness (Galatians v. 16, 25 ; Ephesians v. 18, R.V.M. ; Philippians iii. 3 ; Revelation i. 10).

The *Wind* proclaims the winnowing and searchingness of the Spirit's power (Isaiah xl. 7 ; Ezekiel xxxvii. 9 ; John iii. 8 ; Acts ii. 2).

Rivers proclaim the abundance of the Spirit's supply and the plenitude of His grace (Psalm i. 3 ; xlvi. 4 ; John vii. 38).

The *Dew* shadows forth the refreshing and fertilization of the Spirit's presence (Genesis xxvii. 28 ; Deuteronomy xxxii. 2 ; xxxiii. 13, 28 ; Psalm cxxxiii. 3 ; Job xxix. 19 ; Isaiah xviii. 4 ; Hosea xiv. 5).

The *Water* symbolizes the effectiveness and sufficiency of the Spirit's ministry (Psalm lxv. 9 ; Isaiah xliv. 3 ; John iii. 5 ; iv. 14 ; vii. 37, 38).

The *Clothing* depicts the equipment and strength of the Spirit's endowment (Judges vi. 34, R.V. ; Luke xxiv. 49, R.V.)

The *Earnest* delineates the promise and sample of the Spirit's promise of glory (II. Corinthians i. 22 ; v. 5 ; Eph. i. 14).

Syllabus of
The Dove as an Emblem of the Holy Spirit

Two Books—I. *Productiveness of the Spirit*—Comments by Gesenius, Milton, and Owen—" Moved " (Genesis i. 2)—Involution, Revolution, Evolution—Use of Greek preposition " *Ek* "—Life—Five senses evidence of life—*Love*—" Two souls in sweet account "—*Knowledge*—Carlyle's word—*Reaping*—The Spirit's working in The Acts—Liddon's comment—*Abundance*—Totality of The Spirit in Christ—The Kaiser's method—Wireless telegraphy—II. *Performance of the Spirit*—Shelley's couplet—Five questions *re* Noah's Dove : when ? whence ? whither ? what ? why ?—*When ?* After Judgment—Christ beneath Jordan, after opened heaven, &c.—*Whence ?* From the ark—Spirit from God—Dr. A. J. Gordon's statement—*Whither ?* To the earth—The Son of Man and the Spirit for men—Inadequacy of Arnold's morality and *Spectator's* comment—*What ?* Three sendings of the Dove—Josephus and mud on Dove's feet—View from Stirling Castle—Dove and leaf—Meaning of Hebrew word " *pluckt off.*"—Dove not returning—" *Meno* " *re* Christ—*Why ?* Abated waters—Tennyson on the Dragon Fly—Who is great?—III. *Perfection of the Spirit*—Dr. Dale's Saying —(1) *Dove is clean in nature* (Song of Solomon vi. 9)—Seven things the Spirit is and does—(2) *Dove is gentle in manner* (Matthew x. 16)—" No gall "—" Gall " in New Testament—Meaning of " Gentleness "—(3) *Dove is constant in love* (Song of Solomon v. 12)—Gill's comment—Fruit of the Spirit—What His love is like—The Æolian harp—(4) *Dove particular in food* —Raven *versus* dove—Seven references to the Spirit in Peter's Epistles—(5) *Dove swift of wing* (Psalm lv. 6)—Illustrations of the Spirit's alertness and activity—(6) *Dove beautiful in plumage* (Psalm lxviii. 13)—Doves seen by Miss Whately in Egypt—The faulty canvas—" Cassio makes me ugly "—(7) *Dove social in habit* (Isaiah lx. 8)—" Let us make man "—" Peter, James, and John "—Use of " *meta* " *re* The Spirit—Christ's teaching about The Comforter—Ruskin on a " pause."

THE DOVE

THE dove speaks of the beauty of the Holy Spirit's character. Like the dove, He is gentle, loving, and kind. We recognize this when we pray to Him, and ask Him to—

> "Come as the Dove, and spread Thy wings,
> The wings of peaceful love;
> And let Thy Church on earth become
> Bless'd as the Church above."

The facts of nature and the truth of God's Word are the two best commentaries upon truth. We shall keep these two things before us in the study of the Holy Spirit as the dove.

I. THE PRODUCTIVENESS OF THE SPIRIT.

The first reference to the Holy Spirit in the Bible, represents Him as "moving" upon the chaotic waters (Genesis i. 2). The earth had become "waste and void," by what means we do not know, unless by some act of judgment because of sin committed by Satan and his angels; but we do know that "He created it not a waste" (Isaiah xlv. 18, R.V.), and whenever it is spoken of as being in such a condition it is the outcome of an act of God's judgment upon sin ("Confusion" and "emptiness" in Isaiah xxxiv. 11 are the same words as rendered "*without form*" and "*void*" in Genesis i. 2).

The word "*moved*" as found in connection with the Holy Spirit suggests a bird sitting on a nest of eggs to warm them into life. The Vulgate renders it by "*incubabat.*" Gesenius says of this word, "Figuratively used of the Spirit of God, Who brooded over the shapeless mass of the earth cherishing and vivifying." Milton expresses the same thought when he says:—

> "And chiefly Thou, O Spirit, that dost prefer
> Before all temples the upright heart and pure,
> Instruct me, for Thou knowest, Thou from the first
> Wast present, and with mighty wings outspread
> Dove-like sat'st brooding on the vast abyss,
> And madest it pregnant."

Owen expounds the passage—" The Spirit of God came and fell upon the waters, cherishing the whole, and communicating a prolific and vivific quality unto it, as a dove gently moves itself upon its eggs until it hath communicated vital heat unto them."

The same word as rendered "*moved*" is given "*fluttereth*" in Deuteronomy xxxii. 11, in speaking of the eagle fluttering over her young, as an illustration of God's tender dealing with Israel. The two passages taken together give us the thoughts of the Spirit's action in bringing into life and caring for the life which He has produced. This is specially true in regard to the new life produced in the experience of the believer in Christ, and His sustainment and nurture of that life.

He who knows not the Spirit's operation will not experience the saving of grace, nor the grace of glory. A sense of sin is the starting point in the work of grace. The very first thing the Holy Spirit produces in the soul is a consciousness of the evil of sin. Where this is lacking His grace is wanting. Samuel Rutherford, in writing to one, says : " Many are beguiled with this, that they are free of scandalous and crying abominations ; but the tree that bringeth not forth good fruit is for the fire. The man that is not born again cannot enter the kingdom of heaven. Common honesty will not take men to heaven. Alas, that men should think that ever they met with Christ, who never had a sick night, through the terrors of God on their souls, or a sore heart for sin." A sense of darkness and emptiness is the precursor of light and satisfaction, for the " Spirit moved " are the words which ever go before " Let there be light."

The Greek preposition "*Ek*," which means "*out of*," and is so rendered in John xvii. 6, occurs nine times in the New Testament in connection with the Holy Spirit. Twice it occurs when speaking of the Spirit as the Father of Christ's humanity. Mary is said to be " with child *of* (*Ek.*, out of) the Holy Ghost," and Joseph is told the same by the angel, when he says, " that which is conceived in her is *of* (*Ek.*, out of) the Holy Ghost " (Matthew i. 18-20) ; and twice Christ uses it when He speaks of the necessity of the new birth and its nature, and describes it as being " born *of* (*Ek.*, out of) the Spirit " (John iii. 6-8).

The other passages where the preposition occurs are of interesting moment, and demonstrate in a most interesting way that the best commentary on the Bible is the Bible itself. The following words may be applied to each verse,—Life, Love, Knowledge, Reaping, and Abundance.

Life. The two witnesses described in the Book of the Revelation are slain because of their testimony. Their dead bodies are left exposed in " the street of the great city . . . . where our Lord was crucified "; but they are subjects of miraculous vivification, for we read " the Spirit of Life *from* (*Ek*, out of) God entered into them and they stood upon their feet " (Revelation xi. 11). The similarity of language connects this incident with the valley of dry bones (Ezekiel xxxvii. 1-14). In each case the Spirit of God is the Quickener, Who gives life. As the Spirit of Life caused these dead bodies to live, so He is the One Who has quickened the believer from the death of sin; and as the five senses are practical demonstrations of natural life, so the *hearing* of Christ's voice in obedience (John x. 27), the *seeing* of His saving sufficiency and succour (Heb. ii. 9, 10), the *tasting* of the Spirit's grace and constraining love (Romans v. 5), the *touching* of the hem of Christ's priestly service of power (Mark v. 30; Hebrews vii. 15), and the sweet *smelling* savour of a wholly consecrated life (Romans xii. 1, R.V.), show we have spiritual life.

Love. " If we love one another, God dwelleth in us, and His love is perfected in us. Hereby we know that we dwell in Him, and He in us, because He hath given us *of* (*Ek.*, out of) His Spirit " (1. John iv. 12, 13). The evidence of our love to God is seen in our loving one another, and this love secures the abiding presence of God, and His abiding presence is the token that we find our abiding in Him, and this mutual abiding is the result of the Spirit's ministry, for it is " out of " Him.

One says of love,—

> " Two souls in sweet accord,
> Each for each other caring and each self unheard,
> Bringing life's discords into perfect time;
> True to true feeling, and to nature living,
> Plighting no faith, nor needing proof nor proving,
> Taking for granted, never asking, giving,
> Not doubting, and not fearing ' how ' or ' where ' ?
> Not caring if less bright or young or fair;
> Sure to be ever loved, and sure of loving."

Thus, true love, or love in truth, ever goes out of itself in ministry to the object of its affection. Man's love is the fixing of the heart's desire on some object for its own ends; but the love which is of God fixes its affection upon some object, loves for love's sake, and finds its own satisfaction in the satisfaction of another.

Knowledge. " He that keepeth His commandments dwelleth in Him, and He in him. And hereby we know that He abideth in us, *by* (*Ek.*, out of) the Spirit He gave us " (1. John iii. 24). These words are like a two-armed sign-post, they point onwards to the path of obedience, which leads to the joyful place of the Lord's abiding presence; and they point back to the Source of power which enables us to obey for it is " out of " the Spirit every good thing is accomplished. And as the surveyor of the road knows the places to which the guide-post points, so the believer recognizes the power which enables him to obey, and the consequent safety.

Carlyle says : " Love is ever the beginning of knowledge, as fire is of light." These words are essentially true in relation to the child of God, for the love of the Spirit is the Spring which moves us in the path of obedience, as the mainspring in the watch causes it to go; and as the hands on the dial indicate the motive power within, so our obedience gives us the knowledge that we are abiding in Christ to our joy, and that He is abiding in us to our power.

Reaping. " He that soweth to the Spirit shall *of* (*Ek.* out of) the Spirit reap life everlasting " (Galatians vi. 8). The context clearly indicates that all effective work in the Lord's service, while the end is the believer's reward, owes its origin and completion to the Holy Spirit. Ruskin says: " The detail of a single weedy bank laughs to scorn the carving of ages." God's work in nature proclaims the wonder of His skill, while the best of man's productions manifests his inability to produce like God. The same is true in the realm of Grace : when the Spirit works He is always effective. If we read through the Acts of the Apostles, with this thought in our minds, we shall see the Spirit's effectiveness at a glance. The disciples bear witness to Christ, for " *the*

Spirit gave them utterance" (Acts ii. 4). Philip knew where the anxious eunuch was, for the "*Spirit said unto Philip, go near, and join thyself to this chariot*" (Acts viii. 29). When the work of the evangelist was done, and the Lord wished His servant elsewhere, "*the Spirit of the Lord caught away Philip*" (Acts viii. 39). What gave Peter the assurance that it was the will of the Lord he should preach the Gospel to the Gentiles was, as he says, "*the Spirit bade me go with them nothing doubting*" (Acts xi. 12). The Holy Spirit was the power which made Agabus proclaim with prophetic voice there would be a great dearth, for it was "*signified by the Spirit*" (Acts xi. 28) that this should be so. Stephen, being "*full of the Holy Ghost*" (Acts vii. 55), was able to see the opened heaven and the glorified Christ standing at the right hand of God waiting to receive him. Paul and Barnabas, being "*sent forth by the Holy Ghost*" (Acts xiii. 4), were Divinely commissioned and equipped for their service; and Paul, being "*filled with the Holy Ghost*," was able to see that Elymas the sorcerer was "full of all subtlety and all mischief" (Acts xiii. 9, 10).

Spirit-begotten work, by means of Spirit-qualified workers, in whom the Spirit has operated, must produce a harvest which is lasting. Liddon has well said: "Belief in the Holy Spirit implies an habitual sense of the reality of a spiritual supersensuous world. There is .... a constant and profound tendency to sink under the dominion of materialistic habits of thought, that is to say, to surrender ourselves to the fascination and empire of the bodily senses," And it is only as we have the habitual sense of the "reality of the spiritual," by "belief in the Holy Spirit," that we reap any benefit and are any blessing.

Abundance. "God giveth not the Spirit *by* (*Ek.*, out of) measure" (John iii. 34). There are two thoughts wrapped up in these words: (1) Christ received the Spirit in His *totality* at His baptism. He is seen in a *bodily* shape descending and abiding upon Him. The fulness of the Godhead dwelleth in Him *bodily* (Colossians ii. 9). The Father hath "given all things into" the hand of Christ. (2) The giving of the Spirit to Christ in His Divine personality and totality, is not only for Christ, but also for those who are Christ's, for as Godet says : "God does not give *to* Him *for* Himself only, but for *all* " *;* hence, Christ is not only the One Who is *baptized* with the Spirit, but the *Baptizer* too. Our supply is found in Christ, for in Him we are made full because the fulness of the Godhead dwells in Him (Colossians ii. 9, 10, R.V.) Dr. Maclaren says : "All the fulness of God is in Him, that from Him it may pass into us. . . . The treasure was lodged in the earthen vessel of Christ's manhood that it might be within our reach. He brings the fiery blessing as a Divine life from heaven to earth enclosed in the feeble reed of His manhood, that it may kindle kindred fires in many a heart. Freely the Water of Life flows into all cisterns from the ever fresh stream into which the Infinite depth of that unfathomable sea of good pours itself."

When the Emperor of Germany wants to study a new subject, instead of going to the best book upon it, he sends for the best man. For instance, when he heard of the wonderful discovery made by Professor Röntgen, he wired for him to come to Berlin at once, and, after an interview which extended over several hours, the Emperor had so examined and cross-examined the great physiologist that at the end of the time he knew almost as much about the X-Rays as the inventor himself. Similarly, whenever the Emperor comes to England he gets in touch with experts—especially military and naval experts—and in a short time he astounds even the quickest of them by the rapidity with which he has caught up their ideas, and the tenacity with which his memory holds to the smallest details. In other words, the Emperor seeks his information from living men and not in dead print. Well for us if we seek our blessing in the Living Man at God's right hand, then we shall know the Spirit's personality, power, and presence, to our advancement in the Divine life, and to the effectiveness of spiritual service.

As in wireless telegraphy the essential thing is for the transmitter to be in adjustment with the receiver, so it is equally essential for the receiver of our faith to be perfectly adjusted with the transmitter of God's power, for it is only as we keep in touch with the Spirit by prayerful consecration, that He can accomplish His purpose in and fulfil His will through us.

II. THE PERFORMANCE OF THE SPIRIT.

The Bible is like a majestic mountain, in which, while there is a progressiveness in its elevation, there is also a oneness in its substance.

> " the mountains kiss high heaven,
> And the waves clasp one another."

These words of Shelley may be applied to the unity of the Scriptures, for they kiss heaven in their affectionate testimony, and the Old and New Testaments clasp each other in their revelation. This may be seen in many ways, but it is sufficient for our purpose to ponder over the correspondence between the sending forth of the dove out of the ark by Noah, and the coming forth of the Holy Spirit like a dove and resting upon Christ, as illustrating the mission of the Holy Spirit in this present dispensation. For the sake of brevity and clearness we shall note five questions—When ? Whence ? Whither ? What ? Why ?

When? The sending forth of the dove was after the terrible judgment which had fallen upon the world, because of man's sin. The first time the dove went out of the ark, there was no resting place to be found for the sole of her foot, nor was there the second time, but the third time there was, for she came back no more. Not till the waters of wrath were abated did the dove find a resting place. Now note the correspondence. It was after the Lord Jesus had gone down into the waters of Jordan, after he had been baptized as a sinner by the representative of the law, that the heaven was opened and the Holy Spirit, in the bodily shape of a dove, was seen descending upon Him, and not only alighting upon Him, but, as it is emphasized, " *remaining* " upon Him. " The Spirit abode upon Him." As Godet remarks, " This luminous appearance, then, represents an inspiration which is neither partial as that of the faithful, nor intermittent as that of the prophets." In the old times the Spirit came and went as the dove went to and fro from the ark, but now, since Pentecost, He abides in the believer as He abode on Christ.

Hence, we do not need to ask Him to come, but to recognize His presence, for we are by virtue of the redemptive work of the Lord Jesus, the temples of the Holy Ghost. Of this we must never lose sight, that it is because Christ has given Himself up to death for our sin that He is able to give us the gift of the Spirit. If there had been no Calvary of substitution there would have been no Pentecost of blessing. The Lamb of God must die for us before the Spirit can live in us. He must go through the Jordan of God's judgment against sin, before He can bring us into the Canaan of the fulness of the blessing of the Spirit's endowment.

We may gather from this that the first thing in the mission of the Spirit, is to make known the fact that Christ has accomplished His work of suffering for sin. " Christ *hath* suffered for us " is the Spirit's testimony. Not *is* suffering, but *hath*. The tenses of the Bible have a tension of meaning. The night of suffering is past, the morn of the Gospel has come. The darkness is gone, and the crimson light of the salvation of God shines. The work is done, for the Redeemer rests at the right hand of God, and now, all who rest in Christ rest in His rest, and partake of the benefits of His cross.

Whence ? Noah's dove came forth from the ark. God's Dove came from heaven. There are two thoughts suggested by this. As the dove came forth from the ark, the ark being a type of Christ, so the Holy Spirit, because of what Christ is, and has done, comes forth to the earth of man's iniquity, to tell him of the only ark of salvation, where he can find safety and peace. The lighting of the Holy Spirit on Christ as the Dove proclaims two things, first, He could come as the Dove on the Lamb of God, for there was a correspondence between the spotlessness of God's Lamb and the gentleness of God's Dove. Second, He came upon Christ as the Dove to qualify Him for His ministry, and to act through Him in blessing to others.

There is something significant in that the Spirit comes from the opened heaven. May it not be He comes from heaven to lead to heaven and heavenly things ? When Christ commissioned His disciples to go and preach the

Gospel He told them they had first to tarry till they were "endued with power from on high" (Luke xxiv. 49). This expression, "power from on high," at once suggests that the power is spiritual in its source, character and end. It is not of the earth, earthy, but of the heavens, heavenly. Not of man in his puny inability, but of God in His almighty ability. The late Dr. Gordon, of Boston, once said: "Christianity is beset with three powerful currents which insidiously operate to deflect her from her course. Materialism, which denies or ignores the supernatural and concentrates its heed on ameliorating the outward conditions of human life; criticism, which is clever at analysis and dissection but cannot construct a foundation on which the religious faculty may build and rest; and a fine literary taste, which has greatly developed of late and is disposed to judge of power by force of words or by delicacy of expression." There is but one reply to these attempts to undermine the rock bed of our faith in Christ, and that is, the Christ in the lovingness of His all-satisfying love and His almighty grace, dwelling in the heart and life by the active operation of the Holy Spirit, for heaven's facts are only made known to the faith which is born of Him.

Whither? The dove which came from the ark came to the earth to find a resting place. The Spirit came upon Christ as the Son of Man, for He Himself, in speaking of Himself as the Son of Man says, "Him hath God the Father sealed" (John vi. 27). It is not without significance that the manhood of Christ is specially mentioned when reference is made to the Spirit's coming upon Him. Earth has no sorrow that Heaven cannot cure, because Heaven has come down in the Person of Christ and the Holy Spirit to cure the sorrows of earth. The fact that the Son of God and the Holy Spirit have come into the world, proves beyond all demonstration that the Lord alone can meet the deep necessity of man. Man cannot meet the need of his fellow. Mere morality cannot satisfy the human heart. Ritualism with its gaudy trappings does not remove the ache from the heart, nor the sting from the conscience.

A striking letter appeared some time ago in the *Spectator*, as to the inadequacy of the moral teaching of such a writer as Matthew Arnold to touch and transform the lives of the poor. It says :—

"God forbid that I should decry culture, education—the best stimuli to the imaginative faculties possible; but the fact remains that when all these incentives to the highest human enjoyment and elevation have had their say, there still remains 'the poor man,' whom Matthew Arnold did not know, and if he had known would not have understood. What is to become of him? A million Matthew Arnolds, with such work as *Literature and Dogma*, *Rugby Chapel*, and *Self-Dependence*, could not answer if they cared to. But Jesus Christ can answer, does tell, does care; and even if 'miracles do not happen,' still every day does see the wayfaring man, though a fool, brought into the highway of holiness by the foolish preaching of the Word of God. My complaint against Matthew Arnold and his disciples is that they, never having known bodily privation, the want of common necessaries, the absence of all the alleviations of life, even in devastating sickness, cannot, do not, enter into the all-absorbing joy of belief in a God manifest in the flesh to preach good tidings to the poor. It may even be that your reviewer, in his zeal for Matthew Arnold's reputation, has not known what it is to have a wife lying ill, children hungry, and a broker's man in the house. I have, and I have known the blessedness of a 'Friend that sticketh closer than a brother' at a time like that to save me from despair or self-murder, and to bring me out into a large place. Is it then any wonder that I, reading *Self-Dependence*, or the preface to *Literature and Dogma*, turn almost fiercely upon the smug complacency of Matthew Arnold and his 'culture,' and ask him what does he know of the need of 'the poor' to whom Immanuel came? He is a sweet poet, can weld into harmonious cadences the great words of our language, but when it comes to preaching the Gospel to the poor he is less than the least of believers; the Divine knowledge of man's deepest difficulties does not appear to have touched his comfortable heart. To conclude: the words upon which I based my remarks may be found in *Self-Dependence*, last phrase :—

'Resolve to be thyself, and know that he
Who finds himself, loses his misery,'

which I would paraphrase :—

> ' Resolve to know thy Lord, and know that he
> Who finds the Christ, loses his misery.' "

This is well and truly said. The old question, "Canst thou not minister to the mind diseased?" has never been answered by culture and art, and never will be answered outside the Gospel of the grace of God.

The Spirit of God comes to reveal the Christ of God, Who makes known the love of God, Who secures by His blood the forgiveness of love, the peace of Heaven and the joy unspeakable. God's Dove imparts His nature to the believer in Christ, infuses the life which enobles and the love which inspires. None but Jesus can do helpless sinners good, and none but the Spirit can enable the sinner to trust the Christ Who can meet his need. It is His work to do this, and He delights to do it.

What? What were the results from the sending forth of the dove from the ark, and the coming of the Spirit upon Christ? There were three sendings forth of the dove from the ark. The first time it found no rest for the sole of its foot, and returned to the ark. Josephus says "that the dove came back to Noah with her wings and feet all wet and muddy." May we not take this as illustrative of the fact that in all the missions of the Spirit, from the Fall to the coming of Christ, He always had to bear testimony to man's sin and iniquity. As one stands on the summit of Stirling Castle, the Forth can be seen winding its way on to Edinburgh, so as we stand on the vantage point of God's Word, the black river of man's sin down the ages can be traced, winding on in its hellish course, bringing death and devastation wherever it goes. How often the Spirit of God in the testimony of His Word laments over the sin and wilfulness of man, till in the purpose of grace, Christ identifies Himself in substitutionary love, and speaks of man's sin as "My sin."

The second time the dove came back to the ark it came with an olive leaf in its mouth, which is significantly said to be "pluckt off." The word means, to be freshly torn from the tree. The Hebrew word *Taraph* comes from a root which means to tear in pieces, and is generally used to describe the action of wild beasts in rending their prey to pieces. It is rendered " rent in pieces " in Genesis xxxvii. 33, where Jacob takes it for granted that Joseph has been killed by a wild beast when he sees the blood-stained garments of Joseph. The same root word is given " ravening " in Psalms xxii. 13, where Christ speaks of the wicked who were surrounding Him like a lot of wild beasts. Rotherham translates the verse : " They have opened wide their mouth, a lion *rending* and roaring." Putting these Scriptures together, do they not suggest to us the thought, that as the olive leaf was torn off, and the dove bore in its mouth this emblem of peace, so the Holy Spirit bears testimony to the death of Christ, Who was " cut off " out of the land of the living for our transgressions, and now proclaims that Christ has made peace by the blood of His cross.

The third time the dove went from the ark it did not return. It had found a resting place. So with the Holy Spirit. He had gone to and fro from the presence of the Lord, in Old Testament times, finding no resting place, but when He beheld the One in Whom God delighted, then He rested upon Him. The first three gospels mention that the Spirit descended or lighted upon Christ ; but John adds, the Spirit " abode " upon Him. The Greek word *meno* means to dwell, and is so rendered again and again. God rested after His creative work ; Christ in figure having accomplished His redemptive work, rests in the satisfaction of God (Heb. iv. 10) ; and now the Spirit rests upon Christ, henceforth to find His permanent abode in Him. All His mission emanates from Christ, all His blessings are found in Him, all His instructions are from Him, all His ministry is toward Him, all His unfoldings are about Him, all His aim is to enhance His glory, and all His working in the believer is to reproduce Him.

Why ? The reason why the dove was sent forth from the ark was " to see if the waters were abated " (Genesis viii. 8) ; and the reason why the Holy Ghost came upon Christ was to qualify Him for the great work of redemption which He was sent to do, so from that time we find Him as the faithful Servant in humble dependence upon the Spirit's grace and power. Why is the Holy Spirit given to believers ? For the same reason that the dove came to Noah, and the Spirit came upon Christ. First, to assure us that for us the judgment of sin is past, for the storm has burst upon Christ and has exhausted itself upon Him. Second, to take up His abode in the mystical body of Christ through our union with the Head, and to impart His nature and infuse His grace in every part. Tennyson, in speaking of the change which comes to the dragon-fly when it emerges from its grub state, says :

> " To-day I saw the dragon-fly
> Come from the wells where he did lie.
> An inner impulse rent the veil
> Of his old husk ; from head to tail
> Came out clear plates of sapphire mail.
> He dried his wings : like gauze they grew ;
> Through crofts and pastures, wet with dew,
> A living flash of light, he flew."

Mark how Tennyson makes " the inner impulse " to rend the old husk. It was the life within which brought it into the liberty and sunshine without. The same is true in the Divine life. We can only rise to the dove-like character as we have the fulness of the Dove-like Indweller.

It has been said : " He only is great of heart who floods the world with a great affection. He only is great of mind who stirs the world with great thoughts. He only is great of will who does something to shape the world to a great career. And he is greatest who does the most of all these things and does them best." But who can make these ideals actual ? We need the Doer to do. We require the Actor to act. Who is He ? The Spirit, and the Spirit alone.

III. THE PERFECTION OF THE SPIRIT.

Dr. Dale, in referring to the difference of the revelation of the Holy Spirit in the Old and New Testaments, says : " When we pass from the Old Testament to the New we are in the presence of a great revelation of the Spirit of God as well as of the Son of God." That revelation of the Spirit is twofold. We are told what He is and what He does. In what He is we discover His perfection ; and in what He does we experience His power. We may see His perfection in the names and titles which are given to Him, and also in the emblems and similes which are used to illustrate His worth and work. We shall ponder some of the things which are said of the dove by way of illustration.

The dove is clean in nature. The Bridegroom in speaking to the Bride calls her, " My dove, my undefiled " (Canticles vi. 9). The dove was a clean bird, and as such was allowed to be brought in sacrifice. In using this simile the Bridegroom declared the purity of His Bride. We may use the appellation in describing the perfection of the Spirit. He is the *Spirit of Truth to sanctify* (John xiv. 17), but He is not only the Spirit of Truth to communicate truth's nature, He is also the living expression of it, even as the rays of the sun prove the sun which shines. He is the *Spirit of Grace to beautify* (Acts vi. 5, 8, R.V.), but He is not only the Spirit to make the character beautiful with His grace, He has inherent beauty, even as the fragrance of the flower tells the nature of the plant. He is the *Spirit of Love to intensify* (Colossians i. 6), but He is not only the Spirit of Love to kindle in our hearts the affection of love, He *is* Love, even as the kindly action of the mother proves the love of her heart. He is the *Spirit of Life to fructify* (Galatians v. 22), but He is not only the Spirit of Life to quicken us into the life of spiritual things, He is also the Life itself, even as the fruit of the tree owes its being to the sap. He is the *Spirit of Christ to qualify* (1. Peter i. 11), but He is not only the Spirit of Christ to carry out God's will in us, He is also one with Christ in the spotlessness of His character. He is the *Spirit of Holiness to testify* (Rom. i. 4), but He is not only the Spirit of Holiness to testify, He is also the personification of holiness, even as the fire is the cause of warmth. And He is the *Spirit of Light to clarify* (Ephesians i. 17), but He is not only the Spirit of Revelation to enlighten the mind of our understanding, He is also the Light of Life, even as the flame of the lamp proclaims the oil which causes the wick to burn.

To know the Spirit in the holiness of His nature, in the beauty of His character, in the perfection of His personality, and in the glory of His grace, is to be in touch with a power which is beyond earth, but enables us to fulfil earthly duties in a heavenly manner.

The dove is gentle in manner. Christ in sending forth His

disciples told them to be "Harmless as doves" (Matthew x. 16), indicating the harmlessness and the gentleness of the dove. "One reason that is given for the gentleness of the dove is that the bird has no gall, the gall being considered by the naturalists of old as the source and fountain of contention, the bitterness of the gall being supposed to infuse itself into the spirit." Of one thing we may be sure, there is no bitterness in the Holy Spirit. The word "*gall*" only occurs twice in the New Testament—once in connection with Christ when He was upon the cross, and was offered "vinegar mingled with gall." What an illustration of what the world has to offer—"vinegar and gall, sourness and bitterness." The other occasion when the word was used, was when Peter told Simon Magus that he was in the gall of bitterness and the bond of iniquity. A statement which is true of every one out of Christ, for such are indeed in the gall of sin's misery and in the bondage of the world's tyranny. As the dark cloud shows up the brightness of the bow, so these statements, which refer to the opposite of what the Spirit is, enhance His glory. "The fruit of the Spirit is gentleness." The word gentleness comes from the Latin "*gens*," a clan or family. In the old Roman sense a gentleman was one who was of good family, a well-born man. The words of Christ—"He that is from above is above all"—may be applied to the Spirit, for He is from heaven. Because He is above all He can bear with all, and meet the need of all. As the Psalmist put it long ago, "Thy gentleness hath made me great."

The dove is constant in love. The Bride in the Song of Solomon says of the Bridegroom, in referring to His eyes, "His eyes are as the eyes of doves beside the rivers of water" (Song of Solomon v. 12). Gill, in commenting on these words, says: "Doves by the riverside keep their eyes fixed upon the purling streams; and in drinking, as Pliny observes, do not erect their necks, and lift up their heads, but keeping their eyes fixed upon the water, drink a large draught of it after the manner of beasts. Christ, being sweetly delighted with His own people, has fixed His eyes upon them, and never removes them. He withdraweth not His eyes from the righteous." What is true of Christ is equally true of the

Spirit. His love is constant, pure, and true. As the tree produces after its kind, so the Spirit proves by His productions, His perfection; hence we read, "The fruit of the Spirit is love." David, in lamenting the death of his constant friend Jonathan, says: "Thy love to me was wonderful, passing the love of women" (II. Samuel i. 26). One trait in the love of women is the constancy of their affection, even when they have some grounds for supposing that it is not reciprocated. The love of the Spirit is very similar, only deeper and more real. It is said the reason why the dove is the emblem of chastity is because "it lives in the strictest monogamy, never desiring another mate." Of this we are perfectly sure, from the statements of Holy Writ, the Holy Spirit is constant in His affection for us. His love is like the *air*, free and pure; like the *sun*, warming and healing; like the *mountains*, strong and protecting; like the *sea*, deep and powerful; like the *stream* which moves the mill-wheel, useful and gladdening; like the *wind*, purifying and helpful; and like the *soil* to the tree, nourishing and productive.

Let us keep in touch with the Spirit, then we shall have the trait of his constant love reproduced in us, for it is only as we are in communion with Him that we can become like Him. "One of Frances Ridley Havergal's poems tells of an Æolian harp which a friend sent with a letter describing the wonderful sweetness of its tones. Miss Havergal took the harp and thrummed its seven strings, but there were no thrilling strains, only common music. She read the letter again, and found instructions which she had overlooked at first. Then she raised the window and put the harp under the sash. Now the wind swept over the strings and the room was filled with the melodious strains which no fingers of man could have produced. Only when the breath of heaven blew upon the harp could its marvellous music be brought out. The same thing is true with us in connection with the harp of our spiritual nature. If we attempt with the fingers of our own efforts to accomplish spiritual ends, we shall only end with the wail, "The good I would do I cannot perform"; whereas if we allow, through the medium of prayerful consecration and whole-hearted obedience, the Spirit to have His way with us, He will reproduce His grace, His truth, and love, and gentleness, and constancy.

The dove is particular in food. The very fact that the dove could be offered in sacrifice is proof that it was a clean bird. Two of the characteristics of a clean bird were that it could fly and that it did not feed upon flesh. All grain feeding birds that did not feed upon flesh were clean. The difference between the raven and the dove is plainly seen in the two which were sent out of the ark. The raven did not come back into the ark, it undoubtedly found carrion upon which to feed outside, therefore was content to remain outside ; but the dove was forced by the necessity of hunger to come back to Noah. The Holy Spirit is very particular in the food upon which He feeds. His one aim and ministry is associated with the Word of God. He finds His satisfaction in making known the message God has given Him to reveal. He is the Inditer of the Word, and He is also the Explainer of it.

There are seven references to the Holy Spirit in the Epistles of Peter (I. Peter i. 2, 11, 12, 22 ; iii. 18 ; iv. 14 ; II. Peter i. 21). Four of the references have a distinct bearing on the Word of God ; and in them the Spirit is said to be doing, or to have done, four things, namely—signifying, qualifying, purifying, and moving. *The Spirit signifying*—" The Spirit of Christ in them did signify." The Spirit indited the prophesies of the Old Testament which related to the sufferings and the glory of Christ ; but the amanuenses did not understand the words given to them, so they are said to be " searching " into the meaning of the message after it had been given to them. " Here we have inspired writers studying the meaning of what they themselves had written. If they were prophets on the manward side, they were evidently pupils on the Godward side. With all possible allowance for the human peculiarities of the writers, they must have been reporters of what they heard, rather than the formulators of that which they had been made to understand." *The Spirit qualifying*—" Preached the Gospel unto you by the Holy Ghost sent forth from heaven " (I. Peter i. 12, R.V.) The power by which the apostles were enabled to preach was the Spirit. They spake as He gave them utterance, as well as giving the message they uttered. So that both matter and might came from Him. These are ever the two essential things to recognize, namely, the message of the Gospel, and the might of the Spirit. A Divine message, delivered in Divine Power, for the Divine end, which is, the glory of God in the salvation of men. *The Spirit purifying*—" Ye have purified your souls in obeying the truth through the Spirit " (1. Peter i. 22). Again we are reminded that the Spirit is the Effector of every good work. Cleansing had come to the believers to whom reference is made—on the human side through obedience, and on the Divine side through the Spirit. He alone can separate the defilement from the soul and make it pure. This we recognize when we pray :—

" Holy Spirit, God's indwelling !
All my being's pulses move ;
My unholiness dispelling,
Teach me perfect love.
Cleanse my human, harmful hating ;
Purge my passions and refine ;
All my nature re-creating
By Thy faith and mine.
" Gentle, loving Holy Spirit,
Quell the tumult and the strife ;
Sanctify by Jesus' merit ;
Grant me perfect life !
Only by Thy wise selecting
Can my words and deeds be true ;
Thy immaculate correcting
Maketh me anew.
" Holy Spirit ! In Thy guiding
All my restlessness shall cease ;
In my heart enthroned, abiding,
Bring Thy perfect peace !
Fashion me like Christ in pureness ;
Let my service praise His name :
Nurtured by Divine matureness
I shall be like Him.
" Holy Spirit, my Refiner ;
Light and Comforter within ;
Joy of hope and Prayer's Designer ;
Cleanser of my sin ;
Soul Instructor ; Truth Revealer ;
Teacher of the Living Word ;
Heavenly Helper ; Holy Healer ;
One with Christ the Lord."

The Spirit moving—" Moved by the Holy Ghost " (II. Peter i. 21). These words describe the power which influenced the holy men of old to write the pages of Holy Writ. The word rendered " *moved* " is a very forceful one. Rotherham gives it " *borne along.*" The meaning is to be borne along by a power outside of oneself. The word is translated " *bringing* " when reference is made to the man who was sick of the palsy being brought by his friends to Christ ; it is given " *were driven* " when the apostle recounts how they were driven before the storm (Acts xxvii. 17) ; and it is rendered " *rushing* " when attention is called to the coming of the Spirit on the Day of Pentecost. The meaning of the word at once dissipates the thought that the Word of God evolved from the mind of man. It came from the Inspiring Spirit, Who wrote an inerrant word. Since the Holy Spirit is so closely associated with the Word, and to carry out the simile, feeds upon the truth, how careful we should be to feed upon it too, for the only way to keep in touch with Him and to maintain communion with God is by this means.

The dove is swift of wing. The Psalmist on one occasion said : " Oh that I had wings like a dove : for then would I fly away and be at rest " (Psalm lv. 6). It is said : " The wings are the strength of the dove. Upheld by them she can fly for many hours, so that the birds which are pursuing her cannot take her." The Holy Spirit is equally quick in all His transactions, there is no overtaking, nor taking Him by surprise. If we read through the Acts with this thought in our mind we shall see at a glance His punctuality and alertness. When the Day of Pentecost was fully come He is on the spot to fulfil the promise of Christ ; when Philip's mission is accomplished with the eunuch, at once the Spirit catches him away to another sphere of labour ; when the Church at Antioch prayed about the work of the Gospel in other spheres, and asked whom they were to send, the Spirit responded at once, " Separate Me Paul and Barnabas " ; when the apostles were inclined to go in a wrong direction to a field of labour, at once the Spirit stands in their way and forbids them to go ; and when the Church at Ephesus needed overseers to care for the flock of God, He appointed them. We can quite understand how carefully Eleazer would guard Rebekah as he was conducting her to Isaac, and how he would anticipate her slightest wish. How much more so is the Holy Spirit. He is the Comforter, the Heavenly Paraclete: the One Who is called alongside to assist. He prays with us in our praying, He assists us in our need, He comforts us in our sorrow, He cheers us in our despondency, He guides us in our difficulties, He quickens our faith, He stirs our love, and He brightens our hope.

The dove is beautiful in plumage. " Though ye have lien among the pots, yet shall ye be as the wings of a dove, covered with silver, and her feathers with yellow gold" (Psalm lxviii. 13). Miss Whately has in her *Ragged Life in Egypt* described some of the sights she saw on the flat roofs of the houses in Cairo. Among other things she states, in referring to the flat roofs : " One thing never seemed cleared away, and that was the heaps of old broken pitchers, sherds, and pots, that in these and similar houses are piled up in some corner ; and there is a curious observation in connection with this. A little before sunset, numbers of pigeons suddenly emerge from behind the pitchers and other rubbish, where they have been sleeping in the heat of the day, or pecking about to find food. They dart upwards, and career through the air in large circles, their outspread wings catching the bright glow of the sun's slanting rays, so that they really resemble yellow gold ; then, as they wheel round, and are seen against the light, they appear as if they were turned to molten silver, most of them being pure white, or else very light coloured. . . . It was beautiful to see these birds rising clean and unsullied, as doves always do from the dust and dirt in which they had been hidden, and soaring aloft in the sky till nearly out of sight among the bright sunset clouds."

May we not apply this to God's Dove ? As the sun of the testimony of the truth shines upon Him, how beautiful He appears. Who can with Him compare ? He is allglorious within. There is a story told of a lady artist, who lost an only child. The mother began to paint on canvas the likeness of her child. She reproduced a striking likeness, and then put it away. Some little time after she went to look on the face of her loved one, when, to her surprise, she found a number of blotches on the picture. She touched the painting up, and expected it would be all right. She looked at it again shortly after, and there were the disfiguring marks making themselves seen again. After an examination the artist found the fault was not in the colours, but in the canvas. That canvas is like us, however beautiful the picture of Christ the Spirit produces in our lives, there are sure to appear blotches every now and again; but with the Spirit Himself that can never be, the canvas of His nature is spotless, and it can never be that there shall be anything in Him but perfection. Shakespeare says:—

> " If Cassio do remain,
> He hath a daily beauty in his life
> That makes me ugly."

These words may be applied to the Holy Spirit, the more we know of Him, the more we discover our ugliness, and find out the blotches of our imperfection. But these may be taken by way of contrast. The beauty of the Spirit not only makes us conscious of our unworthiness, but if we get to know Him rightly, we find the beauty of the Spirit is not only a discovering beauty, it is also an imparting beauty. Communion with the Spirit leads to conformity to the Spirit. Moses dwells in the Lord's presence and comes forth with the shining face. The two on the mount are transfigured with Christ. The outsiders, in the days of the early disciples, took knowledge of them, that they had been with Jesus and learnt of Him.

The dove is social in habit. The prophet, in referring to the habit of doves in the East, which fly in large companies, says: " Who are these that fly as a cloud, and as the doves to their windows?" (Isaiah lx. 8). The reference is to the doves who have been away from their apertures in the rocks, and are making their way home. As the dove is a social bird, so the Holy Spirit loves the society of the redeemed. Right through the Word of God there breathes the fact that the Lord loves the company of His own. When God finished the work of creation, He saw there was something needed to complete His ideal, so we find Him saying to the Son and the Spirit,

"Let us make man." The same thing is illustrated in the life of Christ. He was continually seeking the company of those whom He loved. This is specially seen in His action with Peter, James and John. Again and again He took them with Him. They are seen with Him on the Mount of Transfiguration; in the house of Jairus, when He raised the ruler's daughter from the dead; and in the Garden of Gethsemane. How plaintive was His question to His disciples when He found them asleep in the garden, after He had asked them to watch with Him for one hour, as He said: " Could ye not watch with Me one hour ?" The same is true of the Spirit. He loves the communion of saints.

The preposition " *Meta* " only occurs in connection with the Spirit three times in the New Testament, but they are most significant in their occurrence. Christ says He will pray the Father that another Comforter may come, and " that He may abide *with* you for ever " (John xiv. 16). Paul finishes his epistle to the Church at Corinth with the well-known benediction : " The grace of the Lord Jesus, and the love of God, and the communion of the Holy Spirit be *with* you all " (II. Corinthians xiii. 14); and when he wrote to the saints at Thessalonica, and commended them for receiving the Word of God, among other things he said, they received it "*with* joy of the Holy Ghost " (I. Thess. i, 6). These verses suggest a triangle of purpose. The Spirit as the Comforter or Paraclete, is the One Who is called alongside of the believer to assist him, and to meet the emergencies of the pilgrim life.

Four times Christ speaks of the Holy Spirit as " the Comforter," and as such He is the Substitute for Christ, the Divine Presence, the Instructor to teach, the Remembrancer to remind, the Testifier to witness, the Convicter of sin, and the Fulfiller of Christ's promise (John xiv. 16, 26; xv. 26; xvi. 7). And in all these offices He proves the truth of His title—the Comforter or Helper—for

As Christ's Substitute, He is all to us that Christ was;

As the Divine Presence, He is the Supplier of all need;

As the Instructor, **He** is the Unfolder of Christ's glory;

As the Remembrancer, He is the Reminder of our obligations to Christ;

As the Testifier, He is the Witness to reveal what He knows of Christ;

As the Convicter, He reproves the world of their sin by the lives and testimonies of His saints;

And as the Comforter, He is with us to meet every necessity, and to help us in every need.

The Spirit lives for us. He loves to have everything in common with us, hence, as we are in sympathy with Him, we begin to realize what the " communion of the Spirit " is; for as we have fellowship with Him in all the affairs of our life, this in turn leads us to have joy from Him, for obedience to the Spirit is the secret of fellowship with Him, and the consequence is—His joy.

There is a needs be to pause and listen to the Spirit's voice, if we are to know the virtue of His power. In the hum of life's business, we are apt to forget the hush of the Lord's Presence which steals into the spirit through waiting upon the Lord. Ruskin wrote to a young person once some true and terse words; he said: " There is no music in a rest, Katie, that I know of, but there is the making of music in it. People are always missing that part of the life-melody, and scrambling on without counting; not that it is easy to count, but nothing on which so much depends is very easy. People are always talking of perseverence and courage and fortitude; but patience is the finest and worthiest of fortitude and the rarest, too."

> " In every life
> There's a pause that is better than onward rush,
> Better than hewing, or mightiest doing;
> 'Tis the standing still at sovereign will.
> There's a hush that is better than ardent speech,
> Better than sighing, or wilderness crying;
> 'Tis the being still at sovereign will.
> The pause and the hush sing a double song
> In unison low, and for all time long.
> O, human soul, God's working plan
> Goes on, nor needs the aid of man,
> Stand still, and see,
> Be still, and know."

The shining face of Moses was not got by a hurried call at heaven's gate, it was obtained by dwelling in the Lord's presence for forty days. The skill of David in slinging stones was not obtained when he met Goliath, it was got by practice in the wilderness. The blessing of Pentecost came after the tarrying in prayer. If we would know the Spirit's sociability we must tarry in His presence.

Syllabus of
The Seal as an Emblem of the Holy Spirit

The Truth indicated—I. *The Sealer*—The Father's Loving Acts (Ephesians i.)—II. *The Sealed*—Christ's sealing and ours: the similarity and the difference—III. *The Seal*—" As He is, so are we "—IV. *What the Seal implies*—(1) *A Finished Transaction*—Jeremiah's purchase from Hanameel (Jeremiah xxxii. 6-10)—God's transaction with Christ about us—The Old Woman's Statement—(2) *Security* (Job xli. 15)—Two Seals—Three B's—Placard outside the Church—" May no man reverse " (Esther viii. 8 ; Ephesians iv. 30)—" Until "—(3) *Ownership* (Haggai ii. 23)—" We are Christ's "—Merchants marking timber—(4) *Recognition* (II. Timothy ii. 19)—What the Lord knows—Called by name—(5) *Secrecy* (Daniel xii. 9 ; Job ix 7)—The secret life—Owen's comment—(6) *Obligation* (Nehemiah ix. 38)—Two Parties—In Bond—(7) *Authority* (I. Kings xxi. 8)—" *Exousia* " and its use—(8) *Impression*—Outward proof of inward grace—What the Finnish Pastor wanted—The Qualifier—Dora Greenwell's happy comment.

THE SEAL

THE Holy Spirit, as the Seal, shadows forth the truth that believers having been purchased by the blood of Christ, God marks them as His property by the bestowment of the Holy Spirit, Who takes up His abode in them, and witnesses to their acceptance in Christ. Thus the sealing of believers may be summed up as follows : it is the conscious acceptance of believers in Christ, by the assuring grace of the indwelling Spirit, Who witnesses in their hearts to that effect, by means of the Word.

There are four points we shall notice : (1) The Sealer ; (2) the Sealed ; (3) the Seal ; (4) what the Seal implies.

I. THE SEALER.

The Sealer is God the Father. Christ's testimony about His own sealing, as the Son of Man, is, "Him hath God the Father sealed" (John vi. 27). Believers are also sealed by God the Father. In the first chapter of Ephesians, we see the Father's loving acts. He has blessed us in His Christ with all blessing (i. 3); He has chosen us in His love before all time (i. 4); He has predestinated us in His good pleasure to the place of His children (i. 5); He has graced us in His Beloved with all beauty (i. 6); He has enriched us in His grace with an abundant endowment (i. 7, 8); He has revealed to us His secret as to His plan to sum up all things in Christ (i. 9, 10); He has displayed in us His glory in the action of His love (i. 11, 12); and He has sealed us with His Spirit, thus marking us as His own possession (i. 13), for the word in II. Corinthians i. 22 may be rendered, "He hath marked us as His own," and what that mark is, we are told in Ephesians i. 13, namely, "the Holy Spirit of Promise."

We are too apt to forget the Father's work. It is well for us to remember that the Father is the Source of every blessing, Christ the Channel, and the Spirit the Power. The Father gives, Christ does the work, and the Spirit applies. God chooses, Christ procures, and the Spirit quickens.

II. THE SEALED.

Believers in Christ, and believers only, are sealed with the Holy Spirit of promise. As sinners, we are quickened by Him, but as saints we receive Him, for the world cannot receive Him (John xiv. 17), and then He becomes God's seal upon us. As an illustration of this truth, we cannot do better than look at the sealing of Christ, for as John Owen says: "If we can learn aright how Christ was sealed, we shall learn how we are sealed. The sealing of Christ by the Father was the communication of the Holy Ghost in all His fulness to Him, authorizing Him into, and acting His Divine power in all the acts and duties of His office, so as to evidence the presence of God unto Him and appropriation of Him. So in God's sealing of believers He owns them, and gives them His Holy Spirit to fit them for their relations, to enable them unto their duties, to act their new principles, and in every way to discharge the work they are called to do. He gives them the spirit of power, of love, and of a sound mind. And hereby does God seal them."

As to the fact that Christ was sealed, listen to the testimony of John: "John bare record, saying, I saw the Spirit descending from heaven like a dove, and it abode upon Him." At the sealing of Christ as the Son of Man, at His baptism, we see three things: (1) The descent of the Holy Spirit upon Him; (2) the voice of the Father from the opened heaven acknowledging His Son; (3) Christ knew that He was sealed. He had the consciousness that He pleased the Father. So, in the believer's sealing, it is with the Holy Spirit. God by His Word tells us that, as believers, we are accepted in Christ, and He is well pleased with us in Him; and He also acknowledges us in His Word as His children: "Behold what manner of love the Father hath bestowed upon us, that we should be called children of God, and such we are" (1. John iii. 1, R.V.) "Ye are not in the flesh," viz., in our old Adam standing, but in Christ, and as a consequence the Spirit of God dwells in us; and we know that we are thus sealed, for we are assured by the Lord in His Word, that in Christ we are sealed with the Spirit, for "we have received the Spirit of adoption, whereby we cry, Abba, Father; and the Spirit Himself beareth witness with our spirit that we are the children of God" (Romans viii. 15, 16).

There is a difference between Christ's sealing and ours. He was sealed because of what He was in Himself, we are sealed because of what we are in Him.

III. THE SEAL.

The Seal signifies the Holy Spirit. It is not some emotion or experience, but it is the presence of the Holy Spirit in the believer, witnessing to his full acceptance in Christ, telling us by the Word that as Christ is, so are we in this world (1. John iv. 17).

Is He the Son of God? So are we sons of God (1. **John iii. 1**).

Is He beloved of God? So **are we** (1. John iii. **1**).

Is He the Righteous One? So are we in Him (II. Cor. v. 21).

Is He without spot? So are we in Him (S.S. iv. 7).

Did He die on the cross? So did we in Him (Romans vi. 6, R.V.)

Is He raised from among the dead? So are we in Him (Ephesians ii. 6).

Is He accepted of God? So are we in Him (Eph. i. 6).

Is He precious to God? So are we in Him (I. Peter ii. 7, R.V.)

Is He the Holy One? So are we in Him (I. Cor. i. 2).

Is He the anointed of God? So are we (I. John ii. 27).

What more terse and telling statement could be given than the following monosyllables? "As He is, so are we in this world" (I. John iv. 17).

May we indeed be subject to Him Who is the Seal in us of our oneness and blessedness in Christ, and being subject to Him we shall live in the power of these precious facts, namely, what we are in Christ, and what Christ is to us.

IV. WHAT THE SEAL IMPLIES.

1. *Among men a seal signifies a finished transaction.* When Hanameel came to Jeremiah for him to buy the field from him, after having bought it, he had the transaction written in a book (Jeremiah xxxii. 10, margin), verified by witnesses, and then "took the evidence of the purchase, both that which was sealed according to law and custom, and that which was open." There seems to have been two copies of the written contract, one which was signed and sealed, and one which was kept in a public place for anyone to see. But the signing and sealing spoke of a definite transaction between two parties, as parties will say to-day when a legal document is attested— "Witness my hand and seal" (Jeremiah xxxii. 6-14). God uses this transaction of Jeremiah's as a pledge to him, that He will restore Judah again to their own land (Jeremiah xxxii. 15, 44).

A definite transaction was entered into by the Father and the Lord Jesus. The former covenanted to the latter to give to Him those who should believe on Him as a reward of His vicarious toil, as Christ Himself says, "Them which Thou hast given Me" (John xvii. 9); and He in turn covenanted to give to His Father all that His own could never do. And as the rite of circumcision was the seal of the covenant that God made with Abraham (Genesis xvii. 10, 11; Romans iv. 11); so the sealing of the Spirit is the mark of the finished transaction between God and Christ, as to our salvation.

Many of God's saints live an up-and-down experience, simply because they do not believe, or do not recognize the finished work of Christ and their standing in Him. They think that their salvation somehow or other depends partly, if not altogether, on them. They forget this fact, or they are ignorant of it, that man is an utter failure. God tried man in innocence (Adam in Eden), left him to his own conscience (Adam to Noah), tried him under law (children of Israel), and, from first to last, man was a failure; and the crowning proof of the enmity in man's heart is seen as we look at the cross. We see what God thinks of man as we behold the Son of God, groaning, bleeding, suffering, dying, and remember that is what we deserved; but see also how Christ met every righteous claim of God. He satisfied Divine justice by having its sword sheathed in His own heart. He bore the curse of a broken law. He paralyzed the devil and undid his work; by His very death He conquered him that had the power of it. Listen to His cry, "It is finished"; and the proof of it is Christ at God's right hand; and the seal of this fact of the believer's acceptance in Christ is the indwelling Spirit of God. As an old woman said once, "The Father and the Son settled the matter between them about my salvation, and I simply received the benefit of it."

2. *Things are sealed for security*. We read of Leviathan's scales, they "are his pride, shut up together as with a close seal" (Job xli. 15). There is no vulnerable point in them: not even the air can get between them. So those who are united to Christ. Who can separate them from His love?

Man put a seal upon the tomb of Christ when He was buried, to keep His body secure, but He rose and passed through the clothes which swathed Him and the stone of the sepulchre (Matthew xxvii. 66). The seal could not detain Him. During the millennium Satan will be shut up in the bottomless pit and firmly sealed down (Revelation xx. 3). As Lincoln says: " Here the scene is reversed. In Matthew it was the devil up and Christ down, and man's seal used to keep Him down. In Revelation the tables are turned, and Christ is up and the devil is down, and a seal employed to keep him down."

There are three precious B's in God's Word. God has a Bottle for our tears (Psalm lvi. 8), a Book for our thoughts (Malachi iii. 16), and a Bag for our transgressions (Job xiv. 17), and Job says that that bag is sealed up. Yes, our sins are sealed up in a bag, and Satan dare not touch that seal. Christ has put away sin by the sacrifice of Himself. I remember passing a high ritualistic church, near London, a few days before what is called Good Friday, and outside there was a large placard, with these words upon it : " This is the day—Good Friday—when we come together to remember the sins for which Christ died." Now God says, " Your sins and iniquities I will remember no more." Shall we remember what God says He has forgotten ? Rather, let us ever remember Him Who put them away.

We read in Esther viii. 8, that the writing that was written in the king's name, and sealed with the king's ring, may no man reverse. That was the law of the Medes and the Persians, which altered not. In a far higher sense we know that no man or devil can reverse the sealing of the believer with the Spirit by God our Father, for we are sealed until the day of redemption (Ephesians iv. 30). We speak of final perseverance, but how much better is the fact that every true child of God will be finally preserved by God until the day when Christ shall redeem our bodies. How sweet is that little word " until." How often we find it occurring. Looking back in the past, we remember He sought us—like the shepherd did the sheep, until He found us (Luke xv. 4). Thinking of the future, we are confident that He that has begun the good work in us will perform it until the day of Jesus Christ (Philippians i. 6). In the meantime we are to remember Him until He come (1. Corinthians xi. 26) ; occupy as His servants until He come (Luke xix. 13); keep His commandments until His appearing (I. Timothy vi. 14, R.V.); that we may be without offence until the day of Christ (Philippians i. 10). We also know the Antichrist will not be revealed until the hindering power is taken out of the way, viz., the Spirit in the Church (II. Thessalonians ii. 7), and that He will not be satisfied until His enemies become His footstool (Hebrews x. 13).

3. *The thing that is sealed belongs to someone: this implies ownership.*

God's promise to Zerubbabel was, " I will make thee as a signet, for I have chosen thee " (Haggai ii. 23).

The Spirit frequently uses the possessive in reminding believers of their relationship to Christ. All things are ours, because we " are Christ's " (I. Corinthians iii. 23). We are responsible to recognize each saint, whatever his social position may be, because he is " Christ's servant " (I. Cor. vii. 22). When our Lord returns in grace, He will especially look after those who are said to be " Christ's at His coming " (I. Corinthians xv. 23). No believer is to think he occupies a peculiar position in God's grace, for " If any man trust to himself that he is Christ's, let him of himself think this again, that as he is Christ's, even so are we Christ's " (II. Cor. x. 7). The essential thing to give us the right of relationship with Abraham's spiritual seed is, " If ye be Christ's, then are ye Abraham's seed " (Galatians iii. 29). The mark that we belong to our Lord is clearly stated : " They that are Christ's have crucified the flesh with the affections and lusts " (Gal. v. 24); and on the other hand those who are not in the Lord are said to " seek their own, not the things which are Jesus Christ's " (Philippians ii. 21). If we truly recognize the Lord's proprietary right to us, we cannot be out of fellowship with Him, nor with each other.

Bickersteth, in referring to the fact that believers are sealed with the Holy Spirit, says : " The allusion to the seal as a pledge of purchase would be peculiarly intelligible to the Ephesians, for Ephesus was a maritime city, and an extensive trade in timber was carried on there by the shipmasters of the neighbouring ports. The method of purchase was this :

The Seal

The merchant, after selecting his timber, stamped it with his own signet, which was an acknowledged sign of ownership. He often did not carry off his possession at the time ; it was left in the harbour with other floats of timber ; but it was chosen, bought, and stamped ; and in due time the merchant sent a trusty agent with the signet, who, finding that timber which bore a corresponding impress, claimed and brought it away for his master's use. Thus the Holy Spirit impresses on the soul now the image of Jesus Christ ; and this is the sure pledge of the everlasting inheritance."

4. *Things are sealed that they may be recognized by the mark of the seal.* The Hebrew word rendered " *sealed* " in Jeremiah xxxii. 14 is rendered "*marked*" in Job xxiv. 16, and " *stopped* " in Leviticus xv. 3. The connection of these words illustrates their significance. In the latter place the unclean issue marks the man's flesh and makes him unclean, and in the former passage the adulterer marks the house in the daytime, that he may recognize it at night when he comes to gratify his lust, hence, we read, " In the dark they dig through houses, which they had marked for themselves in the daytime."

The Lord stamps His own with the Spirit that He may recognize them, hence, we read, " The foundation of God standeth sure, having this seal, the Lord knoweth them that are His " (II. Timothy ii. 19). Frequently the Lord is said to seal those whom He would recognize. The 144,000 of the twelve tribes of Israel during the time of the tribulation, are a sealed host (Revelation vii. 2-8).

There are things which God says He knows : " He knoweth the way that I take " (Job xxiii. 10) ; " He knoweth our frame " (Psalm ciii. 14) ; " He knoweth them that trust in Him " (Nahum i. 7) ; He knows His sheep (John x. 14). He knows His own. They may not be known by the world ; but in spite of the rubbish of ritualism, formalism, attacks of infidels, unbelief of the world, and the hypocrisy that abounds, God has, and knows His own, and each one of them individually.

" I have called thee by thy name, thou art Mine " (Isaiah xliii. 1). The Lord does not put His people in the bulk, but

c

He names them in particular, and notices their individual characteristics. Abraham, the faithful; Isaac, the peaceful; Moses, the meek; Elijah, the courageous; Daniel, the devoted; John, the beloved; and Peter, the zealous; are all and each known by the Lord and the grace which made them what they were.

5. *A sealed document speaks of secrecy.* When God revealed to Daniel certain things, he is told they are "closed up and sealed" (Daniel xii. 9). God is also said to "seal up the stars" (Job ix. 7). There are secrets about them which He alone knows. The reason why those who are in spiritual sloth cannot understand the things of God is because they are as a sealed book to them (Isaiah xxix. 11). The Bridegroom, in speaking of His Beloved, says: "A garden inclosed is My Sister, My Spouse, a spring shut up, a fountain sealed" (Canticles iv. 12). The fountains were sealed to keep out the dust of the desert, as well as to declare ownership. The believer's life is said to be "hid with Christ in God" (Col. iii. 3). The word "*hid*" might be rendered "*secret*": it is rendered "*secretly*" in John xix. 38. The "hidden" or "secret" man of the heart (1. Peter iii. 4) loves to keep in the secret chamber of the Lord's presence, and to do all things there as unto Him (Matthew vi. 4, 6, 18). The sealed heart loves to keep in touch with the Spirit, for it knows He is the Secret Force to move in all things, for as John Owen says: "God's sealing of believers is His gracious communication of the Holy Ghost unto them, so to act by Divine power in them as to enable them unto all the duties of their holy calling, evidencing them to be accepted with Him both to themselves and others, and asserting their preservation unto eternal salvation." Men may wonder that God's people can be what they are, but they would cease to wonder if they only knew the Spirit as He is.

6. *A sealed document indicates obligation.* When Nehemiah recognized the obligation of Israel as God's servants to serve Him, we hear him saying: "We make a sure covenant, and write it, and our princes, Levites and priests, seal unto it; now those who were at the sealing (margin) were Nehemiah," &c. (Nehemiah ix. 38; x. 1). Each of the covenanting parties

The Seal

to a deed is mutually responsible to fulfil his several contracting duties. In relation to the Holy Spirit, there is God's part pledging to bring us through to the glory, hence, the Spirit in relation to us is called "The Holy Spirit of Promise," as the "Earnest of our inheritance" (Eph. i. 13), and there is our part not to "grieve the Holy Spirit of God," because we are sealed with Him unto the day of redemption.

When a case sealed by the British Government, which is destinated to Canada, has to pass through the United States, the latter power will respect the former's seal and see that the case is safely delivered. It would be a violation of international treaty and courtesy for the bonded article to be disturbed. Believers are destinated to the glory, and while passing through this world are bonded in the government of grace, and the Lord will see we are safely delivered to the place of His purpose in Christ. The sealed ones are responsible not to deface the seal, nor mar the work of the Spirit by grieving Him, but to keep in simple and wholehearted obedience to the word of His direction.

7. *A seal indicates authority.* Wily Jezebel knew when she took the king's seal and sealed the letters she sent to the elders of the city where Naboth lived, that they would recognize the stamp of the king's authority (1. Kings xxi. 8). The same thought is embodied in Haman's action in sealing with the king's ring, which Ahasuerus had given to him, the mandate which meant the slaughter of the Jews (Esther iii. 12), and the counter-mandate of the king for the Jews to defend themselves against Haman's iniquitous proposal (Esther viii. 8-10). Daniel sealed up in the lions' den expresses the same thought of authority (Daniel vi. 17).

There is one Greek word, "*exousia*," often translated "power," which means authority. It is rendered "*authority*" in Luke xix. 17, "*liberty*" in 1. Cor. viii. 9, "*right*" in Hebrews xiii. 10, "*jurisdiction*" in Luke xxiii. 7, "*strength*" in Revelation xvii. 13, and "*power*" in Matthew xxviii. 18. If the passages are looked at, it will be seen that authority is the better word in each case. To want authority in the things of God for authority's sake, is to miss the authority that is sought, but to be under the authority of the Lord for His glory's sake is to have His authority behind us. Simon Magus wanted the "*power*" ("exousia") of the Spirit for his own display (Acts viii. 19), but on the other hand there are certain rights which the Lord gives His own. For instance, He gives them the "*right*" ("exousia") to the Tree of Life (Revelation xxii. 14). He gives them "*power*" ("exousia") to become the children of God (John i. 12), and also "*authority*," for the authority which the Lord has given to us is the Holy Spirit (Mark xiii. 34), as the apostle intimates when he says to the Corinthians, "The *power* ('exousia') which the Lord hath given me to edification" (II. Cor. xiii. 10). The presence and operation of the Spirit are the authority for our actions, not that He is given that we may use Him, but He is given that He may use us, and thus through us demonstrate His authority, even as the herald has the authority of the king when he acts according to the king in his authority, and therefore has the king in his authority.

8. *The seal leaves an impression upon the wax which corresponds to it.* The outward evidence of the sealing with the Spirit is the resemblance between Him and those sealed. We have no right to say we have the Spirit of Life if we have not the life of the Spirit. The Spirit of Truth is seen in the truth of the Spirit. The Spirit of Love is manifest in the love of the Spirit. The Spirit of Grace is evidenced by the grace of the Spirit. The Spirit of Humility is made known by the humility of the Spirit. The Holy Spirit is revealed in the holiness of the Spirit. The translation into the kingdom of God's dear Son (Colossians i. 13) is demonstrated by the transfiguration into His character (II. Corinthians iii. 18), where the Spirit dwells His love is seen. Life from the Spirit is followed by the walk in the Spirit (Galatians v. 25).

Look not at the Spirit within to find Him, but look at the Christ without, and He will find you. We have not to feel the pulse of our experience, but to keep our hearts in touch with Him by our obedience. "I want to know more of the Spirit's power, the power I once had," said a Finnish pastor to me in New York. "What hinders?" I asked; "there is a cause for every effect!" "Yes, I know." "Is there any sin?" I asked. "Yes, there is one thing I do not want, yet I often want it, and I want the Lord to take away the want!" "He will give what you want, if you honestly ask Him," I said ; " but remember this, there will be no consecration and power till there is cleansing ; and when you are cleansed He will be to you all you need by looking, not at the Spirit Who fills, but to Christ the Filler and Qualifier."

We need to emphasize this latter, for many are looking the wrong way. Dora Greenwell puts it happily when she says : " Faith saves us, but how ?—by making us aware of Christ, Who saves. Faith does not make things what they are, but shows us them as they are in Christ. Certain systems lay a pressure upon the subject side greater than the spirit of man is at times able to bear ; working out all things from the depths of individual consciousness as if truths were not there at all until they are manifestly there for us. Happy for us if Christ can look there and find His own image reflected, however faintly, but we must look at Him, at the sun in the heavens, not at the sun in the lake, its broken and ever-varying reflection."

Syllabus of the Holy Anointing Oil

The Spirit's Pre-eminence—I. *The Composition of The Holy Anointing Oil*—Seven Particulars (Exodus xxx. 22-25)—The Best—The " Pure Myrrh " of the Spirit's Excellence—Characteristics of Myrrh—The " Sweet Cinnamon " of The Spirit's Grace—What the Spirit does—The " Sweet Calamus " of the Spirit's Worth—Lacordaire's remark—The " Cassia " of the Spirit's Righteousness—Alexander Balfour and business—The test—The unpentecosted member of the P.L.—The " Oil Olive " of the Spirit's presence—Passover secures Pentecost—The " Shekel " of the Spirit's word—Eve's three blunders—Obedience—How the Christian became an agnostic—The Holy Anointing Oil of the Spirit's holiness—What the Spirit *is* and does—The use of " *Epi* " in relation to Christ and believers—" The Seven Trumpets "—The little girl and the pillow—II. *Prohibitions concerning the Holy Anointing Oil* (Exodus xxx. 32, 33)—(1) Not to be put on man's flesh—The spiritual having absolute sway—A worker drifting from the dynamic of the Spirit to the demoniac of the devil—Ambrose's question to the knight—Three blighting tendencies of the times—The Word of God *versus* the voice of carnal reason—Frank Crossley's testimony—Selfish ends in spiritual things—Judas and Simon Magus—F. Crossley on " legitimate means "—" The weaker part "—The investure which makes invisible—False sentimentality *versus* true practicality—G. Macdonald's words—" He do nothing : he very holy man "—(2) The anointing oil not to be put on strangers—Godet's comment—(3) No imitation of the holy ointment allowed—Flippant expressions—Cases in point—III. *The Application of the Holy Anointing Oil* (Exodus xxx. 26-29)—The anointed tabernacle and Christ *re* The Spirit of Jehovah—Scotch body's testimony—The anointed ark and Christ *re* The Spirit of Wisdom—Demosthenes and Cowper on wisdom—The anointed table and Christ *re* The Spirit of Understanding—What God said to the mother about her child—The anointed lampstand and Christ *re* The Spirit of Counsel—Andrew Bonar's comment on the lascivious woman and the peace offerings—The anointed incense altar and Christ *re* The Spirit of Might—" Bite bigger, Billy "— The anointed altar of burnt offering and Christ *re* The Spirit of Knowledge—Browning's poem—Hawker's comment— What it means to know Christ—Bishop Fisher's testimony— The anointed laver and Christ *re* The Spirit of the Fear of the Lord.

THE HOLY ANOINTING OIL

Exodus xxx. 22, 23-33.

THE holy anointing oil is pre-eminently a type of the Holy Spirit in His personal worth, and in the perfection of His graces. As there was none to be made like it, so there is none who can be compared to Him. He excels in His excellence. He is supreme in His superiority. He is unique in His holiness. He is majestic in His might. He is, like Christ, the chiefest among ten thousand and the altogether lovely. We say of Him and to Him :

" O Thou, of Comforters the best,
O Thou, the soul's most welcome Guest,
O Thou, our sweet repose ;
Our resting-place from life's long care,
Our shadow from the world's fierce glare,
Our solace in all woes.

" O Light Divine, all light excelling,
Fill with Thyself the inmost dwelling
Of souls sincere and lowly ;
Without Thy pure Divinity,
Nothing in all humanity,
Nothing is strong or holy."

I. The Composition of The Holy Anointing Oil.

Nothing was left to the concept of Moses ; Jehovah gave him distinct and specific directions, which he was responsible to carry out. The spices are named, the weight of each given, the weight to be employed specified, the way the spices were to be mixed, the oil with which the spices were to be blended, and the name by which the compound was to be called. Let us notice the several details and ponder their spiritual significance.

There are seven particulars given about this oil. There were to be four specified spices in certain proportions, mingled with a hin of oil olive ; the spices were to be principal ones, and they were to be weighed "after the shekel of the sanctuary."

The spices were to be the best. The word "*principal*" is of frequent occurrence in the Psalms, and is rendered "*excellent*" (Psalm cxli. 5), "*head*" (Psalm xxiii. 5), "*top*" (Psalm lxxii. 16), "*beginning*" (Psalm cxix. 160), and "*chief*" (Psalm cxxxvii. 6). The spices were to be the best. There was to be nothing second-rate or inferior. Everything was to be of the best. How true this is of the Holy Spirit! He is excellent in His Divine personality, for He is the Spirit of God, God the Spirit. He is the Head of the things of the mystical body of Christ, for He gives to each member as He wills. He is the beginning of the spiritual life, and the chief, having the supervision of all the graces and gifts of the Gospel, even as Eleazer was the steward of Abraham, who carried out his commissions, sought out Rebekah, showed her the jewels of his master, got her to be the wife of Isaac, and conducted her safely to one who was waiting to receive her to himself. In whatever way we think of the Lord Jesus and the Father, the Holy Spirit is the Mover, the Revealer, the Executor, the Initiator, the Originator in all.

The " Pure Myrrh " of The Spirit's Excellence. "Pure myrrh," or as Rotherham renders it, "*self-flowing myrrh.*" Myrrh was obtained in one of two ways: by making an incision into the tree, or by the gum which exuded from it. It was the latter which was used, because of its purity and because it came freely from the tree without the act of man. The word "*pure*" is rendered "*liberty*," and is specially associated with the year of jubilee. (Leviticus xxv. 10 ; Isaiah lxi. 1 ; Jeremiah xxxiv. 8, 15, 17 ; Ezekiel xlvi. 17.) There is nothing forced about the Holy Spirit, nor in the realm of grace into which He brings those who are Christ's. The Spirit goeth where He listeth, and makes those free whom He enlisteth. Walking in the Spirit, there is no fear of being fettered by the flesh nor fretted by fear. As the song in the lark makes it soar, so the Spirit in the believer

THE HOLY ANOINTING OIL

lifts him into the blue of heaven's joy, into the sunshine of God's love.

The reference to myrrh in Scripture indicates its properties, and suggests its spiritual significance. The oil of myrrh is *purifying in its application*, as used by the women of the court of Ahasuerus (Esther ii. 12). Myrrh is *fragrant in its smell*. The king in His grace and beauty and influence, as typified in His garments being anointed with the oil of gladness, is said to "smell of myrrh" (Psalm xlv. 8). And frequently we read of "sweet-smelling myrrh" (Canticles v. 5, 13), and being "perfumed with myrrh" (Proverbs vii. 17; Canticles iii. 6). Myrrh is *rare in its finding*. It grew "in Arabia around Saba." The bride, in speaking of the rarity, beauty and exclusive excellence of her Beloved, exclaims of Him: "A bundle of myrrh is my well-Beloved" (Canticles i. 13). Myrrh is *costly in its price*. When the wise men brought their treasures to the infant Christ as expressing their homage and affection for him, among those treasures were "gold, frankincense and myrrh" (Matthew ii. 11). Myrrh is *soothing in its use*. When they at the cross would mitigate the pain of the suffering Saviour they offered Him "wine mingled with myrrh" (Mark xv. 23), but He would not receive it. Myrrh is *preventive in its nature*. The secret disciple Nicodemus rendered a service to the body of his Lord when he would preserve it by the "hundred pounds' weight" of "myrrh and aloes" (John xix. 39). One other thing we may notice about myrrh which is not mentioned in the Scriptures: it is *bitter in its taste*. Fausset says of the wine which was offered to Christ on the cross, "it was embittered by myrrh."

Every one of these points finds its counterpart in the gracious personality and work of the Holy Spirit. He is the *Purifier* to fit us for the fellowship of our Divine Lord and Master. He is the *Inspirer* of our worship, and makes it ascend to the Lord as an odour of a sweet smell. He is the *Exceller* Who alone can make us to be rare, peculiar and above the natural, for

"Every virtue we possess
And every conquest won,
And every thought of holiness,
Are His alone."

He is the *Gift* of priceless worth, which Christ has purchased and given by and through the price of His own peerless death. He is the *Comforter*, Who soothes by His presence, sympathizes with His love, and cheers in His grace. He is the *Preserver*, Who shields by His environment and endues in His power; and He is the *Tester*, Who often in His providential dealings with us leads us into suffering and trial, that the spiritual life may be toned up, and that He by so doing may make the sweet the sweeter, the light the brighter, and the glory the more glorious.

The " Sweet Cinnamon " of The Spirit's Grace. The cinnamon is the aromatic inner rind of the " *Laurus cinnamomum.*" This spice is only mentioned in two other places in the Old Testament. Once in calling attention to what the Beloved compares His Bride when He speaks of her as a " garden enclosed," and enumerates the different things found in the garden, and among them speaks of " spikenard and saffron, calamus and cinnamon." The Beloved bids the winds to blow upon this garden, that " the spices thereof may flow out." Whereupon the Bride responds by saying, " Let my Beloved come into His garden and eat His pleasant fruits " (Canticles iv. 12-16). The other place where the word occurs is in Proverbs vii. 17, in speaking of the strange woman who is made to say, as she seeks to entice her victim, " I have perfumed my bed with myrrh, aloes and cinnamon." Gesenius derives the word cinnamon from " *quun,*" " *quaneh,*" " *cane,*" the idea being that of *standing upright*. Dr. Strong says it is " from an unused root, meaning to erect, cinnamon bark, as in upright rolls." The cinnamon is described as being " sweet," or as it might be rendered, " cinnamon of spice." The same word is given " *spices* " in Exodus xxx. 23, and " *sweet odours* " in Esther ii. 12. It signifies that which is fragrant.

All this proclaims the perfuming and satisfying grace of the Holy Spirit. He is the *Producer* of the graces of the Christian life, which rejoice the heart of Christ and makes Him appreciate what they are and do, even as He did the act of Mary's love in anointing Him for His burial. He is the *Perfumer*, Who makes the resting-place of God's love in

Christ to be fragrant with the fellowship of God's care, even as Christ fed the seated and hungry multitude with bread which had been in His gracious hands. He is the *Erecter*, Who makes the believer to be erect in the rectitude of His inspired Word, even as the psalmist says, " He leadeth me in the paths of righteousness " ; and He is the *Sweetener*, Who will make the temper fragrant with the grace of patience and forbearance. Charles Swain says of a good temper :

> " A charm to banish grief away,
> To free the brow from care—
> Turns tears to smiles, makes dulness gay,
> Spreads gladness everywhere.
> " As smiles the rainbow through the cloud
> When threatening storm begins,
> As music 'mid the tempest loud
> That still its sweet way wins.
> " As springs an arch across the tide
> When waves conflicting foam,
> So comes the seraph to our side,
> The angel to our home."

The way to conquer a bad temper is to be conquered by the Spirit ; and the way to obtain a good temper is to be ever tempered by the gracious Spirit. No one ever sought His aid by prayer but was made gentle by His power. He who would be sweet must be sweetened.

The " sweet calamus " of The Spirit's worth. We cannot be dogmatic as to what special spice is here indicated. It was evidently a fragrant cane. " A scented cane is said to have been found in a valley in Lebanon, reed-like, much-jointed, and very fragrant when bruised." The Hebrew word is rendered " *stalk* " in speaking of the " seven ears of corn . . . . upon one *stalk* " (Genesis xli. 5) which Pharaoh saw in his dreams. The same word is rendered " *branch* " in describing the lampstand and its branches : " His shaft and his *branch* " (Exodus xxxvii. 17). It is also rendered " *reed* " and " *cane* " in Isaiah xlii. 3 and xliii. 24. In the latter passage God charges His people with not having brought Him " sweet *cane*," and in the former it is said, " a bruised *reed* shall He not break." Newberry says of the spiritual significance of this spice : " Calamus is the pith—sweet and fragrant also. Emblematic of the Spirit of Christ in all His internal thoughts, feelings and affections." Men deal with the surface of things, and often form an opinion of a thing or a person by what they see, but the Spirit searcheth the heart and goes into the depths. "The Spirit searcheth all things, yea, the deep things of God" (1. Corinthians ii. 10). Lacordaire overheard one say in a Paris restaurant : " I cannot believe in God, because I believe only in what I understand."

Whereupon Lacordaire remarked : "There is one who does not believe in God, because he does not understand Him ; nor does he understand why the same fire melts the butter and hardens eggs, yet he eats an omelet."

How different is the child of God ! He knows he cannot understand all that God is, any more than a child can understand the business of his father, but he knows God knows, and to know that He knows is all he cares to know. Tell a man of the world that he is to rest his heart on the bosom of God and he does not understand what you mean, but tell a tired tried believer and he at once rests and is content, and sings with you as on his way he goes :

> " Be still, my soul, thy Father loveth thee ;
> Fret not, nor murmur at thy weary lot ;
> Though dark and lone thy journey seem to be,
> Be sure that thou art ne'er by Him forgot.
> He ever loves ; then trust Him, trust Him still ;
> Let all thy care be this—the doing of His will.
> Canst thou not trust His rich and bounteous hand
> Who feeds all living things on sea and land ?
> Be thou content."

To know the sunshine of the Spirit's care and love is to have a talisman which turns every care into a blessing, and every rough place in life into a Bethel.

The " cassia " of The Spirit's righteousness. There is a good deal of uncertainty as to what spice is meant by cassia. Its origin is doubtful, but if the derivation suggested by Robertson be correct, it springs from a root which signifies " to cleave," and also " to stoop " and to " bow down." Newberry says it is the " outer bark " of an aromatic plant, and is expressive of the gentleness, sweetness and excellence of the external character and conduct. The same Hebrew word only occurs in one other place (the "cassia" spoken of in Psalm xlv. 8 is a different word), namely, in Ezekiel xxvii. 19, where reference is made to the merchandise of Dan and Javan : " Bright iron, cassia, and calamus were in thy market." We can at least make a practical application of the spiritual meaning in the last association, for is there not a need in our trafficking in the markets of men, in the outer things of life, that we should be so under the sway of the Spirit that nothing mean, shoddy or unrighteous should characterize us ?

One of the grandest testimonies ever given to a Christian merchant was one given by a customer of the late Alexander Balfour, of Liverpool. He said : " When an order was given it was carried out exactly as if he were acting for himself. Of course, I could not but stick to him."

It may be asked, " What main principle should actuate a Christian business man ?" I believe with the one who has said : " All business practices and methods are to be tried, not by the prevailing customs of the trade or profession, but by the Spirit of Christ." This applies to all, to every sphere in life. I once asked a Christian to do a piece of work in order to help him, but he did it so badly and lazily that I vowed I would never employ him again ; and I once bought an article from a certain member of the Pentecostal League, which turned out to be so poorly done that when I meet him in meetings and in the street, I have to pray against a feeling of contempt which arises in my heart. The one thing which shall keep us right and true is ever to be acting under the Spirit of God ; then we shall give and get value for money. The Lord will be consulted and served, then our motto will be, not how to *get on*, but how to *keep in* with Him, and if we keep in with Him we shall get on with our fellows.

The " oil olive " of The Spirit's presence. The basis of the anointing oil was olive oil, or, as the Scripture says, " *oil olive* " ! that is, the oil to be used was that which was obtained by bruising, which at once suggests that before we could have the blessing of the Spirit's anointing there must be the bruising of Christ's atonement. Pentecost is made possible by **the Passover.** Calvary secures the coming of the Spirit.

I do not intend to dwell upon the uses of oil as mentioned in Holy Writ now, but shall hope in a subsequent chapter to refer to this most suggestive topic. But by type, emblem and illustration, we are reminded that Christ's work for us secures and precedes the Spirit's work in and through us. Our Divine Isaac is offered up before Eleazer is sent forth to get a bride for the Beloved Son. The Rock must be smitten before the water gushes out. The burnt offering is mentioned before the meat offering mingled with oil. Jordan must be passed before Canaan is entered. Christ goes beneath the waters of baptism, typical of His baptism on the cross, before Heaven is opened and the Spirit descends. He spoke of His exodus in death, on the mount of transfiguration (Luke ix. 31), before He went to Olivet and told of the Spirit's coming (Luke xxiv. 49). The blood comes first in the cleansing of the leper and in the consecration of the priests, then the oil on the blood (Lev. xiv. 14 ; Exodus xxix. 7).

The " shekel " of the Spirit's word. Not a single thing was left to the caprice or thought of Moses. The quantity of the spices and the standard weight were all determined by God Himself. We must be careful to use God's weights for His things. What God says, and not what we think, must ever be the weight to weigh our actions. One command of the Lord was that " Thou shalt not have in thy bag divers weights " (Deuteronomy xxv. 13) ; that is, a heavy one to buy with and a light one to sell with. Is it not a fact that too often the maxim of the world is, " Get as much as you can for your money, never mind how the article is obtained ; and sell as high as you can, never mind who suffers ?" It is thought by some that the shekel of the sanctuary was double the weight of the ordinary weight. Whether that was so or not we do know this, that God's thought about things is always beyond the most lofty of man's. " My thoughts are not your thoughts." Men are doing to-day what Eve did long ago with the Word of God : they *take from, add to* and *alter.* The Lord told our first parents they were to eat of every tree of the garden *freely,* but Eve took from the Lord's word when she said to the tempter, " We may eat of the fruit of the trees of the garden " (Genesis ii. 16 ; iii. 2). She omitted the word *freely*, and thus cast a reflection on God's character. Eve added to the word of the Lord when she said she was prohibited from "*touching* the tree." The Lord had said nothing about touching the tree, but that they were not to eat of it (Genesis ii. 17 ; iii. 3) ; and Eve altered the word of the Lord when she referred to the consequence of disobedience by saying, "*Lest* ye die," whereas the Lord had said, "Thou shalt *surely* die." (Genesis ii. 17 ; iii. 3).

Whenever any have failed to comply with the Lord's direction it has meant the loss of blessing or the prevention of it. Naaman got no cleansing from his leprosy so long as he followed the "I thought" of his own reason, but as soon as he obeyed the Divine fiat to wash in Jordan then he was cleansed. Saul was commissioned to "utterly destroy" Amalek, but he spared the goodly for the Lord's service, and the consequence was he lost his kingdom and was slain by the hand of one of the race he had spared. The man of God out of Judah was told to do a certain service in a certain way, but he listened to the old prophet of Bethel, and met an untimely death as the result of his disobedience.

Let me give a practical illustration. I knew a Christian man who went right in the face of the Lord's command, "Be ye not unequally yoked together with unbelievers," by going into business with a man who was an agnostic. What was the consequence ? It was not long before he began to read books which engendered doubt in his mind and unbelief in his heart, and ultimately he gave up all we hold dear in the Christian faith. Let any one fail to weigh his actions with the weights of the sanctuary and at once he will get wrong.

Certainly we must accept what the Lord says about the Holy Spirit, for as all the spices were weighed according to the sanctuary weight so all the Holy Spirit is, in His efficient graces, must be determined by what the Lord says of Him in His word. The Lord knew what He was about when He told His disciples to "tarry in Jerusalem till they were endued with power from on high." He knew they could only have power by the Holy Spirit coming upon them ; power to suffer, power to serve, power to worship, power to live, power to hear, power to witness, yea, all that was requisite to life and godliness. The same thing is true now; we have no might for anything apart from the Holy Spirit in His almighty efficiency.

The " holy anointing oil " of the Spirit's holiness (Exodus xxx. 31). The composition when completed was called " The holy anointing oil," because of the sacred use to which it was devoted, and it typifies the Holy Spirit in the holiness of His character as He equips believers for the service of God. The different titles which are given to the Holy Spirit are significant of what He does. He is *" the Spirit of God,"* therefore, God the Spirit in His Deity and omnipotence (Ephesians iv. 30); He is the *" Spirit of Christ,"* for He is given by Christ and speaks of Him (1. Peter i. 11); He is the *" Spirit of Life,"* for He is the communicator of the life of God and the sustainer of the spiritual life (Romans viii. 2); He is the *" Spirit of Truth,"* in opposition to everything that is false and untrue, and as indicative of all that is true and real (John xiv. 17); He is the *" Spirit of Grace,"* as the bestower of all the graces of the spiritual life, and as the inspirer of all that is gracious (Zechariah xii. 10); He is the *" Spirit of Power,"* as opposed to all that is weak and inefficient, and as the enabler to every good (Acts i. 8); and He is the *" Spirit of Holiness,"* or the *" Holy Spirit,"* because He alone can sanctify and make us like Himself (Romans i. 4).

By way of illustration let us take a few sentences in the New Testament where the Spirit is said to be " the Holy Spirit," and briefly note by the connection how holiness of heart and life are suggested.

" Sanctified by the Holy Ghost " (Romans xv. 16). He is the One Who separates from all evil, and to the Lord Himself, even as the refiner removes the dross from the silver and stamps the image of the King upon it.

" Joy in the Holy Ghost " (Romans xiv. 17). Joy is a grace which only lives in the realm of holiness, even as the bird lives in the air and the fish in the water. As we are in the realm of the Spirit, we possess His joy.

" Temple of the Holy Ghost " (1. Corinthians vi. 19). The body of the believer is the abode of the Spirit, hence we are holy because He is, even as the magic wand of the legend

silvered all the cave. "The *temple* of God is holy, and such are ye" (I. Corinthians iii. 17, R.V.M.)

"*Keep by the Holy Ghost*" (II. Tim. i. 14). The Spirit is the safe depository and the guard which preserves what the Lord has entrusted to the believer, namely, the Gospel with which he is to trade, even as the treasure in the Bank of England is guarded by the guard outside and locked vaults within.

"*Partakers of the Holy Ghost*" (Hebrews vi. 4). As the child partakes of the nature and traits of its parents, even so believers, by virtue of their spiritual birth, possess the nature of the Holy Spirit; they know this in increasing power as they are found in the line of God's will, even as the current of electricity is transmitted through the wire at headquarters.

"*Moved by the Holy Ghost*" (II. Peter i. 21). The holy men were used as instruments to be the channels through which the Spirit acted in writing the Sacred Records. Being what they were, He could use them as He did. They were borne along by Himself as a ship is moved by the wind filling the sails.

"*Praying in the Holy Ghost*" (Jude 20.) As the atmosphere is the medium by means of which we are able to converse the one with the other, so as we pray in the Spirit we make known our requests unto God.

"The anointing oil" is distinctly specified as being such. It was specially poured upon Aaron, the high priest. As the oil of anointing was poured upon the priest, so the Holy Spirit, as the Sanctifier and as the Consecrator, rested upon Christ and rests upon believers, qualifying for the service of God. The Greek preposition "*epi*," rendered "*upon*" and "*on*" in the New Testament, occurs fifteen times. Seven times the Holy Spirit is referred to in connection with Christ.

1. As the *Begetter* of Christ's holy humanity, *originating*, hence He is said to "*come upon*" Mary (Luke i. 35).

2. As the *Descending One, acknowledging*, hence, He was seen "descending *upon* Him" (Mark i. 10).

3. As the *Heavenly Dove, sealing*, hence, He was seen "lighting *upon* Him" (Matthew iii. 16).

4. As the *Attesting Witness, confirming*, hence, John the Baptist was assured that as the Spirit "abode *upon* Him," He was the Son of God (John i. 32, 34).

5. As the *Abiding Power, remaining*, hence, the Spirit came, but He was also the One remaining *on Him* (John i. 33).

6. As the *Anointing Grace, sending*, as Christ Himself says, " The Spirit of the Lord is *upon* Me, because He hath anointed Me to preach the Gospel " (Luke iv. 18).

7. As the *Beloved Enabler, qualifying*, for God says of Him, " I will put My Spirit *upon* Him " (Matthew xii. 18).

Nine times the Holy Spirit is said to be, or to come, upon believers. As the *Former of Character*, " The Holy Ghost being *upon* him " (Luke ii. 25), was the secret of Simeon being " just and devout." As the *Communicator of Power*. Christ's promise to His disciples was, " Ye shall receive power, the Holy Ghost coming *upon* you " (Acts i. 8). As the *Fulfilment of Promise*. The Spirit sat *upon* each disciple as they waited for the fulfilment of Christ's promise (Acts ii. 3). As the *Giver of Vision* the Spirit was to be poured " *upon* all flesh," that the young men might " see visions " (Acts ii. 17). As the *Opener of Lips*, for the promised Spirit was to be " *on* My servants . . . . . and they shall prophesy " (Acts ii. 18). As the *Gift of Love*. When Peter spake the word in the house of Cornelius " The Holy Ghost fell *on* all them which heard the Word " (Acts x. 44). As the *Baptism of Grace*, as Peter testifies when he recounts what took place in the house of Cornelius, which was but a fulfilment of what John the Baptist had preached, hence, as he says, " The Holy Ghost fell *on* them " (Acts xi. 15-17). As the *Witness Bearer*, for as soon as " the Holy Ghost came *on* " the disciples at Ephesus they " spake with tongues and prophesied " (Acts xix. 6). As the *Consoler in Suffering*, for the " Spirit of Glory and of God resteth *upon* " those who are evil spoken of for the sake of Christ (I. Peter iv. 14).

The one powerful and practical fact which impresses one, as the Scriptures are pondered, is the supernatural power of the Spirit fitting for service in the daily round of life. The Spirit coming upon and resting upon us is essential in order to make us thoughtful for others, to form the character after Christ, to sweeten the words of our tongues, to fulfil the duties in the home, to make us obedient to the Word, and to make our witness effective. I have a good deal of sympathy

The Holy Anointing Oil

with the reply which was given to a professing Christian who was greatly concerned about the subject of prophecy, but was not careful in bringing up his children. He asked a servant of Christ one day:

"Pray, sir, what is your opinion of the seven trumpets?"

"I am not sure," was the reply, "that I understand your question, but I hope you will comprehend mine. What think you of the fact that your seven children are growing up without God and without hope? You have a Bible-reading in your house for your righteous neighbours, but no family prayer for your children."

After all, we need to come back to this simple and fundamental fact, there is no royal supply of power known by those who are not found on their knees in prayer. One night the mother of two little girls was away at bedtime, and they were left to do as they would. "I am not going to pray to-night," said Lilian, when she was ready for bed. "Why, Lillian!" exclaimed Amy, with round eyes. "I am not going to. There isn't any use." So she tumbled into bed. Amy knelt and prayed. The little prayer finished and the light extinguished, Amy crept into bed. There was a long silence; then Lillian began to turn restlessly, giving her pillow a vigorous thump and saying, crossly: "I wonder what is the matter with this pillow?" Then came a sweet little voice from Amy's side of the bed: "I guess it's 'cause there isn't any prayer in it."

A few minutes more of restlessness, and Lillian slipped out of bed and knelt in prayer. Then all was quiet and peaceful, and the two little girls slept.

There will always be restlessness and discontent when prayer is wanting, but they who wait on the Lord shall not want any good. Praying always we prevail always. Meeting God at the mercy seat, we shall never lack the mercy and might which are only obtained there.

II. PROHIBITIONS REGARDING THE HOLY ANOINTING OIL.

The prohibitions were three in number. The holy anointing oil was not to be put upon man's flesh, nor upon a stranger, neither was anything to be made like to it (Exodus xxx. 32, 33).

1. *The anointing oil was not to be put upon the flesh of man*—" Upon man's flesh shall it not be poured." Man's nature has become contaminated by sin and corrupted by iniquity, hence, it is always looked upon as being the seat and source of evil. The apostle sums it up when he says, " I know that in me, that is in my flesh, there dwelleth no good thing." The flesh in relation to the believer is regarded as dead in the death of Christ, and he is viewed from the Divine standpoint as not being in the flesh but in the spirit, that is, in the nature in which the Holy Spirit takes up His abode (Romans viii. 9). The significance of the anointing oil *not* being put on man's flesh, is, *the spiritual having absolute sway to the exclusion of the fleshly.* Let us look at a few ways in which the Spirit of God is not made to serve fleshly ends, for let it be said with fear and trembling, there is a possible danger of the most spiritual things being perverted to a wrong end, as an experienced worker recently said to the writer, in speaking of one who up to a certain point was possessed by the Spirit : " Unmistakably the worker was under the power of the Spirit up to a certain time, and then I could only account for her words and behaviour, as applied to one possessed by a demon, for it was the flesh and not Christ."

When the spiritual is not made subservient to the natural, the holy oil is not on the flesh. The opening lines of Tennyson's Holy Grail represent to us the monk and knight of the Round Table, questioned by the aged Ambrose as to what set him on the quest after the Holy Grail :—

" ' Was it earthly passion crost ?'
' Nay !' said the Knight, ' for no such passion mine ;
But the sweet vision of the Holy Grail
Drove me from all vainglories, rivalries
And earthly heats.' "

The vision of the Christ, through the Spirit's enlightening grace, is the one thing to blind to " all vainglories," to kill all " rivalries," and quench all " earthly heats." If we had a clearer vision of the real unseen, the unreal seen would not attract. The sight of Christ ever blinds to the sights of earth.

The three blighting influences of the present day are,

love of ease, love of pleasure, and love of money. Alas! that any of the redeemed should not obey the Lord's injunction to "seek first the kingdom of God." But this is so, when pleasure keeps away from the prayer-meeting, the love of money kills generosity, and the love of ease makes the lover indolent. These shall not prevail, if the Spirit's anointing is upon us, for He will give us to see, as Stephen did being full of the Spirit, the beauty of Christ.

When the Word of God is authoritative in our hearts, and we do not follow the voice of carnal reason, then the Spirit is not hindered by man. The late Frank W. Crossley, of Manchester, in recounting the special blessing he received when he sought by earnest prayer the anointing of the Holy Spirit, says :—" The beginning of the matter was quite a new appetite for His Word. I hungered for it, and ate it up as never exactly before, then to prayer, and then this blessing . . . more especially has come now the desire to get other souls into the blessing, and the sense of commission and direction to speak to them."

It has always been, and always is, an indication of knowing the Spirit's power, when we honour His Word. We cannot honour Him without honouring His Word. The truth of the Gospel is not contrary to reason, but it is *above* reason, therefore we do not go by reason, but by revelation. Cowper well says :—

"'Tis Revelation satisfies all doubts,
Explains all mysteries except her own,
And so illuminates the path of life,
That fools discover it, and stray no more."

In reading through the Acts of the Apostles, one of the many things which impress and attract is the responsiveness of the early Christians to the Word of God. What is the cause ? Is it not found in the words of Acts i. 2 ? There we read, " He through the Holy Ghost had given commandments," and in the Spirit's power they kept the commandments. The commandments had come *through* Him, they were to be performed *in* His power, and *to* Himself. He who has only the light of reason has a farthing rushlight to guide him, but he who has revelation has the light of the sun to lighten and cheer, to warm as well as lead.

The anointing of the Spirit is resting upon us when we do not allow spiritual things to serve selfish ends. I am more and more convinced that we need to have the flame of a pure motive burning on the altar of our hearts. We condemn Judas because he, under the plea of caring for the poor, wanted the money from the sale of the ointment that Mary put on Christ. We discountenance Simon Magus because he wanted to possess the Spirit's power for his own aggrandisement. But does not something similar happen when we want spiritual blessing for our own selfish comfort? when we want the Spirit's power for our own purpose? F. W. Crossley, in addressing a meeting once in the West of London, used these burning words :—" How are we to attract the most people into this earthly and yet heavenly paradise? That is a much-vexed question. What, for example, are legitimate means? or what is legitimate bait? I confess I am somewhat familiar with the flies and worms in use among fishers of men. . . . I believe I know of only one safe kind. We must be the bait ourselves, and be willing to be gobbled up. We must not come decked with gold or costly array . . . . if we accept service in the ranks of the lowly-hearted Master. . . Reality first and last. If this is forgotten people will turn on us and say, properly enough, that they would rather be real and in hell, than humbugs in heaven. But this, thank God, is not the alternative. As a matter of fact the humbugs will all be in hell, and the real folks in heaven. Let us be real, *i.e.*, really like the Master, filled with His love and self-sacrifice, and we shall soon prove a very catching lot. *No other bait will be wanted if the Spirit of Jesus is seen in His followers.*"

And that Spirit will be seen as the Spirit's anointing is known, for self can have no place where He is in possession, for there is only one thing that fills the heart of the one thus possessed, and that is what does He desire. " I charge you," says the bride to the daughters of Jerusalem, " that ye stir not up, nor awake my Love, till He please " (Cant. iii. 5). What pleases Him will please us, if we are in fellowship with Him.

The Holy Anointing Oil

The anointing of the Spirit is resting upon us when we do God's work in God's power and not in the strength of human energy. There is a beautiful sonnet addressed by Lowell to William Lloyd Garrison, in which he speaks of his noble services to suffering humanity as a cleaving to the fortunes of the weaker part :—

> " He saw God stand upon the weaker side,
> That sank in seeming loss before its foes ;
> .   .   .   .   .
> therefore he went
> *And humbly joined him in the weaker part.*"

God always stands upon the side of those who are weak, and joins Himself to him who is of the weaker part, for the weakness is the condition in which His power is found. It was when we were " without strength " that Christ died for the ungodly ; it was to the impotent man that Christ displayed His omnipotence in making him whole ; it is to those who have no might that He giveth power ; it was Gideon's feeble men who experienced Jehovah's conquering might ; it was when Jehoshaphat appealed for God's power that he got the victory over his enemies ; it was when Daniel was helplessly shut up in the lion's den that he experienced the deliverance of Heaven ; and it was when Paul was weak that God made him strong. Our weakness is always the fit displayer of His might. Dr. Maclaren has well said : " The Holy Ghost is the only real power for service. Why have we not this power ? *Because we are not willing to be made invisible by the investure.*" This *investure* always makes invisible, as in the case of Gideon, we read, " the Spirit of the Lord *clothed* (margin) Gideon " (Judges vii. 34). That investure was the secret of Gideon's success. He first conquered Gideon, then He conquered through him.

There are three great principles taught us in the New Testament in relation to Christian work : (1) We have to do with spiritual things, things which are supernatural in their origin and nature. (2) The spiritual things can only be made known and conveyed to others by means of spiritual power, that power being the power of the Holy Spirit ; and (3) that the Holy Spirit works through spiritual agencies, that is, through those who have spiritual life, and who are in fellowship with Himself.

The anointing of the Spirit always expresses itself in a practical way, and not in a false sentimentality. George Macdonald represents one of his characters, as having a great regard for the clergy, the " church," and certain ritualistic observations, but who nevertheless was hard, and cold, and cruel, and he rightly says : " What religion is there in being convinced of a future state ? Is that to worship God ? It is no more religion than the belief the sun will rise to-morrow is religion. It may be a source of happiness to those who could not beleive it before, but it is not religion. Where religion comes that will certainly be likewise, but the one is not the other."

What he means to say is, that practical religion is the act of the life prompted by the heart of love, and not a mere assent to certain propositions of truth. The fact is, he who truly believes the truth lives it out truly.

Too often the foundations of truth get covered up with the additions of superstition, like the foundation piles of a pier covered with mussels and sea-weed. Fancy such a superstitious apprehension of holiness as the following :—

An Arab dragonman was once asked what constituted the sanctity of a certain Moslem saint,—

" What does he do ?"

" He do nothing ; he very holy man !"

There is a spurious holiness which looks at itself with a self-satisfied complacency, and criticizes others with a critical spirit of censure, such persons need to remember one thing, that whenever the Spirit is said to come upon individuals, He came upon them to communicate blessing to others, and not for the endued to retain blessing for themselves.

2. *The anointing oil was not to be put upon a stranger.* The stranger was one who was outside the pale of Israel's blessing, hence, all Gentile Christians are reminded they were strangers to the covenant of promise (Ephesians ii. 12). The stranger in a typical sense is one who is unsaved—a stranger to God. Very significantly Christ says of the world in relation to the

Spirit, "Whom the world cannot receive, because it seeth Him not, neither knoweth Him" (John xiv. 17). Godet says: "It was not owing to any arbitrary action that, on the morning of the day of Pentecost, the Spirit descended on one hundred and twenty persons only, and not on all the inhabitants of Jerusalem: the former only had undergone the indispensable preparation."

3. *No imitation was to be made of the anointing oil.* It was sacred. The typical meaning is this, there is not to be anything which savours of imitation in the things of God. God abhors imitations. When man in the energy of the flesh tries to imitate and substitute the human for the Divine, it comes very near the sin of blasphemy against the Holy Spirit. That sin is attributing to the devil what belongs to the Spirit, but this sin is attributing to the Spirit what belongs to the devil. Briefly put, the following are a few examples of unholy imitations. How often believers say a thing is of the Spirit when it is only self-will. A person says he is led of the Spirit, when all the while he is having his own way.

In these days we find many taking the name of God as a cover for sin. People profess to be so holy that they cannot sin, no matter how deeply they may go into sin. The sin they commit, no matter how devilish and fleshly, is not sin, but a product of the Holy Spirit. One such modern cesspool is bracketed under the name of the carnality of Christ, when " holy " women are so lewd and abandoned that they believe Christ has illicit intercourse with them, as their minds think Him to the act.

Substituting human energy in God's work for the Spirit's might and calling it His work, is another form of imitating the Holy Oil. How often we find the organization of man running things, instead of the operation of the Spirit moving things. Meeting in a place of worship and never worshipping God. Found on bended knees and not bowed in spirit. Words coming out of the lips which have no response in the heart. Let us beware lest we grieve or quench the Spirit in any way, for while He makes allowance for human infirmity, **He will not allow the substitutes of man to take the place of Himself.**

III. THE APPLICATION OF THE HOLY ANOINTING OIL.

We shall confine this section of our meditation to the tabernacle, in its association with the holy anointing oil. " And thou shalt anoint the tabernacle of the congregation therewith, and the ark of the testimony. And the table and all his vessels, and the candlestick and his vessels, and the altar of incense. And the altar of burnt offering with all his vessels, and the laver and his foot " (Exodus xxx. 26-28).

The psalmist in speaking of God's glory in the temple of nature says : " In His temple every whit of it uttereth His glory " (margin—Psalm xxix. 9). This is true also of the tabernacle. There is not a single thing but speaks of Christ in some way and emphasizes the fact that Moses wrote of Him. Take only the furniture mentioned in the verses above. The tabernacle proclaims the incarnation of Christ— the One Who tabernacled among us ; the ark made of shittim wood overlaid with gold, and the gold blood-sprinkled mercy-seat with the cherubim and glory speak of His mediatorial work as the God-man ; the table of shewbread tells of His intercommunication between the Father and us as the basis of Fellowship, the one with the other ; the lampstand of His light-giving grace points to His ministry in making known to us what the Father is in Himself ; the incense altar of His gracious and fragrant ministry is typical of Him as the Mighty Intercessor in ministering to our need ; the burnt offering shadows forth the altar of His finished and glorious offering whereby God is glorified and we are accepted before Him ; and the laver of His wondrous Word speaks of Him as He reveals defilement and then removes it.

There are four ways in which we may view the life and ministry of Christ. We may think of Him in relation to the Father as John does, as the Sent One doing the Father's will ; we may ponder His path as Mark does, as He serves humanity in meeting its need ; we may muse upon the kingly worth of His beautiful character, as Matthew does ; and we may think of Him as the Man anointed with the Holy Spirit going about doing good, as Luke does. We specially think of Him in relation to the Holy Spirit, as set forth in the anointing of the different vessels of the tabernacle.

There are three ways in which almost every truth of the Bible is represented to us, namely, by type, by prophecy, and in its fulfilment. The first is the root of promise, the second is the tree of Divine utterance, and the third is the fruit of minute fulfilment. I purpose treating this subject in this threefold way. First, noting the seven vessels enumerated; then noting a correspondence between the prophecy of the Holy Spirit and Christ in the sevenfold delineation given to us in Isaiah xi. 2; then seeing how each has its distinct fulfilment in what is said of the Holy Spirit and Christ in the New Testament.

The Anointed Tabernacle—" Thou shalt anoint the tabernacle." The tabernacle is typical of Christ as the One Who tabernacled among us, and its anointing signifies that He became what He was by the Holy Spirit. As the Angel said to Mary: " The Holy Ghost shall come upon thee. . . . . therefore that holy thing which shall be born of thee shall be called the Son of God." The Divine testimony was, " The Spirit of Jehovah shall rest upon Him " (Isaiah xi. 2), and when He was baptized " the Spirit " was seen " descending upon Him " (Mark i. 10). The Spirit as the Spirit of Jehovah proclaims God in covenant relationship with man, and especially with the Man of men Who came to act on behalf of men. The covenant of grace, unlike the covenant of works, is not between God and man, but between God and Christ, He undertakes for us and we take the benefit. As the Scotch body said, " God and Christ have undertaken my salvation between them and I get the benefit." His public ministry for us began at the waters of Jordan and ended at the judgment of the cross; began at the opened Heaven and finished in the opened grave; but not a step did He take till He was sealed with the Spirit. None knew so well as He the necessity for the Spirit's equipment.

The Anointed Ark—" Anoint the . . . . ark of the testimony." The ark is typical of the combination of Deity and humanity which is found in Christ. The Son of Man and the Son of God—one Person. There are nine things in connection with the ark, the acacia wood, the gold, the mercy-seat, the blood, the glory, the cherubim, the manna, the budding rod, and the tables of the law, every one of which has its fulfilment in Christ. The incorruptible wood of His peerless humanity, the unsurpassed worth of His glorious Deity, the propitiatory value of His Divine atonement, the precious blood of His finished work, the express image of His effulgent glory, the satisfied cherubim of His approving justice, the complete fulfilment of His perfect obedience, the budding rod of His unique life, and the suitable manna of His adaptable grace. The apostle in speaking of God's estimation of the life and work of Christ says, He is the embodiment of the wisdom of God (see 1. Corinthians i. and ii.), hence, we are not surprised to hear that the Spirit rested upon Him as the "Spirit of Wisdom" (Isaiah xi. 2). Demosthenes says: "The end of wisdom is consultation and deliberation." And Cowper:

> "They whom truth and wisdom lead
> Can gather honey from a weed."

These sayings find their confirmation and illustration in Him upon Whom the Spirit of Wisdom rested. Christ ever consulted His Father's will, and every act was the result of deliberation. There was nothing hasty, empty, nor thoughtless about Him. The consequence was, He ever got the honey of blessing from every weed of trial. Take but one incident in His life, namely, His temptation in the wilderness. "He was led by the Spirit into the wilderness"; yea more, He was not only led to the temptation, but led all the way through, as the Revised Version of Luke iv. 1 says: "Led by the Spirit *in* the wilderness." We are not surprised He met the enemy as He did and routed him so completely. It is always the case, when we act after consulting the Word of the Spirit and deliberate in His grace.

The Anointed Table—"Anoint the table." The typical significance of the table is, the fellowship there is between God and man by means of Christ, Who is the Bread of Life. The table of shewbread is so called because "the bread of faces" was placed upon it for seven days, as though to feed God, then the priests ate it in the holy place; thus Jehovah and the priests had communion (Exodus xxv. 30; Leviticus xxiv. 5-9). The Spirit as the "Spirit of understanding"

(Isaiah xi. 2) rested upon Christ, hence, He had the capacity to distinguish that which brought satisfaction to His Father and met the need of man, for the root meaning of the word translated "understanding" is to separate or distinguish; as Gesenius says, "to discern, to mark, to understand, all of which depend on the power of separating, distinguishing, discriminating." Job says : "Cannot my taste (margin, " palate ") *discern* perverse things ?" (Job vi. 30). "Give Thy servant an understanding heart .... that I may *discern* between good and bad " (1. Kings iii. 9) ; in each case the word denotes the power to separate the precious from the vile. When Christ left the place of temptation the first thing that is said of Him is, "He returned in the power of the Spirit .... and He taught " (Luke iv. 14, 15), and one thing He ever did in His teaching was, not to give in an indiscriminate way the secrets of the Kingdom. "To you is given to know the secrets of the Kingdom "(Matthew xiii. 11) He said on one occasion to His disciples ; and on another occasion He did not commit Himself to some who professed to believe on Him, because He discerned they were not true in their avowal (John ii. 24, 25). He was ever ready to meet the need of the honest seeker, like He did Nicodemus, as is indicated in the Revised Version of John iii. In the end of the second chapter He did not commit Himself to those who were not true, but in the beginning of the third chapter we read, "Now there was a man," &c. He did commit Himself to him, as is evident in what He said to him. He was always ready to give to the needy heart, and He gives in the Spirit's grace and power.

If there is one thing more than another to which we need to give heed, it is to obey the injunction "to discerningly approve the things that differ " (Newberry, Phil. i. 10) ; and among the practical things, is this, God appreciates *what we are* more than *what we do*. "An anxious, earnest Christian woman was crying to God for service, and wondering why she was tied up in her home and unable, like other women, to go out and reach a broader sphere. Her bright little girl was playing beside her and calling in vain to the pre-occupied mother to help her with her doll, which had lost a finger, and which to her was the central object in life. Again and again she came to the mother with her little trouble, and the mother fretted and worried with her own spiritual need, pushed her off, and at length rather harshly sent her away and told her not to bother her, as she was busy with higher things. Wearied and disappointed the little one went off alone in a corner and sat down with her broken doll and cried herself to sleep. A little while after the mother turned round and saw the little rosy cheeks covered with tears and the little wrecked doll lying in her bosom, and then God spake to her and said: ' My child, in seeking some higher service for Me you have broken a little heart of Mine. You wanted to do something for Me. That little child was the messenger I sent, and that little service was the test I gave you. He that is faithful in that which is least is faithful also in more, and he that is unfaithful in the least is unfit for the greater.' " He answers our cry as we answer the cry of others.

The Anointed Lampstand. The anointed lampstand is typical of what Christ was and the testimony He bore, in the power of the Spirit, as the Light of the world. The light from the seven-branched lampstand was the only light in the holy place. It was sufficient to reveal the glories of that holy place, and the beauty of the furniture therein. We read that " whatsoever maketh manifest is light " (Ephesians v. 13), and Christ was ever doing this. No one can read through His life without being impressed with the shining forth of His glory.

His works manifested His almighty power. Death yields its prey, the sea owns His sway, demons obey Him, and none can say Him nay when His mandate is issued.

His words manifested His Divine origin. He spake as never man spake, for the simple reason He was more than man.

His humility was manifested in His absolute fitness for the exalted position of the throne of glory, for He alone is qualified to occupy the highest place who has first served in the lowest.

His compassion was manifested in His glorious mercy.

THE HOLY ANOINTING OIL 63

Mercy's highest function is to meet the need of the most abject and destitute, and surely He did this.

His love manifested His lowly grace. His words about the Father's heart throbs for the prodigal, and the home provision for his need are unveilings of His own acts. He did what He taught.

His holiness manifested His beautiful character. He was all-beautiful without because He was all-glorious within.

He Himself manifested the splendour of God, for He is the brightness of His glory.

We do not wonder when we read, " The Spirit of counsel " (Isaiah xi. 2) was upon Him, for the Holy Spirit was the oil feeder of His life and testimony. The Hebrew word translated " counsel " in Isaiah xi. signifies both the possession and impartation of counsel. Christ had both. He not only had the possession of " the counsel of the Lord " which " standeth for ever " (Psalm xxxiii. 11), but He was able to give infallible guidance to all who sought His aid. The word translated " counsel " is rendered " advisement " in calling attention to the advice the lords of the Philistines received regarding David (1. Chronicles xii. 19 ; 1. Samuel xxix. 2-4). No one ever listened to the advice given in the teaching of Christ but found it true and reliable. John would call down fire from Heaven upon some upon whom he looked with disfavour, but before he did so he asked his Lord's advice, and at once his fiery spirit is quenched in the rebuke, " Ye know not what manner of spirit ye are of." Peter, acting on his own authority, cuts off the ear of the servant of the high priest. Self-action brings injury to others. Christ's action ever ministers health and happiness.

Light ever does one of two things : it attracts or repels. Many animals and insects love the dark. Christ in His life and testimony attracted and repelled. He attracted the children, but He repelled the religious professor. Why did He repel the latter ? Because he was untrue. Christ ever counsels us that the outer garb of profession will not do for the inner worth of grace. Dr. Andrew Bonar says upon the peace offering and the lascivious woman's action thereto : " Few ordinances were more blessed than these peace offerings.

Yet, like the Lord's supper with us, often were they turned to sin. The lascivious woman in Proverbs vii. 14 comes forth saying: " I have peace offerings with me; this day have I paid my vows." She had actually gone up among the devoted class of worshippers to present a thank offering and had stood at the altar as one at peace with God. Having now received from the priest those pieces of the sacrifice that were to be feasted upon, lo! she hurries to her dwelling and prepares a banquet of lewdness. She quiets her conscience by constraining herself to spend some of her time and some of her substance in His sanctuary. She deceives her fellow-creatures, too, and maintains a character for religion, and then rushes back to sin without." Is there nothing of this in our land? What means Christmas mirth after pretended observance of Christ being born? What means the sudden worldliness of so many on the day following their approach to the Lord's table? What means the worldly talk and levity of a Sabbath afternoon or evening after worship is done?

As Christ was able to be all He was because enabled by the Spirit, as He says, " The Spirit of the Lord is upon Me," so let us be energized in that same power. Mulock says, " Be loving and you will never want for love; be humble and you will never want for guiding." This is perfectly true, but there is something before these effects, and that is the great cause; hence, we would say, " Be in the love of the Spirit, that you may be loving, and in His grace of humility, that you may be humble."

The Anointed Incense Altar—" Anoint . . . . the incense altar " (Exodus xxx. 27). The incense altar is typical of Christ in the excellence of His person as our great High Priest, as He acts in His intercessory ministry at the right hand of God. But there is a sense in which it may be applied to Christ as the Anointed of God in His life, as He went about doing good (Acts x. 38). His life was one hallowed benediction, and went up to God as a sweet-smelling savour. The secret of that life is found in " the Spirit of might " (Isaiah xi. 2) which rested upon Him. The maxim of the world is might is right, and this too often means might setting on one side the right. With Christ might was to do good. He had the might to do the right. How significant are the words, "He went about doing good." Shirley says :—

"Only the actions of the just
Smell sweet and blossom in the dust."

The actions of the Just One were ever sweet and blossomed. We have only to follow one of the many lines of His actions, and that is to mark the references where He is said to be "moved with compassion." The loathsome leper stirs His *healthful compassion* to touch him with the touch of His cleansing life; the weeping mother calls forth His *sympathetic compassion*, and He gives the dead son back with His resurrection life to comfort her; the hungry multitude urge Him to supply with His *providing compassion* the bread which satisfied their need; the sightless men, with their urgent cry, led Him to go to them with His *powerful compassion*, which He exercises as He opens their eyes; the prodigal in his pain and penury causes Him to act with *intense compassion* as He hurries with quick steps to meet him; the sinning woman condemned by men excites His *forgiving compassion*, for He assures her He does not condemn her; and the excited publican, hiding in the sycamore tree, makes His *arresting compassion* seek his salvation.

There is, as Goldsmith says, "the luxury of doing good." He who does good to others brings more and most good to himself. Two ragged boys, barefooted, were going along one of the streets of New York. One was perfectly happy over a half-withered bunch of flowers which he had just picked up. "I say, Billy," said he, "wasn't somebody real good to drop these posies just where I could find them? And they're so pooty and nice. Look sharp, Billy, mebbe you'll find something bineby." Presently the boy exclaimed : "Oh, jolly, Billy, if here ain't 'most half a peach! And 'tain't much dirty, either. 'Cause you hain't found nothin' you may bite first." Billy was just going to take a little taste of it when his companion said : "Bite bigger, Billy. Mebbe we'll find another 'fore long." That boy had a kind heart, and he showed his goodness in his generous kindness. We can do something, for is not the poor world needing the Bread of Life? We are sure of this, anyway, if in obedience to our

Lord we give the blessed food of the Gospel, that whether it is received or not, we are in Him a sweet-smelling savour.

The Anointed Altar of Burnt Offering. The altar of burnt offering is typical of Christ in His devotion to the Father's will, even unto death. The six offerings are unmistakably types of Christ in His life and death. The following words sum up: manifestation, substitution, redemption, communion, consecration, and joy.

Manifestation. The meat offering, proclaiming Christ in the purity of His nature.

Substitution. The sin offering, speaking of Christ's enduring the wrath of God as the Sufferer for sin.

Redemption. The trespass offering, typical of Christ Who died for our sins, that we might be released from their guilt and government.

Communion. The peace offering, setting forth how the fellowship severed by sin is restored by means of the death of Christ.

Consecration. The burnt offering, proclaiming Christ as He delighted to do His Father's will, and thus brought delight to Him, as He glorified Him on our account.

Joy. The drink offering represents Christ in the joy of His heart doing the will of God, and the joy God found in the death of His Son, for wine rejoiceth the heart of God and man (Psalm civ. 15).

We are told that Christ "through the Eternal Spirit offered Himself without spot to God (Hebrews ix. 14). Ponder the last two words, " to God," for they explain the Godward aspect of the work of Christ. Browning in one of his poems makes Christ say, as He proclaims one aspect of His work to Eve :—

> " And shall your sins
> Have sunken to all Nature's heart from yours,
> The tears of My clean soul shall follow them
> And set a holy passion to work clear,
> Absolute consecration. In My brow
> Of kingly whiteness shall be crowned anew
> Your discrowned human nature. Look on me
> As I shall be uplifted on a cross
> In darkness and eclipsed and anguished dread,
> So shall I lift up in My pierced hands."

By means of His pierced hands He not only throws back the dominator of hell, but He lifts up to the delight of Heaven. He places the believer in the unsullied light of Heaven and makes him to be as He is. Hawker has well said: " The Christian should dwell at the cross as one who has passed through it, not as one who hopes to be saved by it. It is from the fields of the promised land that we regard the dark depth of this Jordan ; but the more steadily we gaze the more clearly do we understand the perfect completeness of our salvation, and the fearful cost at which it was gained by the Son of God. . . . The crucifixion is the great event of this world's history ; the only one which reveals the whole character of God ; the most awful, the most blessed ; the sharpest sword of justice there glitters in the brightest beams of love."

The Christ of sacred prophecy says : " The Spirit of knowledge " (Isaiah xi. 2) should rest upon Him. The Spirit as " the Spirit of knowledge " acts upon Him from God, making Him do His will, and acts through Him to others that they, too, might know the Divine purpose. This is aptly seen in the last prayer of Christ for His disciples, when He says, " This is life eternal to know God and Jesus Christ, Whom He hath sent," and to know Him, as the One Who glorified God on earth. To know Him is to possess the *panacea* to meet every ill in life, to have the *key* to unlock every difficulty, to hold the *helm* to guide the bark of our being through the shoals of temptation, to possess the *test* by which every action is to be tried, to have a *lubricator* to oil the wheels of service, to have a *supply* to meet every emergency, and to have a *harmonizer* which ever feeds the heart with joy. Bishop Fisher expresses what it is to know Christ and God in the sense indicated. When he came out of the Tower of London and saw the scaffold on which he was to be beheaded, he took out of his pocket His Greek Testament, and, looking up to Heaven, exclaimed : " Now, O Lord, direct to some passage which may support me through this awful scene." He opened his Testament and his eyes alighted upon the words, " This is eternal life." He instantly closed it and said, " Praised be the Lord, this is sufficient for me and for eternity."

The Anointed Laver. The laver is typical of the Word of God in its cleansing power. When the Holy Spirit speaks of the purpose of Christ in loving the Church He says, " Christ loved the Church and gave Himself for it, that He might sanctify and cleanse it with the washing (margin, R.V., " laver ") of water by the Word " (Ephesians v. 25, 26). The laver is not only typical of the written Word, but also of the Living Word. Both the written Word and the Living Word are called " the Word of God." The anointed laver specially speaks of Christ as the One Who, in the power of the Spirit, was the living expression of all that is found in the Scriptures. Christ's action and attitude regarding the Word of God are most marked. He *treated* it reverently, He *obeyed* it thoroughly, He *followed* it fully, He *rested* upon it implicitly, He *loved* it supremely, He *kept it faithfully*, and *reproduced* it constantly. The Spirit of the " fear of the Lord " (Isaiah xi. 2) was ever the spring of all His actions. " The love that fears, and the fear that loves," were the beautiful textures which were woven into all the life of Christ.

There is a remarkable Scripture in Hebrews v. 7 which refers to Christ's fear. It says : " Who in the days of His flesh, having offered up prayers and supplications with strong crying and tears unto Him that was able to save Him out of (margin) death, and having been heard for His Godly fear " (R.V.) The flame of fear fed by the fuel of love was ever burning on the altar of Christ's heart. There was no such thing as tormenting fear with Christ, but there was the subjective fear of service lest He should fail in fulfilling the work of His Father, hence, the constant retirement in prayer ; and there was the filial fear of affection, lest as the Son He should fail to delight in the will of God when called to suffer in the agony of Gethsemane, hence, His strong crying and tears. Oh, for a like fear as we work out our salvation, for we are called to do it " with fear and trembling." We too, like our Lord, must fall back upon Divine resources, for if we would have the Spirit to work in us to will and work of His good pleasure we must work with Him in earnest prayer and an intense faith.

Syllabus of
The Anointing as an Emblem of the Holy Spirit

"As for you the Anointing"—I. *Anointed to honour*—"Expedient" *versus* "profitable"—"The Support"—II. *Anointed to sanctify*—The Holy One makes holy—Violets from Santa Barbara—III. *Anointed to minister*—"Minister unto Me," &c.—The priestly word for service in the New Testament—The character and comprehensiveness of priestly service—Moule on "worship"—IV. *Anointed to see*—Spirit's thorough work—"Touch up" or a "burn off"—"*Blepo*"—Consequence of the Anointing—V. *Anointed to know*—"*Chrisma*"—Seven "we knows"—Shakespeare on the bane of ignorance and the blessing of knowledge—VI. *Anointed to do good*—A triple designation—Obtainment, retainment by maintainment—Richard Cecil's prescription—Herbert's saying—VII. *Anointed to stand*—Meaning of "stablisheth"—Five things the Anointing makes stedfast—"Stand fast, Craig Ellachie"—VIII. *Anointed to rule*—The Anointing One in the heart—The difference in the two men—IX. *Anointed to receive*—God's anointed got the best—Minister in Brooklyn—Vinet's illustration—What George Müller did—X. *Anointed to save*—Seven words of command—Luminary of character—"Holding forth"—"Snatching"—"Saved by the hair of his head"—The Spirit of Brainerd and Alleine—XI. *Anointed for healing*—Does God heal sickness now?—Reasons why we may expect healing—The woman from Perth Amboy—XII. *Anointed to preach*—The Jubilee—The devil in a pulpit—Result of Spirit's working—"Lapsed masses" or a lapsed Church?—XIII. *Anointed for victory*—Peter before and after Pentecost—XIV. *Anointed to die*—Mary and Judas—Charles Kingsley on selfishness—What George Müller saw the brother lacked—The Anointer and the Anointing—Two men at St. Louis—House filled with the odour.

THE ANOINTING

THERE is so much said about anointed persons and things, which may be taken to typify the Spirit's grace and work, that it is profitable to meditate further upon the topic in a separate study.

"As for you, the Anointing" (1. John ii. 27, R.V.), so says the Spirit in calling attention to the special privilege and responsibility of those who are His recipients. The practicality of the truth is clearly indicated and enunciated in the purpose for which different things and persons were anointed.

I. ANOINTED TO HONOUR.

One of the many things that God did for Israel, as stated in Ezekiel xvi. 6-15, is, "I anointed thee with oil"; and Satan in his privileged position before his fall is called "the anointed cherub" (Ezekiel xxviii. 14). Among other things the Psalmist recounts of the Lord's doings for him, is, "Thou anointest my head with oil" (Psalm xxiii. 5); and the Lord had to reprove Simon for his want of courtesy when commending the woman of the city, "My head with oil thou didst not anoint, but this woman hath anointed My feet with ointment" (Luke vii. 46). Jehovah has honoured Christ in anointing Him with the oil of Gladness above His fellows (Hebrews i. 9).

There are two things we need, namely, we need the atonement to save, and the anointing to sanctify. Christ said it was "expedient" that He should go away, otherwise the Comforter would not come (John xvi. 7). It was not a matter of expediency, but of profit. The Greek word rendered "*expedient*" would be better rendered "*profitable*." The word is a compound one, made up of the primary preposition "*sun*" signifying union, and "*phero*" a primary verb meaning to bear, thus "*sunphero*" means to bear or bring together, hence to be advantageous. The word is translated "*brought together*" in Acts xix. 19, "*good*" in Matthew xix. 10, "*better*" in Matthew xviii. 6, and "*profitable*" in Matthew v. 29, 30. The profit of Christ's going away and the bestowment of the Spirit in consequence, is manifold. His going away, was, by the way of the Cross, the triumph of His resurrection, His ascension to the throne, and the Father's presence ; and the result would be the Spirit's ministry in the making of Christ's death the death of sin, the causing us to know the victory of His resurrection, and the consciousness of the ascended throne life in fellowship with the Father. Honoured indeed are those who have " the Support," as Godet translates the words " the Comforter." To have Him with us as the Divine Companion, and within us as the Dynamic Consecrator, is to have ample and abiding support.

II. ANOINTED TO SANCTIFY.

" Moses took the anointing oil, and anointed the Tabernacle and all that was therein, and sanctified them " ; and he also anointed Aaron and his sons to " sanctify " him and them (Leviticus viii. 10-12, 30) ; and of believers in Christ it is said, " Ye have an unction (an anointing, R.V.) from the Holy One " (1. John ii. 20). As the holy anointing oil made everything holy which it touched, so the Holy One is the One Who makes holy. We have no inherent holiness. We are holy as we are possessed by the Holy Presence. We are holy in His holiness, loving in His love, strong in His strength, tender in His tenderness, patient in His patience, calm in His peace, and consecrated in His consecration. Get out of touch with Him by neglecting prayer, and the fragrance of His presence is wanting.

I picked up a small note book one day, and as I opened it a delightful fragrance of violets greeted me. I could not think at the moment how the book could smell so sweet, then I remembered a friend had given me some violets at Santa Barbara, on the Pacific Coast, and I had pressed some of them between the leaves of the book. I also sent some of the violets in a letter on a journey of 7,000 miles to England, and nearly a year after the friend said, " I have kept those violets in my handkerchief box, and they still shed forth their fragrance." Thus the things which the violets touched were made like themselves, sweet. So the Spirit imparts His character to those who are permeated by His holiness and sweetened by His grace.

III. ANOINTED TO MINISTER.

Of Aaron and his sons it was said : " The anointing oil of the Lord is upon you " (Leviticus x. 7). The various things which Aaron and his sons were to do typify what believers are called upon to do in the exercise of their holy priesthood. The " priest who was anointed " is continually referred to (Leviticus iv. 3, 5, 16 ; Numbers iii. 3) as the one who had the right to act ; and only those who are made priests through faith in Christ have the true qualification to worship God, whether it be in sanctified praise or in religious service. Continually we read in the Book of Leviticus " *The priest shall.*" No less than over a hundred times does the sentence occur, and these do not include the equivalent expression, " *he shall.*"

Further the Lord says of Aaron and his sons : " Thou ... shalt anoint them, and consecrate them, and sanctify them, that they may minister unto me in the priest's office " (Exodus xxviii. 41). The Hebrew word rendered " minister " is a primary one, and means to attend as a menial or a worshipper, and as such to contribute, to minister, to serve, and wait on another. Many are the suggestive and typical associations of the word. The priests were elected, clothed, consecrated, and anointed to minister unto the Lord, as He Himself frequently says—" Minister unto Me in the priest's office " (Exodus xxviii. 1, 3, 4, 41 ; xxix. 1, 44 ; xxx. 30 ; xl. 13, 15). They were not to minister to themselves, nor to the office, but to Jehovah Himself. The priests were to minister " before the Lord," that is, in the consciousness of His holy and hallowing presence (1. Chronicles xxiii. 13) ; they were to minister " in the name of Jehovah," that is, under His authority and as He Himself would act (Deuteronomy xviii. 5, 7) ; and in their work the priests were called to **wash themselves before they came near to the altar of burnt**

THE ANOINTING

offering (Exodus xxx. 20), indicating that cleansing is a prelude to worship. All these have their counterpart in the priesthood of believers.

When we turn to the New Testament we find the same thing is emphasized. There are two main ideas embodied in two different associations, namely, there is the service of the slave; and there is the service of the worshipper. In each of the following Scriptures, the words "*ministry*," "*service*," "*serve*," and "*worship*" are all relative, and speak of priestly service done to the Lord. It will be observed that the association of these sentences of Holy Writ touch every part of our life, Godward, selfward and toward others. Such a ministry in its priestly worship is a *body-presented ministry*, for to present our bodies to the Lord is our "reasonable" (spiritual) *service* (Romans xii. 1); it is a *God-concentrated ministry*, for His demand is "Him only shalt thou *serve*" (Matthew iv. 10; Luke iv. 8); it is a *love-rendered ministry*, for we are to "*serve* Him without fear" (Luke i. 74); it is a *Christ-concentrated ministry*, as Paul expresses it, "Whom I *serve*" (Acts xxvii. 23); it is a *pure-conscience ministry*, as the apostle could testify, "God, Whom I *serve* .... with pure conscience" (II. Timothy i. 3); it is a *saints-helping ministry*, for we are to "*minister*" to each other in spiritual and carnal things (Romans xv. 27; II. Corinthians ix. 12; Philippians ii. 17); and it is a *God-pleasing ministry*, for we are "to *serve* God acceptably with reverence and godly fear" (Hebrews xii. 28). It will be noticed there is no talk in this priestly service, but there is continued practice. The question naturally arises, who is sufficient for these things? The Spirit says those who answer to the true circumcision are those who glory in Christ Jesus, who *worship* God in the Spirit, and have no confidence in the flesh (Philippians iii. 3).

"Worship God in the Spirit," or as Dr. Moule gives it and comments: "We who by God's Spirit worship, doing priestly service in a spiritual temple in a life, love and power, which is ours by the presence of the Holy Spirit." In His power alone is it possible for us to give to the Lord such a ministry. Without the anointing there cannot be the worshipping which is honouring to the Lord.

IV. Anointed to See.

Christ's solemn counsel to the lukewarm Church of Laodicea was, " anoint thine eyes with eyesalve that thou mayest see " (Rev. iii. 18). The word anoint, " *egchrio*," is a compound one, derived from " *en*," which means in, and " *chrio*," which means to smear, hence, its meaning to *rub in*. A mere placing on is not sufficient, there must be a rubbing in—a thorough work. No half measures will suffice, there must be a drastic and definite act till the shortsightedness is removed. Contact with the Spirit is the only remedy for the blindness which is born of self-complacency and self-sufficiency. A pastor, who had been a coach-painter, was once relating his experience, how the Lord dealt with him in searching him to the very foundations of his being; and in the course of his testimony said : " I used to be a coach-painter, and when the people used to bring their buggies to be renovated, we would ask them, ' Do you want a touch up and a varnish, or a burn off and a thorough job.' So when the Holy Spirit dealt with me in a very definite way He made a thorough job of it. There were no half measures." Such a work means a smarting of soul, a humbling to the spirit, and prostration in the dust to self, but it leads to the mount of vision, where we can see God.

" That ye may *see*." The word rendered " *see*," " *blepo*," is variously rendered, namely, " take heed," " beholdest," " look," " saw," " see," " seen," " beware," " perceive," and " regardest." Let us weave into the texture of our study a few Scripture sentences where " *blepo* " is found, as illustrating how the Spirit works by means of the loom of His Word to bring home to us the outcome of His holy anointing. Anointed by the Spirit we shall see the glorified man at God's right hand, which shall make us exclaim, " We *see* Jesus " (Hebrews ii. 9). Anointed by the Spirit, we shall estimate the seen unreal and the real unseen at their true value, and we shall say, " the things which are not *seen* are eternal " (II. Cor. iv. 18). Anointed by the Spirit we shall apprehend the possibility of falling and thus avoid the probability of it by obeying the word, " Let him that thinketh he standeth, *take heed* lest he fall " (I. Corinthians x. 12). Anointed by the

The Anointing

Spirit we shall guard ourselves by vigilance and prayer in response to Christ's injunction, "*take ye heed*, watch and pray" (Mark xiii. 33). Anointed by the Spirit we shall know the evil of a heart of unbelief, and thus "*take heed*" lest there be in us an evil heart of unbelief (Hebrews iii. 12). Anointed by the Spirit we shall be conscious of the weakness of ourselves and when we "*behold*" a mote in a brother's eye, be quick to discern it is but the reflection of the beam in our own eye (Luke vi. 42). Anointed by the Spirit we shall be alert to look after the inner sphere of our spiritual life and thus "*look* to ourselves" (II. John 8). Anointed by the Spirit we shall not be discouraged by our weakness for we shall "*see* our calling" that God takes our weakness for the display of His glory (I. Corinthians i. 27). Anointed by the Spirit, we shall know we are responsible to have an all round life, and thus "*see*" that we "walk circumspectly" (Eph. v. 15). Anointed by the Spirit we cannot do other than "*take heed*" to build the right material on Christ the Foundation (I. Corinthians iii. 10). Anointed by the Spirit, we shall "*beware*" of those who would lead us away from our Lord and astray from His truth (Philippians iii. 2); and anointed by the Spirit, we shall be careful to keep in the gathering of the saints and be helpful to others, and this with a growing intensity as we "*see* the day" of Christ's return "approaching" (Hebrews x. 25).

V. Anointed to know.

"Ye have an *unction* from the Holy One, and ye know all things.... But the *anointing* which ye have received of Him abideth in you, and ye need not that any man teach you; but as the same *anointing* teacheth you of all things, and is truth, and is no lie, and even as it hath taught you, ye shall abide in Him" (I. John ii. 20, 27). The word "*chrisma*," rendered "*unction*" and "*anointing*" in the above Scripture, means to rub with oil, and is typical of the consecrating power of the Spirit. The consequence of this anointing is a spiritual insight into Divine things. With startling abruptness we read, "Ye know all things." He teacheth and thus gives us to know. Some of the things which we know as the result of His teaching are specifically stated. Take but seven of the "*we know's,*"* by way of illustration. *A wonderful passage crossed and its proof*—" We know we have passed from death unto life because we love the brethren " (1. John iii. 14). No longer in the death realm of sin, but in the Divine realm of the Saviour, and the proof of it, love to all the saints. *A wonderful Person known and His followers*—" Hereby *we* do *know* that *we know* Him, if we keep His commandments " (1. John ii. 3). The companions of the King are those who obey His royal behests. The badge of loyalty is the insignia of royalty. *A consuming passion and conscious assurance.* " Hereby *we know* that we are of the truth and shall assure our hearts before Him " (1. John iii. 19). With the fire of love burning on the altar of our hearts, we shall have ignited within us the flame of confidence in the Lord's presence. *A mutual abiding and the precursor which brings it*—" Hereby *we know* He abideth in us " (1. John iii. 24). The forerunner of obedience brings the believer into the palace of the Lord's presence, and the Lord in His Spirit responds in His power, and the result is a personal acquaintance with the Divine. *A double blessing found in the will of God*—" If *we know* that He hear us, whatsoever we ask, *we know* that we have the petitions desired of Him " (1. John v. 15). The hands that open the door of heaven's blessing are the hands of confident faith and responsive love. *A Keeper and the kept*—" We *know* that whosoever is begotten of God sinneth not, but He that was begotten of God keepeth him " (1. John v. 18, R.V.) Christ is the One that *was* begotten, and the believer is the one that is begotten. *The Coming One and the conformed*

---

* There are two different words rendered "*know*" in John's Epistle. The one signifying the knowledge of a person's personal observation, and the other meaning a personal relationship between the one knowing and the object known. When in Los Angeles some time since, I had observed the orange groves and the fruit on the trees in their tempting beauty and apparent lusciousness ; but one day in walking among the fruit trees I was invited to help myself to the fruit, which I did, and then I knew the difference between a packed orange and a plucked one. In the first instance I had the knowledge of observation, but in the second instance I had the knowledge of personal **acquaintance and experience.**

ones—" *We know* that when He shall appear we shall be like Him " (1. John iii. 2). The expectation of seeing the glorified Christ and being like Him, shall have its consummation when He shall come for His own.

These are but a few of the many things which come to those who are taught by the Anointing One. Shakespeare says :—

"Ignorance is the curse of God,
Knowledge the wing whereby we fly to Heaven."

We may alter the lines to say :—

To know Christ is the blessing of God,
For by Him the Spirit leads to God Himself.

VI. Anointed to do Good.

The Spirit of God has summed up the life of Christ in the following pregnant word—" God anointed Jesus of Nazareth with the Holy Ghost and with power, Who went about doing good, and healing all that were oppressed with the devil, for God was with Him " (Acts x. 38). Is there not a sequence and a consequence in the way the Word denotes how the Spirit operated in the Man and Servant—Jesus ? Character is implied in the Holy Spirit coming upon Him. The Holy One of God corresponded to the Holy Spirit, the result was " power," namely, ability to do ; then the climax, " for God was with Him." Character, power, fellowship—character like God's, power in God, and fellowship with Him. Such a Being could do no other than good, and no devil could stand before Him. Like the springtime life He made everything glad and glorious, and like a mighty avalanche He swept all evil before Him.

We cannot, apart from Christ, expect any such blessing and to be any such blessing, but we can in Him. The one glory of the gospel is, God gives what He demands, and then commands what He gives. The Spirit was given to Christ because of what He was in Himself, the Spirit is given to us because of what we are in Him. But on the other hand, is there not a suggested significance in the association of the Spirit's power and the doing good ? The Cause of the good done, and the deliverances effected, was the Anointing, but on the other hand the retention of the Spirit's power was because of the good accomplished. The obtainment of the Spirit's power was essential to overcome the devil's power, and the doing good; but the retainment of the Spirit's blessing was the use of the power bestowed. Many complain they do not retain, well it is because they do not maintain. The obtainment is first, then the retainment by the maintainment.

Richard Cecil on one occasion went to see a lady who was a great professor, but she was very miserable. He found her sitting over the fire. She asked him to sit down, but he would not. He said, "I will not, I know what is the matter. Get up, put on your bonnet, and try and do some good." She did as she was told, and she was soon a different woman. When she met Mr. Cecil a short time after, she said, "Oh, you could not have done me a greater favour than tell me to do some good. Good has come to me in doing good to others." Herbert says, "Help thyself and God will help thee." That is only part of a truth, God helps us to help others, and when we help others we help ourselves.

VII. Anointed to stand.

"Now he which stablisheth us with you into (margin, R.V.*) Christ, and hath anointed us, is God" (II. Corinthians i. 21). There may be two things indicated here which are distinct, but as in the next verse the Seal and Earnest as referring to the Spirit (the seal becomes the earnest) are intimately connected, so the reason why the saints were stablished was because they were anointed, for certainly the reason why God anoints is that He may confirm us.

The word "*stablisheth*" means to make firm, stedfast. It is derived from a word to be stable, and this again is derived

---

* The Greek preposition εἰς (into) is more expressive than ἐν (in), even as a plant may be in the ground and yet need to be planted into it. In my garden in Bristol I observed one day one of the rose trees was looking sickly. Upon examination I found the roots were not well into the ground. I immediately took it up carefully and imbedded it into the ground. Rootage is essential to foliage, flower and fruit.

THE ANOINTING

from the base of a word which is expressed by our "*basis.*" The Greek word is "*basis,*" and is translated "*feet*" in Acts iii. 7. The word "*stablisheth*" is rendered "*confirm*" in Romans xv. 8, and "*established*" in Hebrews xiii. 9 ; and the word from which it is derived is translated "*sure,*" "*firm,*" "*in force,*" and "*stedfast*" (Romans iv. 16 ; Hebrews iii. 6 ; vi. 19 ; ix. 17).

Here again the best commentary on the Bible is the Bible itself. Let us work in, like productive soil into the ground of our meditation, the rich loam of God's truth. The Anointing will give *the confidence of faith*, so that we shall hold fast " our confidence *stedfast* unto the end " (Hebrews iii. 14), and thus be like a firm lighthouse which shines with steady flame amidst all the howling storms. The Anointing will bestow *the outlook of hope*, so that we shall hold fast " the rejoicing of the hope *firm* unto the end " (Hebrews iii. 6), and thus be like a betrothed maiden who looks out with ardent gaze for the return of him who is the object of her heart's affection. The Anointing will give *the diligence of love*, so that the life is not wanting in the graces which beautify and constitute the Christian character, thus the " calling and election " of grace will be made " *sure* " (II. Peter i. 10), even as the several parts of a chorus make a harmonious whole. The Anointing will brace *the sinews of testimony*, so that its feet will be " *stablished* in the faith " of God's truth (Colossians ii. 7), and thus be like a brave warrior in an impregnable position ; and the Anointing will invigorate *the heart of consecration* by causing it to be " *established* with grace " (Hebrews xiii. 9), and thus cause it to be like a beautiful and fragrant garden.

Ruskin, in referring to the war-cry of the Clan Grant, which is " Stand fast, Craig Ellachie,"* and the influence of the home surroundings of the Scotch soldier as he thought of his highland home, says, " How often among the delicate

---

* " In one of the loneliest districts of Scotland, where the peat cottages are darkest, just at the western foot of the Grampians which encircles the sources of the Spey and the Dee, the main road which traverses the chain winds round the foot of a broken rock called Crag, or Craig Ellachie. It is darkened by a few pines, and crowned with a flush of heather. It is a type of Clan Grant, and has its influence upon those who belong to the district."

Indian palaces, whose marble was pallid with horror, and whose vermillion was darkened with blood, the remembrance of grey rocks and purple heaths must have risen before the sight of the Highland soldier; how often the hailing of the shot and the shriek of battle would pass away from his hearing, and leave only the whisper of the old pine branches, ' Stand fast, Craig Ellachie!'" Our Craig Ellachie is Calvary's rugged mound which ever reminds us of Him Who stood amid the storms of Heaven and Hell and Earth for us; and when we would flinch or falter the Spirit reminds us of the Captain Who fell in death for us, that we may stand fast and by His power He makes us strong to this end.

VIII. ANOINTED TO RULE.

"They anointed David King over Israel" (II. Sam. v. 3). The man of God's selection was elected by the people to be their ruler. A true king is not one who occupies the place of authority merely, he has the ability to answer to what the office demands. To have a royal place and palace, and not royal power and dignity is to be in a sorry plight and position. In the Book of Proverbs, the following are said to be the true traits of God's kings: They are Divinely appointed (Proverbs viii. 15), they are haters of wickedness (Proverbs xvi. 12), they are righteous in life (Proverbs xvi. 12, 13), they are powerful in action (Proverbs xx. 2, 8, 26), dependent on mercy (Proverbs xx. 28), friendly to the true (Proverbs xxii. 11), and considerate of the needy (Proverbs xxix. 14). Let us, by the Spirit's consecrating grace, be true to the appointment of grace, haters of evil, right in life, powerful in testimony, dependent on Christ, friendly to the upright, and helpers of the needy.

There is one realm where all may rule, and that is in the realm of the inner man. The wise man wisely says, " Better .... he that ruleth his spirit than he that taketh a city " (Proverbs xvi. 32). When the domain of the inner life is ruled there is no difficulty about the outworks of the soul and body. For this, there is a needs-be for the strengthening of the Holy Spirit that Christ may dwell in the heart (Eph. iii. 16). Mark, it is the Christ, the Anointing One, Who is to dwell in the heart. We must be ruled if we are to rule. Christ must dwell in the heart for this. What is meant by the heart? The heart stands for the will, hence, the sinner has to acknowledge Jesus as Lord and believe in Him with the heart as such (Romans x. 9, R.V.); the heart stands for the affection, hence, Paul said to the Philippians regarding their love for him, " Ye have me in your heart " (Philippians i. 7); and the heart stands for the mind, hence, " the eyes of the heart " need to be " enlightened " to understand spiritual things (Ephesians i. 18, R.V.) When Christ rules in our will to will, in our affection to love, and in our mind to think, the citadel of our being is fully occupied.

The difference between trying to rule ourselves and being ruled by the Spirit is well illustrated by the following incidents. I remember Ned Wright, the converted burglar, telling me that soon after he was converted one of his old companions challenged him to fight. Ned had to exercise all his will power to keep down the old fighting spirit as he was taunted and tantalized. At last he exclaimed, " I wish I was only unconverted for five minutes, I would soon give you what for!" The volcano of the smouldering fires was within, and wanted to flame out in tempestuous outburst. In contrast, I remember seeing a child of God sneered at, howled at, taunted, and gibed by a lot of young fellows in New York City. They did their utmost to provoke him. All the while the man quietly clapped his hands and smiled at his persecutors, exclaiming the while, " Bless the Lord! The Lord bless you!" At last, in utter desperation, one of the fellows said to the others, " Come away, what can we do with a fellow like that?" The smile conquered the scowls, and the reason of the smile without was the sweetness within. The Spirit of God can conquer us if we are willing to be conquered, and He alone can do it.

IX. ANOINTED TO RECEIVE.

" Unto thee have I given them by reason of the anointing " (Numbers xviii. 8). Aaron and his sons being God's anointed ones were privileged to receive and enjoy certain things. We have a long list of the things which belonged to God's anointed

F

ones. Certain of the sin-offerings, trespass-offerings, meat-offerings, heave-offerings, wave-offerings, the best of the oil, wine and wheat, the first ripe things, the firstfruits of all things, and every devoted thing in Israel (see Numbers xviii. 9-20). The best of everything was brought to the Lord by the Israelites, and He in turn gave the specified things to His anointed ones.*

May we not say, those who have the anointing of the Holy Spirit get God's best ? I remember a minister in Brooklyn telling me that there came a distinct crisis and epoch in his life and ministry when he received the enduement of the Spirit for service, and when He received the Spirit as the Administrator in his inner life. How many there are who keep on a low level experience in the spiritual life when they might have God's best.

> " God has His best things for the few
> Who dare to stand the test,
> He has His second choice for those
> Who will not have His best."

Many long for God's best and try to obtain the same, but they go the wrong way about it. They try to detach themselves from the crutches upon which they are leaning, or they endeavour to reach an ideal which is too high for them, or they struggle to get rid of the grave clothes which bind them. The secret of detachment is attachment. Vinet well says, " The first thing is to attach oneself, detachment comes afterwards. The chrysalis covering in which the butterfly was imprisoned only breaks and falls away when the insect's wings have grown—it is by opening that these burst their melancholy integuments. We only detach ourselves from the world when we have learned to know some-

---

* How differently many professing Christians act in the things of God now. The smallest coin in the realm is put into the collection in too many instances. Many of God's servants who can ill afford it have to pay their own travelling expenses when asked to conduct meetings. Too often they are treated, as Duncan Matheson once said, " like angels," who do not need a cup of cocoa to warm them on a cold night, nor money to meet out of pocket expenses and the wear and tear of clothes, &c.

thing of a better. Till then we are but capable of disappointment and weariness, which is not detachment."

When we receive what the Lord has to give, we do not want what the world has to offer. The receptive life is the reproducing life. " Ye shall receive power, the Holy Spirit coming upon you." The received Spirit brought the required power. Of George Muller it has been said, " He brought everything to God and God into everything " ; and it is when God is in everything that everything is brought to God. And what before was never accomplished by our futile efforts and toil, He now accomplishes.

X. ANOINTED TO SAVE.

" Thou shalt anoint him to be captain, that he may save My people " (1. Samuel ix. 16), is the Divine word regarding the setting apart of Saul as King of Israel. We shall be saved and used as we know the Spirit's might. " The power of His might " (Ephesians vi. 10) is the strength which is requisite in order to put on the armour of God, and " the Lord the Mighty Man of valour " (Septuagint version of Judges vi. 12), being with us, who can stand before His presence ?

There is a sense in which we are to save the people. We are saved to save. The responsibility of the Lord's people in relation to those who are not His, is clearly enunciated in many ways. We should have the "*pray*" of intercession (Matthew ix. 38), the "*go*" of preaching the gospel (Mark xvi. 15), the "*look*" of compassion (John iv. 35), the "*save*" of definite action (Jude 23), the "*shine*" of holy character (Philippians ii. 15), the "*holding forth*" of the Word of Life (Philippians ii. 16), and the "*pulling*" of distinct deliverance (Jude 23).

Let us briefly look at the last three. (1) The "*shine*" *of character.* The word "*shine*" would be better rendered "*luminaries*," that is, light-bearers. Shining like stars amid the gloom. It means the world sees us as lights. The word is rendered "*may be seen*" in Matthew vi. 5, "*appeared*" in Matthew ii. 7 and Mark xvi. 9, in speaking of the star that the wise men saw and the appearing of Christ to Mary. The character which is luminous with the loving and holy Christ, like Christ Himself, cannot be hid. (2) The "*holding forth* *of Christ.* Christ is the Word of Life to hold forth in faithful testimony. The attractability of His loving and life-giving personality is the Only One to draw humanity. The word "*epecho*" means to hold on, hence it is rendered "*take heed*" (1. Timothy iv. 16), to retain, hence it is translated "*stayed*" (Acts xix. 22), to pay attention, hence it is given "*gave heed*" and "*marked*" (Acts iii. 5 ; Luke xiv. 7), and to offer to, hence the meaning in Philippians ii. 16. There is life in the Christ we offer. This is the only message to which we are to hold, to stay with, to pay attention to, for it alone contains the message that is the power of God unto salvation. (3) The "*save*" of "*pulling*"—"Save with fear, pulling them out of the fire" (Jude 23). This is no light and easy task. The word "*pulling*" means a violent, strenuous, forceful act, as the Revised Version indicates—"*Snatching* them out of the fire. The word is used of a wolf catching and carrying off a sheep (John x. 12), of Satan catching away the seed of the Word (Matthew xiii. 19), and of the Lord taking away His own to be with Himself (1. Thessalonians iv. 17). A sudden, forceful and decisive act is meant. In this way it is necessary to act when the sinner is in danger of the fire of sin, the fire of hell and the fire of God's wrath. Isaac Marsden was talking to a lad on one occasion, who had a "shock of curly hair". The lad was timid and inclined to run away, when Marsden put out his hand and took hold of his curly hair and held him fast. Meantime he spoke to him of the Christ Who loved him and the devil who dominated him. All the while he talked he gently pulled the lad to the communion rails, and there led him to Christ. He was not only converted, but became a preacher of the gospel, and used to often say afterwards, "Isaac Marsden brought me to Christ by the hair of my head." Oh, for more of such holy work! We want the spirit of Brainerd, who said, " I care not where or how I live, or what hardships I go through, so that I can gain souls to Christ." Saintly Alleine was of the same spirit. He said, " I am insatiably greedy of the conversion of souls."

The qualification for all this is the unction of the Holy One. The difficulties should not daunt us, for He can do what we cannot. When He bids us do, we dare to do all He tells us, leaving the results with Him.

XI. ANOINTED FOR HEALING.

" Is any sick among you ? Let him call for the elders of the Church ; and let them pray over him, anointing him with oil in the name of the Lord, and the prayer of faith shall save the sick, and the Lord shall raise him up " (James v. 14, 15). This is a most controverted passage of Scripture. Some of the Lord's servants say it does not apply to-day, while others say it does.* Without touching upon the controversy, we may look at the following question, " Have we any Scripture warrant or reasons for expecting God will heal sickness ? Yes, there are several. Because of what the Lord *is*. He is Jehovah Ropheca, the Lord that healeth (Exodus xv. 26). We may expect the Lord to heal because of what Christ has

---

* My friend, B. McCall Barbour, of Edinburgh, gave an all round view of the subject some time since, in the following :—

" I. Does God heal to-day ? Yes ! (Hebrews xiii. 8).

" II. Does God *always* heal ? No ! (II. Corinthians xii. 9).

" III. What are the conditions for healing ? (*a*) That it is God's will to do so ; (*b*) that we are right with Him to receive it.

" IV. How does God deliver in sickness ? (*a*) By removal of it ; (*b*) by strengthening to bear it (I. Corinthians x. 13 ; II. Corinthians xii. 9).

" V. Does God ever use means ? Yes ! (Isaiah xxxviii. 21 ; John ix. 6, 11 ; Acts xix. 11, 12 ; I. Timothy v. 23 ; James v. 14).

" VI. What is the right attitude of the believer in sickness ? (1) To say, ' It is here '—face the fact. (2) To ask, ' Why is it here ?' (*a*) natural neglect ; (*b*) spiritual chastisement (Hebrews xii. 6) ; (*c*) to manifest the works of God (John ix. 3). (3) To ask, ' Lord, what wilt Thou have *me* to do ?' (Means or no means—' Thy will be done.')

" VII. What is the wrong attitude of the believer in sickness ? (1) That of ' Christian Science,' which says it does not exist and *tries* to ignore it. (2) That which excludes God from the case—for all that comes to the believer, who is in His will, happens by God's permission (Proverbs iii. 5 6). (3) That which says we must *always* take means, and shuts out the possibility of God healing apart from means. (4) That which says we must *never* use means ; for God, Who has provided such, may have many purposes to fulfil for His glory and our good in requiring us to use them."

done upon the Cross. Like every blessing, healing comes through the atonement. He has "borne our sicknesses, as well as our sins and sorrows" (Isaiah liii. 4, R.V., margin). We may expect the Lord to heal because of the Spirit's indwelling. The indwelling Spirit is said "to quicken our mortal bodies" (Romans viii. 11). Mark, not our dead bodies, but "mortal bodies." Because of the Lord's promise we may expect healing. No plague shall come nigh the dwelling of the one who dwells in God (Psalm xci. 10), and He says, "The prayer of faith shall save the sick." The Lord has healed in the past, as we have record in the Scriptures. He healed Abimelech, Miriam and Hezekiah (Genesis xx. 17; Numbers xii. 14; II. Kings xx. 5, 8), and others in answer to prayer. And we may expect the Lord to heal because He is doing it.

There are many questions which arise. Such as, Does the Lord always heal in answer to prayer? No. Sometimes the Lord takes His servants home by sickness; and sometimes He has compensating grace to give, as in the case of Paul, who gloried in his bodily weakness. Would the elders be justified in refusing to anoint with oil a sick one who sent for them? No, they certainly would not. While conducting a Bible reading at a place on Staten Island, I was asked, with others, to anoint a sister who had come from her home in Perth Amboy. She had risen from a sick bed with difficulty. She was a calm, unemotional woman. I anointed her with oil, and then placed my hands upon her head, pleading the death of Christ's atonement. I quietly and earnestly prayed for her restoration to health. After I had prayed for a short time, I felt as though an electric shock went through my body to hers, and like the woman in the gospel, she "knew" she was healed. In other cases, there has been no feeling, and in others there has been no apparent answer. The Lord can heal, He has healed, He may heal, He does heal, and He may not heal.

Ours not to question why,
Ours to trust or die.

He will not meet the speculation of experiment, but He does meet the simplicity of expectation.

XII. ANOINTED TO PREACH.

Christ's opening words as He entered upon His ministry were, " The Spirit of the Lord is upon Me, because He hath anointed Me to preach the gospel to the poor," &c. (Luke iv. 18, 19). The reference is to the year of Jubilee. The happenings of that year have their correspondence in the gospel. As that year began on the day of atonement (Lev. xxv. 9), so the death of Christ is the basis of the good news of the gospel (I. Corinthians xv. 3). As the Jubilee was a time when the poor had the lost inheritance restored to them (Lev. xxv. 25), so the gospel proclaims to those who are destitute because of sin, the grace which enriches through the poverty of Christ's becomingness in His life and death (II. Corinthians viii. 9). As the Jubilee heralded liberty to those who were in the slavery of bondage (Leviticus xxv. 50) so the gospel brings out of the prison house of sin's darkness into God's marvellous light (Acts xxvi. 18).

"Anointed to preach." An old tradition has it that the devil on one occasion was preaching, and one of God's servants detected who the preacher was, and chided him for his assumption and presumption, whereupon the devil replied, " You need not fear, it will do no good for there was no power with it." A gospel without power is non-effective. Of the apostles it is significantly stated, " They preached the gospel unto you with the Holy Ghost sent down from heaven " (I. Peter i. 12); and Paul declares the secret of his effective ministry was " the effectual working of His power " (Eph. iii. 7). There are three things which are evident to the most casual reader of the Acts of the Apostles, and these are, that the Word of God was preached, that great opposition was raised where it was not received, and there were evident results of the Spirit's working. Trace through the Acts for proof. Acts ii. 41, " three thousand " saved ; Acts iv. 4, " five thousand " believed ; Acts vi. 7, the disciples multiplied and a great company of the priests were obedient to the faith ; Acts viii. 6, the multitudes gave heed to the gospel ; Acts ix. 35, " all " that dwelt in Lydda and Sharon turned to the Lord ; Acts x. 44, all in the house of Cornelius received the Spirit through Peter's ministry ; Acts xi. 21, " a great number believed "; Acts xiii. 44, the whole city gathered to hear the Word of God ; Acts xiv. 1, a great multitude believed ; Acts xiv. 21, " many disciples " were made as the effect of the preached gospel ; Acts xvi. 5, the Churches " increased in number " ; Acts xvii. 6, the world was said to have been turned upside down by the preaching of Paul and Silas ; Acts xviii. 8, people of important position were saved, such as the Chief Ruler Crispus and many of the Corinthians ; and the cause of the revival at Ephesus is said to be because the Word of God prevailed (Acts xix. 18-20). Do such facts correspond to the life of the Church to-day ? One has said, " We often hear of discussions on the ' lapsed masses.' " Why have the masses of the people lapsed from the Churches ? Perhaps the more correct way of putting it would be, Why have the Churches lapsed from the masses ? The answer is not far to seek, it is because they have lost the driving power which alone could keep them abreast of the masses, even the baptism of the Holy Spirit.

XIII. Anointed for victory.

" The yoke shall be destroyed because of the anointing " (Isaiah x. 27) is God's promise to Judah regarding the oppression of the Assyrian. The promise speaks of the power which does away with the yoke. The Spirit is the One Who can break every yoke. There is no one who better exemplifies the difference He can make than Peter, if we ponder what he was before Pentecost and after. Before Pentecost Peter was *self-authorized*, hence he says, " I go fishing " (John xxi. 3) ; after Pentecost he was *God-energized*, as is seen on the memorable day when the Spirit took possession of him. In the one instance he was like a plank floating on the ebb tide of circumstances, and in the other instance he was like an Atlantic liner going against wind and tide. Before Pentecost Peter was *self-resourceful*, as is evidenced by his boastful assertion to Christ, when he said, " Though all shall be offended, yet will not I " (Mark xiv. 29) ; but after Pentecost he was *God-dependent*, for he confessed to the lame man as to earth's resources he had " none," but bade him in the name of Jesus to rise and walk (Acts iii. 6). In the former case he was like an inflated bladder, but in the latter he was like an electrified arm through which the power flowed. Before Pentecost Peter was "*If-burdened*," for he greeted Christ upon the water by "If it be Thou bid me come to Thee" (Matt. xiv. 28); but after Pentecost he was *Scripture-certain*, for, on the Day of Pentecost, he appealed to what was stated in Holy Writ (Acts ii. 16-31). He was harried by the hounds of his own reason in the former case, and was harnessed to the chariot of God's truth in the latter. Before Pentecost Peter was *self-acting*, as when he cut off the ear of the servant of the high priest (Luke xxii. 50) ; but after he was *Christ-actuated*, as is evidenced in his address before the Council (Acts iv. 8-12). In the first instance he was swayed by the impulse of self, but in the second he was moved by the Spirit of God. Before Pentecost Peter was *cowardly* in denying his Lord, but after he was *courageous* in the boldness of the Spirit (Acts iv. 13). Before Pentecost he was *swearing*, when he denied his Master with oaths and curses (Matthew xxvi. 74) ; but after he was *praising* God with the rest of the disciples (Acts iv. 24-31). Before Pentecost he was *warming himself* at the world's fire (Luke xxii. 55) ; but after he had the *inner fire* of the Spirit's baptism (Acts ii. 14).

What a difference! The Spirit's anointing makes all the difference. It means courage instead of cowardice, contentment instead of murmuring, triumph instead of defeat, love instead of jealousy, prayer instead of prayerlessness, progress instead of stagnation, testimony instead of dumbness, usefulness instead of sloth, cleanness instead of defilement, holiness instead of worldliness, and Christ instead of self.

XIV. ANOINTED TO DIE.

Mary of Bethany was the only one who grasped the fact that Christ came into the world to die. Doubtless she had learned the secret while sitting at the feet of Christ, and the consequence was she got and preserved (as the word "kept" in John xii. 7 means) with careful attention the box of costly ointment, and by its use anticipated His burial. Godet in commenting on Mary's act and Judas's attitude has well said,

"Jesus ascribes to the act of Mary precisely that which was wanting to the view of Judas, a purpose, a practical utility. 'It is not for nothing, as thou chargest her, that she has poured out this ointment. She has to-day anticipated My embalming.'"* The loving heart purpose was wanting in Judas, while Mary was having fellowship with her Lord.†

While there was no reference to the Spirit's anointing in Mary's act, nor typical significance in her loving expression, yet we may take it as illustrating the Spirit's work as enabling the believer to die to the old life. It is not natural to die to the old life. Charles Kingsley significantly said, "If you wish to be miserable think about yourself, about what you want, what you like, what respect people ought to pay to you, what people think of you, and then to you nothing will be pure. You will spoil everything you touch; you will make sin and misery for yourself out of everything which God sends you; you will be as wretched as you choose." This is one of the worst phases of selfishness,—the rest will go with this,—and the one to which we need to die. The positive unction of the Spirit will deliver us from the poisoning uncleanness of the self. After all the lack of the positive grace is the open door to admit all of self. "What do I most lack in your judgment?" said a brother to George Müller. He promptly replied, "Your greatest lack is the grace of graciousness." The grace of the Spirit is the cure for gracelessness.

The cure for every ill is the incoming of the Spirit in power, enthroning Christ in the heart. "Strengthened with

---

* "She is come beforehand to anoint My body to the burying" (Mark xiv. 8).

† What a series of contrasts we have between Mary and Judas. She had a box of precious ointment, he had a bag of parsimonous greed; she gave three hundred denaries for her gift, he sold his Master for 30 pieces of silver; she had a loving heart, he had a coveteous one; he complained of her "waste," but he was a "son of waste" (the word "perdition," in John xvii. 12, is the same as "waste" in Mark xiv. 4); he professed to care for the poor, but she cared for her Lord; the ointment she gave was "very precious" (Mark xiv. 3), his complaint was very provoking; her name, like the ointment, is fragrant, his betrayal is obnoxious; and she had kept the spikenard in loving anticipation of Christ's burial, he carried the bag to his discredit.

might by His Spirit in the inner man that Christ may dwell in your heart by faith" is the Divine word. Mark, the strengthening is, "that *the* Christ" (the definite article is in the original), that is, the Christ *as* the Christ. When we have the Anointer we have the Anointing. Two Christians in the City of St. Louis came to the writer at the close of a meeting and said, "We want this filling of the Spirit about which you have been speaking." I found they were cleansed and yielded, but had no consciousness of their need being met. They prayed and asked for what they wanted, but were not satisfied. At last I said, "Won't you take the Filler and thus get the Filling?" They did and went away, not occupied with their experience, but taken up with Christ.

What was the result of the broken box of spikenard in Mary's case? "The house was filled with the odour of the ointment." Likewise when there is brokenness of spirit there is the odour of the grace of humility, and after all, humility is the highest form of holiness, for it is

—" that low, sweet root,
From which all heavenly virtues shoot."

Syllabus of

The Oil as an Emblem of the Holy Spirit

I. *Oil in the wounds*—The activity of the Good Samaritan—God's decisive work—Verbs in passive voice and aorist tense—II. *Oil in the lampstand*—Seven lights in the home—Mothers of Washington, Chrysostom and Wesley—The scold taken out—What Georgia's shining did—III. *Oil in the branches*—Interpretation of Zechariah iv.—A quotation—" The supply "—Question to lady in New York—Three S's—IV. Oil in a cruse—" Is thy cruse of comfort wasting ?"—George Macdonald's saying—Sustained—Play upon the word " comfort " in II. Corinthians i. 3-7, R.V.—V. *Oil in a pot*—A threefold debt—" Lord unctionize our pastor "—The work of the Spirit in Korea—What the Korean Christians did—VI. *Oil on the face*—The tramp and William Pennefather—George Müller and the 23rd Psalm in his face—" Sin makes us ugly, but the grace of God makes us good looking "—The boy and his teacher—A spoonful of sunshine—" Ten cents of glory divine "—The Transformer—VII. *Oil on the ear*—Oil on the blood—Bible reading on the " ear "—Message on the tombstone—VIII. *Oil on the hand*—A. A. Bonar's comment—Bible reading on the " hand "—Seven whatsoevers—Phidias and the hair—What Wm. Burns said to the lady—IX. *Oil on the foot*—Bible reading on the " feet "—The wood sorrel—X. *Oil on the head*—Words on pouring—The Spirit " upon "—" Epi " with the accusative—Spirit's illumination—The agnostic and his " soulless universe " and Adolphe Monod's " All in Christ "—XI. *Oil in, and on, the meal-offering*—Typical meaning—Kellogg's comment—XII. *Oil from the olive*—Geikie on " Beaten " and pressed oil—The oil press of Gethsemane—The coloured man's 'Varsity—" You need more oil in your vessel."

THE OIL

IN many places where oil is mentioned in the Old Testament, the reference is to the holy anointing oil or ointment. We shall not refer to these, but confine ourselves to one line of thought in thinking of oil as an emblem of the Spirit, namely, the places where oil was found as illustrative of the Spirit's ministry.

I. OIL IN THE WOUNDS.

The whole being of the Good Samaritan was active in his compassion for the man who fell among thieves. The Good Samaritan had legs of mercy, for he came where the wounded man was ; he had eyes of kindness, for he saw him ; he had a heart of love, for he had compassion upon him ; he had hands of help, for he bound up his wounds ; he had self-denial, for he put him on his own beast ; he had supporting grace, for he brought him to an inn ; he had loving care, for he took care of him ; he had gracious forethought, for he provided for his future ; and he had a ministry of healing, for he poured into his wounds oil and wine (Luke x. 30-37). All this speaks of the greater Good Samaritan, Who ever ministers to us the oil of the Spirit and the wine of His joy.

The old life of sin leaves many wounds, but He Who was wounded for us can heal our wounds. If the sin-scars are not removed, the sin-fester is cleansed by the oil of the Spirit's presence. "Such were some of ye," says the Lord, in reminding the saints at Corinth of their former associates in iniquity ; but He also says, " but ye are washed, but ye are sanctified, but ye are justified in the name of the Lord Jesus, and by the Spirit of our God " (1. Corinthians vi. 11). Washed by the blood of Christ, justified in Him Who is the righteousness of God, and sanctified by the Spirit. Godet tersely points out that these acts are Divine, and that the verbs are passive as well as being in the aorist tense—"The verbs which express the two facts of justification and sanctification are in the passive, for they signify two Divine acts. . . . the two verbs in the aorist* can only refer both of them to a deed done once for all, and not to a continuous state." The Spirit of God always does clean and definite work. There is no parleying with Him.

II. Oil in the Lampstand.

The golden lampstand was made for a specific purpose, namely, to illuminate the holy place of the Tabernacle. The cause of the light was the oil—" Oil for the light " (Exodus xxv. 6 ; xxxv. 8, 14, 28 ; xxxix. 37 ; Numbers iv. 16). As the light was to give light in the holy place, so there is one place which should ever be sacred to the child of God, and that is, his own home. The home is the place where the light needs to shine most. As there was a sevenfold light given by the seven lamps of the lampstand, so the Spirit will produce by His grace the light of love in the heart, the light of gentleness in the manner, the light of graciousness in the bearing, the light of holiness in the life, the light of righteousness in the action, the light of helpfulness in the service, and the light of faithfulness in the testimony.

The Spirit emphasizes the necessity of first showing " piety at home " (1. Timothy v. 4) ; and that fitness to rule in the house of God's assembly is evidenced in being able to rule well one's own home (1. Timothy iii. 4). If the context of the above Scriptures is studied, it will be found that the former refers to the children in their attitude towards their parents, and the latter speaks of the rule of the parents over their children. Who can tell the influence of a mother's consistent and gentle life ? It was said, " George Washington commanded the forces of the United States, but Mary Washington commanded George. Chrysostom's mother made his pen for him." The mother of the Wesleys shaped their characters by her prayers and holiness, and behind her was the unseen working of the Spirit.

There is no one needs the oil of consecrating grace so much as a parent, for

" Children know,
Instinctive taught the friend and foe."

---

* The aorist tense in Greek refers to some definite act in the past.

The children are quick to notice inconsistencies, and keen to appreciate the kindliness of Christian behaviour. A lady who had a dreadful temper, and used to scold her husband and children, prayed for the Holy Spirit to come into her heart and take the temper away, and He did. About two weeks afterward she overheard her children as they were talking at their play, when one said to the other, " Don't do that. If you do mother will scold." " No, she won't," was the reply, " the Lord has taken all the scold out of her." He will do the same for all who will let Him.

While travelling in Canada some years ago, I came across the following in tract form, which illustrates how we can, each of us, by the Spirit, shine for Christ :—

Georgia Willis, who helped in the kitchen, was rubbing the knives. Somebody had been careless and let one get rusty, but Georgia rubbed with all her might ; rubbed and sang softly a little song.

" In the world is darkness,
So we must shine,
You in your small corner,
And I in mine."

" What do you rub at them knives for ever for ?" Mary said. Mary was the cook.

" Because they are in my corner," Georgia said brightly. " ' *You in your small corner,*' you know, ' *and I in mine.*' I'll do the best I can—that's all I can do."

" I wouldn't waste my strength," said Mary. " I know no one will notice."

" Jesus will," said Georgia, and then she sang again,—

" You in your small corner,
And I in mine."

" This steak is in my corner, I suppose," said Mary to herself, " If that child must do what she can, I s'pose I must. If He knows about knives it's likely He does about steak," and she broiled it beautifully.

" Mary, the steak was very nicely done to-day," Miss Emma said.

" That's all along of Georgia," said Mary, with a pleased red face, and then she told about the knives.

Miss Emma was ironing ruffles, she was tired and warm, " Helen will not care whether they are fluted nicely or not," she said, " I'll hurry over them " ; but after she heard about the knives she did her best.

" How beautiful my dress is done," Helen said, and Emma, laughing, answered, " That is owing to Georgia " ; then she told about the knives.

" No," said Helen to her friend who urged, " I really cannot go with you this evening. I am going to prayer-meeting ; *my corner* is there."

" Your corner ! What do you mean !" Then Helen told about the knives.

" Well," said the friend, " If you will not go with me, perhaps I will with you," and they went to the prayer-meeting.

" You helped us ever so much with the singing this evening,"—That was what their pastor said to them as they were going home,—" I was afraid you wouldn't be there."

" It was owing to our Georgia," said Helen. " She seemed to think she must do what she could, if it was only knives." Then she told him the story.

" I believe I will go in here again," said the minister, stopping before a poor little house. " I said yesterday there was no use, but I must do what I can." In the house a sick man was lying. Again and again the minister had called, but he wouldn't listen to him ; but to-night he said, " I have come to tell you a little story." Then he told him about Georgia Willis, about her knives and her little corner, and her " doing what she could." And the sick man wiped the tears from his eyes and said, " *I'll find my corner too ;* I'll try to shine for Him." And the sick man was Georgia's father. Jesus, looking down at her that day, said, " She has done what she could," and He gave the blessing.

" I believe I won't go to walk," said Helen, hesitatingly. " I'll finish that dress of mother's ; I suppose I can if I think so."

" Why, child, are you here sewing ?" her mother said ; " I thought you had gone to walk."

"No, ma'am; this dress seemed to be in *my corner*, so I thought I would finish it."

"In your corner," her mother repeated in surprise; and then Helen told about the knives. The door bell rang, and the mother went thoughtfully to receive her pastor. "I suppose I could give more," she said to herself as she slowly took out the ten dollars that she had laid aside for missions. "If that poor child in the kitchen is trying to do what she can, I wonder if I am! I'll make it twenty-five."

And Georgia's guardian angel said to another angel, "Georgia Willis gave twenty-five dollars to our dear people in India to-day."

"Twenty-five dollars," said the other angel, "Why, I thought she was poor?"

"Oh, well, she is, but her Father in heaven isn't, you know. She did what she could, and He did the rest."

"But Georgia knew nothing about all this, and the next morning she brightened her knives and sang cheerily:—

"In the world is darkness,
So we must shine,
You in your small corner,
And I in mine."

III. OIL IN THE BRANCHES.

Zechariah had a vision of a golden lampstand with seven branches and lamps, and a bowl on the top. The lampstand was connected with two olive trees, which poured their oil into the bowl by means of two tubes and two branches (Zechariah iv. 1-3, 11-14). That the oil has distinct reference to the Holy Spirit is clearly stated in Zech. iv. 6, and is beyond all question. *Historically*, the reference is to Joshua and Zerubbabel, who were qualified to execute the work of the temple. *Prophetically*, there is a forecast to the two witnesses, who are energized by the Spirit to witness for the Lord during the time of the great tribulation (Revelation xi. 4); and *typically* or *emblematically* we see there is a beautiful illustration of the ministry of grace now. Many are the typical interpretations given of this vision, we beg to give yet another because of its continuity of thought. The two olive trees are

G

emblematic of the twofold revelation of God in Christ, as Light and Love; the tubes and branches " through " (margin, " by the hand of ") which the oil is emptied out are typical of the mediatorial and priestly work of Christ, by means of Whose atonement and priesthood the Spirit comes to us (Zechariah iv. 11, margin); the bowl into which the oil flows as a reservoir for the branches which fed the lamps is emblematic of the Risen Lord Who lives as the Christ (the Anointer) to supply the Spirit; the oil in the branches typifies the indwelling consecrating Spirit; and the oil as the cause of the light is the secret of the Spirit's manifested grace.

The one thought we emphasize is the constancy of the Spirit's supply. One has well said on this: " The oil represents God's fulness for all our need. How does it come? Not by clumsy human mechanism, but by living contact with the two living trees. The oil is ever flowing from the two living Trees, and if the golden pipes are adjusted, and the flow unhindered, and the obstacles removed and the tubes open at both ends, God is continually feeding us, continually filling us. Just as the blood from our heart flows through the veins and arteries to every extremity of our body, flowing without our thinking, flowing when we sleep as well as when we awake, flowing every moment and keeping us alive; so the life of God every moment is pouring through our being, and because He lives 'we shall live also.' That is the perfect ideal of life in the Holy Ghost, not having to go and get a blessing; not having to turn the power on, but keeping in such abiding fellowship, He in us and we in Him, that life will be continually imparted to us, and we shall be continually reflecting it in our life as 'burning and shining lights.' This is the highest type of Christian life. All the struggles, all the efforts, all the seekings, strivings and strainings are preparatory to this, but this is where we want to reach, where we want to rest; not trying to climb the heavens, and, by the slow beating of our wings, reach a higher plane; but, like the soaring bird who is there already and just stretches out its mighty pinions and floats all day long in the blue heavens, so God would have us dwell in God, abide in the heavenlies and have His life ever flowing through us."

Paul expresses this thought twice in his epistles by the word "*supply*" in Ephesians iv. 16 and Philippians i. 19. The word signifies a furnishing upon, a further supply, a constant addition, as the life in the body constantly operating keeps it all alive. " The *supply* of the Spirit of Jesus Christ " means, as Moule says, " A developed presence in me of the Holy Ghost, coming from the exalted Saviour, and revealing Him, and applying Him."

What does this mean practically? It means that Christ is such a living Reality by the Spirit that He satisfies our hearts. " Are you satisfied?" I asked a lady one day in New York. " I am saved," she replied. " Are you satisfied?" " I am saved, I tell you." " Yes," I replied, " I know you said you were saved, but are you satisfied?" " I don't want to answer that question." Instead of being put off, I repeated the question. Then, with a look of unrest and dissatisfaction, she replied, " No, I am not satisfied." How many believers there are like her. When believers go to worldly amusements and questionable places to slake their thirst, it is proof positive that they are not satisfied. What is the reason? The order of the three S's of Deuteronomy xxxiii. gives the answer, namely, saved, separated, satisfied. It is happy to be saved as Israel was, better to be separated as Joseph, but the satisfied life is to be like Naphtali, who was satisfied with the favour of the Lord (Deuteronomy xxxiii. 29, 16, 23).

IV. OIL IN A CRUSE.

One of the most touching things in the life of Elijah was when he went to the widow of Zarephath to be sustained by her in the time of great famine. He must have been surprised to find all the resources she had to sustain him were a " handful of meal in a barrel and a little oil in a cruse," and yet we know he did not look to her alone, for he said, " Thus saith the Lord, the God of Israel, the barrel of meal shall not waste, neither shall the cruse of oil fail, until the day the Lord sendeth rain upon the earth " (1. Kings xvii. 12-16). On the Divine side the incident speaks of God's power and grace to meet the need of His people; and on the human side the lesson is, we conserve what we have by giving it away. We have so little because we give so little. The way to obtain fresh water in the tank is to turn the tap on, and the way to keep our spiritual life fresh, is to share what we have with others.

" Is thy cruse of comfort wasting ? rise and share it with another,
  And through all the years of famine it shall serve thee and thy brother ;
Love Divine will fill thy storehouse, or thy handful still renew ;
Scanty fare for one will often make a royal feast for two.
" For the heart grows rich in giving, all its wealth is living grain ;
  Seeds, which mildew in the garner, scattered, fill with gold the plain.
Is thy burden hard and heavy ? Do thy steps drag wearily ?
Help to bear thy brother's burden ; God will bear both it and thee.
" Numb and weary on the mountains, would'st thou sleep amidst the snow ?
Chafe the frozen form before thee, and together both shall glow.
Art thou stricken in life's battle ; many wounded round thee moan ;
Lavish on their wounds thy balsams, and that balm shall heal thine own.
" Is the heart a well left empty ? None but God its void can fill ;
Nothing but a ceaseless fountain can its ceaseless longing still.
Is the heart a living power ? Self-entwin'd, its strength sinks low ;
It can only live in loving, and by serving love will grow."

George Macdonald says, " If I can put one touch of a rosy sunset into the life of any man or woman, I shall feel I have worked with God." Such a desire is Spirit-born and maybe Spirit-formed, for He never puts a desire into the heart but what He waits to make it live in action. It is one of the glories of the gospel, that the ideals of grace can be realized by the Grace Who gives the ideals. He promises to make His precepts performances. God made His word true in Elijah's case. He sustained His servant through the widow, and the widow sustained herself in sustaining him ; but it was all " according to the word of the Lord " (1. Kings xvii. 16). The word " *sustain* " (1. Kings xvii. 9) is rendered " *nourish* " (margin, Ruth iv. 15), " *feed* " (1. Kings xvii. 4), and " *guide* " (Psalm cxii. 5) ; reading those words with His assurance in Psalm lv. 22—" Cast thy burden on the Lord, and He shall *sustain* thee "—we have His guarantee that He will nourish, guide, feed, and sustain, as we do the like to others. Paul expresses the same thing when he says, "The God of all comfort, Who comforteth us in all our affliction, that we may be able to comfort them that are in any affliction, through the comfort wherewith we ourselves are comforted of God. For as the sufferings abound unto us, even so our comfort also aboundeth through Christ. But whether we be afflicted, it is for your comfort and salvation, or whether we be comforted, it is for your comfort, which worketh in the patient enduring of the same sufferings which we also suffer; and our hope for you is steadfast; knowing that, as ye are partakers of the sufferings, so also are ye of the comfort" (II. Corinthians i. 3-7, R.V.) It will be noticed how the Holy Spirit plays upon the word "comfort," which occurs ten times in these five verses, and which, by the way, is a cognate word,* and is used of the Spirit as The Comforter. The one thought which we emphasize and repeat is, the apostle was able to have fellowship with others in their affliction to their comfort, because he was comforted by the God of all comfort, and he in turn was comforted as He gave comfort.

V. OIL IN A POT.

Elisha, like Elijah, is associated with oil, a vessel and a woman in need. The woman was in a great strait. Her husband is dead, her sons are about to be removed into captivity because of a heavy debt she cannot pay. Elisha wants to know what she has in the house, and she replies, "Thy handmaid hath not any thing in the house, save a pot of oil." Then the man of God instructs her to go and borrow all the empty vessels she can obtain, then to shut the doors, and to pour out of the pot of oil. She poured out of her scanty resource till every vessel was filled. Then she was instructed to sell the oil and pay her debt, and to live with her

---

* "*Parakaleo*" means to call near, alongside to help, and is rendered "*comforteth*," "*comfort*," "*comforted*" in II. Cor. i. 4, 6. "*Paraklesis*" has the same thought, one near to solace, and is rendered "*comfort*" and "*consolation*" in II. Corinthians i. 3, 4, 5, 6, 7. "*Parakletos*" is the word which is applied to the Spirit and Christ. To the former as the "*Comforter*," and to the latter as the "*Advocate*" (John xiv. 16, 26; xv. 26; xvi. 7; I. John ii. 1).

sons on the residue (II. Kings iv. 1-7). As with the other references to oil, so with this, we emphasize one point, namely, her debt was paid by using the oil she had, and the consequences were, her sons were saved from bondage, her credit was enhanced, and she had sufficient to meet the need of her sons and herself afterwards.

There is a threefold debt which rests upon every child of God, viz., we owe obedience to God (the word "*duty*" in Luke xvii. 10 is rendered "*owed*" in Luke vii. 41), we owe love to our brethren (the word "*ought*" in 1. John iii. 16 ; iv. 11 ; is translated "*owe*" in Romans xiii. 8), and we owe the gospel to those who have not heard it, as Paul says, "I am a *debtor* both to the Greeks and to the Barbarians" (Rom. i. 14). How can we meet our liability? Only in one way, and that is by the unction of the Holy Spirit. An aged saint in New York used to often pray for me as together we sought the Spirit's power before preaching the gospel, by the following petition, "Lord, unctionize Thy servant." How much dear Pulis's prayer meant to his pastor he never knew, but the pastor knew the need and always said, "Amen."

One of the most remarkable movements of the Spirit in modern times is the work of grace in Korea. Twenty-five years ago there were no Christians in Korea ; to-day* there are 250,000 followers of Christ, or one convert per hour for every hour of the day and night since the first missionary set foot on Korean soil twenty-five years ago. That result has been achieved on the human side by the distribution of the Bible, earnest prayer, personal service, and self-denial. At one Conference an appeal was made for days of service during the following three months, when a remarkable scene followed. A merchant said, "I am going to do this work continually, but I will devote my entire time to it one week each month." A boatman said he would give sixty days during the three months to the Lord. So one after another the offers of service came, till there were 2,721 days of service promised, or the equivalent of one man preaching Christ continually for close upon seven-and-a-half

---

* June, 1910.

years. The self-denial of the Korean Christians is equally devoted. At the World's Missionary Convention, held in Edinburgh, June, 1910, the following facts were reported : " Already the total offerings of the Korean Church amount to over £25,000 annually, the value of which may be judged from the fact that the smallest Korean coin is of the value of one-fortieth of an English penny, while the wages of the labouring man in America and Korea show a disparity of seven and one-half times against the Korean. Therefore, if the gifts of the Korean Church were translated into terms of modern purchasing power, they should be multiplied sevenfold. The Koreans are heroically undertaking the cost of constructing their church buildings, and Christian school houses, while at the same time doing splendid service in the support of pastors and teachers. Korean men have been known to sell their oxen, and hitch themselves to the plough, that chapels might be built ; to mortgage their own houses that mortgages might be removed from the Houses of God ; to sell their crops of good rice, intended for family consumption, purchasing inferior millet to live upon through the winter, and giving the difference in the cost for the support of workers to preach among their own countrymen. Korean women have given their wedding rings and even cut off their hair that it might be sold, and the amount devoted to the spread of the gospel." When the Church at home acts in a like spirit we may expect the Spirit to act in a like manner to what He has done in Korea. When we use the oil of grace which He has placed in the cruse of our being, we shall find blessing coming to our loved ones, our obligation to pass on the gospel which the Lord has entrusted will be fulfilled, and we ourselves shall find such a residue of blessing which will be beyond all human expression.

VI. OIL ON THE FACE.

Among the acts of God's ministry in Psalm civ., He is said to give " oil to make " man's " face to shine " (verse 15). A shining face is indicative of inward grace. The word " *shine* " is used of the light given forth by the lampstand (" seven lamps shall *give light*," Numbers viii. 2), and of the fire kindled on the altar ("neither do ye *kindle* fire on Mine altar," Mal. i. 10). There is warmth in a kindly glance, and encouragement in a smiling face. "Kindness is a language which the deaf can speak and the dumb can understand." A tramp on one occasion looked up into the kindly face of the late William Pennefather and said, "You, with heaven in your face, will you help a poor fellow." A farmer said of George Müller, "I was going up Ashley Hill one morning, when I met George Müller walking towards the City. Had I not known him, I should have said he was a gentleman of leisure and without a care, so quietly did he walk, and so peaceful and stately was his demeanour. The twenty-third Psalm was written in his face." The inward grace lit up his face. The lack of the inward grace is the reason why many have not a shining face. I remember hearing an old Methodist local preacher say once, "Sin makes us ugly, but the grace of God makes us good looking." Another incident to the same effect. Two boys were playing in a park, when the teacher of one of them passed by. Said one of the boys to the other, "That is my teacher, and she is the most beautiful woman I know." "I don't admire your taste," replied the other boy; "why, she is old, and her face is full of wrinkles!" "Well, but she comes to our house and speaks to me of Jesus, and her face shines with love and tenderness, and it is beautiful." Her heart had the glory within, and she could not help manifesting it, and the boy could not help seeing it. There are a great many Christians who want what the little girl said she took when she was eating her milk sop. The sun shone in it when she put the spoon into her mouth, and she exclaimed, "Oh, ma! I have eaten a whole spoonful of sunshine." Another little girl, being sent to a store in America to get 10 cents. worth of chloride of lime, forgot what she was sent for, and startled the man behind the counter by asking for "10 cents. worth of glory Divine." The glory Divine is the only power that can make us manifest the Divine glory. Sunshine in the countenance is the result of the Spirit in the heart. If we are filled with the Spirit our faces will shine, and the poor perishing world, deluded by the shams and hypocrisies around them, will see beauty and power in us who profess to know the grace of God.

The way to obtain the transfigured life is plainly stated in II. Corinthians iii. 18, " We all with unveiled face reflecting as a mirror the glory of the Lord are transformed (or 'transfigured,' the same word is used of the transfiguration of Christ) into the same image from glory to glory, even as from the Lord the Spirit " (R.V.) When a covering is over a mirror, the person cannot see himself who is looking at it, but when it is removed he can. Believers are as mirrors, and should be as uncovered mirrors, and the Lord is the One Who is looking at us, and as the mirror reflects the person so we are to reflect Christ. The Remover of the veils which hinder Christ being seen and the Transformer is the Spirit, and as we allow Him to do His work, we shall be like Moses, whose face shone, though he wist it not (Exodus xxxiv. 29); like Stephen (Acts vi. 15), and the early disciples, for the Council took knowledge of them that they had been with Jesus (Acts iv. 13).

VII. OIL ON THE EAR.

Having first put the blood of the trespass offering upon the ear of the cleansed leper, then the priest was to put " upon the blood " the consecrating oil also (Lev. xiv. 17). First the blood of atonement then the oil of consecration. That is always God's order. Christ in His vicarious death answering for our sins to our salvation, then the Spirit in His vital grace enabling us to answer to God's word in obedience to our blessing.

The anointed ear denotes the believer answering to God's voice in His word by the Spirit's power. The hearkening ear of obedience (Exodus xv. 26), the bored ear of love's willing service (Exodus xxi. 5, 6), the exclusive ear of consecration's devoted separation (Psalm xlv. 10), the attentive ear of fellowship's ardent attention (Psalm lxxviii. 1), the wakened ear of the disciple's constant instruction (Isaiah l. 4), the opened ear of faith's progressive walk (Isaiah l. 5), and the marked ear of the sheep's following of Christ (John x. 27), are only possible as we are empowered by the Spirit's consecrating grace. In a beautiful English churchyard is a small grave remarkable for its simplicity. On the simple tombstone are these words: " Freddy ?" . . . . " Yes, Father !" Oh! to say " yes " to everything that the Lord commands, then we shall be what the little girl said constituted a Christian, " It is just to do what Jesus would do."

VIII. OIL ON THE HAND.

The cleansed leper had the oil put on the thumb of the right hand as well as the ear (Leviticus xiv. 17). The saintly Andrew A. Bonar, in his commentary on Leviticus, in his own terse and trite way says of the oil upon the leper, " The oil is put on the man's ear—' Lord, I will hear for Thee.' And on his right hand—' Lord, I will act for Thee.' And on his right foot—' Lord, I will walk up and down, to and fro, for Thee.' The priest then pours all that remains of the oil on his head, that as it ran down in copious streams over all his person, he might hear every drop say, ' Thou art His that saves thee.' "

The hand is the symbol of action, hence, again and again the hand of the Lord stands for what He does (Exodus xv. 6 ; Deuteronomy iv. 34 ; Joshua iv. 24 ; I. Kings xviii. 46 ; Job xii. 9 ; Matthew viii. 3, 15 ; Acts iv. 28 ; Acts xi. 21). Right through the Scripture the hand is the representative of what a man is called upon to do or does, thus we have the privileged hand of Joseph's responsibility (Genesis xxxix. 4, 6, 8, 22 ; xli. 42), the stretched hand of Moses' relegated power (Exodus viii. 5 ; ix. 22 ; xiv. 21), the supervising hand of Ithamar's priestly service (Exodus xxxviii. 21), the uplifted hands of Aaron's vicarious blessing (Leviticus ix. 22), the generous hand of loving help (Deuteronomy xv. 7, 8, 11), the persevering hand of Joshua's prowess (Joshua viii. 26), the used hand of Gideon's victory (Judges vi. 36, 37 ; vii. 14, 15), the overcoming hand of David's bravery (I. Chronicles xx. 6), and the communicating hand of the apostles (Acts xi. 30).

There are seven " whatsoevers " which cover the whole ground of the believer's actions. Earnestness should be the spirit of our actions—" Whatsoever thy hand findeth to do, do it with thy might " (Ecclesiastes ix. 10). Responsiveness to Christ is the sphere of our actions—" Whatsoever He saith unto you, do it " (John ii. 5). Devotion to Christ proves our friendship to Him—" Ye are My friends, if ye do whatsoever I command you " (John xv. 14). Thoroughness is the extent of our consecration—" Whatsoever ye do in word or deed, do all in the name of the Lord Jesus " (Colossians iii. 17). Heartiness to the Lord should be the soul of our actions— " Whatsoever ye do, work heartily as unto the Lord " (Col. iii. 23, R.V.) Reward is the outcome of sowing " unto the Spirit "—" Whatsoever a man soweth, that shall he also reap " (Galatians vi. 7) ; and the glory of God is to be the end of all our actions—" Whatsoever ye do, do all to the glory of God " (1. Corinthians x. 31).

It is related of Phidias, the great sculptor, that when someone objected to his taking so much pains with the hair of one of the statues in a temple, because no one would see it, he replied, " The gods will see it !" When we also labour in the consciousness of the Lord's presence, we shall do all, seen and unseen, as to Himself and for His glory. " Are you going to China to win souls ?" asked a lady of Wm. Burns. " No, madam," was his reply, " I am going for the glory of God." God's glory includes our good and others' blessing. Again, we remind ourselves that the possibility of all this is only as the unction of the Holy One is known. Christ acted in the power of the Spirit in all His ministry, how much more do we need Him to operate through us, as the apostle says, " I labour also striving according to His working which worketh in me mightily " (Colossians i. 29).

IX. OIL ON THE FOOT.

" Oil .... on the great toe of the right foot " (Leviticus xiv. 17). The foot is the symbol of the walk or life, hence, we read the wicked " speaketh with his feet " (Prov. vi. 13). Speaking feet are often referred to by the Holy Spirit, that is, in many places where feet are mentioned truths are illustrated. We have the shod feet of Israel's separation from Egypt (Ex. xii. 11), the cleansed feet of the priest's holy service (Exodus xxx. 19), the claiming feet of Israel's possession of the land (Joshua i. 3), the uncovered feet of Joshua's humble submission (Joshua v. 15), the victorious feet of Israel's great triumph (Joshua x. 24), **the preserved feet of God's kept** saints (I. Samuel ii. 9), the sure feet of God's equipped people (Psalm xviii. 33), the privileged feet of God's enriched possessors (Psalm xxxi. 8), the firm feet of the rock-established dwellers (Psalm xl. 2), the turned feet of the quickened one's walk (Psalm cxix. 59), and the beautiful feet of the gospel ambassador's testimony (Isaiah lii. 7; Rom. x. 15; Ephesians vi. 15).

" Walk in the Spirit " (Galatians v. 16) is the Divine injunction as to the sphere and secret of the spiritual life. The wood sorrel, one of England's beautiful wild flowers, grows among the trees in some parts. The plant has shining green leaves, and its flower is a transparent bell with white veins. When it is gathered roughly, or the evening dew falls, or the rain comes, the flower closes and droops, but when the air is calm and bright it unfolds itself in all its loveliness. Like this sensitive flower so is the walk in the Spirit. Let the cold dews of worldliness or the rough hand of sin disturb it then the spiritual life droops, but let the child of God keep in the warmth of Christ's love and the atmosphere of prayer, then the walk that pleases God is evident.

X. OIL ON THE HEAD.

After the priest had placed the blood and oil on the different members of the cleansed leper, the rest of the oil was poured upon his head (Leviticus xiv. 18); Moses did the same with the anointing oil upon the head of Aaron at his consecration to the priesthood (Leviticus viii. 12); and under different circumstances and for different offices we find oil poured upon the head and always with the underlying thought of consecration to some given end (I. Samuel x. 1; xvi. 13; I. Kings i. 39; II. Kings ix. 6; Psalm xxiii. 5). When we turn to the New Testament we find several references to the pouring forth of the Spirit. The word " *cheo*," to pour, is found in several combinations, such as " *Katacheo*," which means to pour down, as when the woman anointed Christ (Matthew xxvi. 7); again, there is " *Ekcheo* " and " *Ekchuno*," which mean to pour out, which is frequently found in association with the Spirit, and is rendered " *pour out*" (Acts ii. 17, 18 ; x. 45), "*shed forth*" (Acts ii. 33), "*shed abroad*" (Romans v. 5), and "*shed*" (Titus iii. 6) ; and there is also "*Epicheo*," which means to pour upon, as when the Good Samaritan poured the oil and wine on the wounds of the wounded man (Luke x. 34). When the pouring out of the Spirit is referred to, it has distinct reference to the gift of the Spirit as the bestowment of power for sanctification and service, as the Lord had promised aforetime (Isaiah xliv. 3 ; Joel ii. 28, 29 ; Zechariah xii. 10). But in addition to the above we find the preposition "*epi*" which only occurs with the accusative case, and signifies one object coming towards another object with distinct intention, thus God makes His sun " to rise *on* "all with the intention to bless all (Matthew v. 45). Again and again the Spirit is said to " come *upon* Christ " with the distinct intention to qualify Him for service (Matthew iii. 16 ; xii. 18 ; Mark i. 10 ; Luke iv. 18 ; John i. 32, 33) ; and the same thing is true of the Lord's people, thus the Spirit was to come upon Mary to beget within her the humanity of Christ (Luke i. 35), He was upon Simeon enabling him to wait for Christ (Luke ii. 25), He was to come upon the disciples that they might " be endued with power " (Luke xxiv. 49 ; Acts i. 8), He came upon the disciples at Pentecost and qualified them to witness to Christ (Acts ii. 3, 17, 18), and in the after days it was the same (Acts iv. 33 ; x. 44 ; xi. 15 ; xix. 6), His regenerating and renewing work is because He comes upon us (Titus iii. 5, 6), and He rests upon us to encourage and strengthen when we are reproached for the sake of Christ (1. Peter iv. 14).

Remembering the head is the seat of thought and stands for the mind, we can understand how much is suggested by the oil upon the head. The Spirit illuminates our mind that we may understand the spiritual things of His spiritual realm ; He inspires our thoughts that we may think God's thoughts after Him ; He controls our intellect that we may ponder His purposes ; and He cultivates our minds that we may be wise and skilful, like Bezaleel and Aholiab (Exodus xxxvi. 1), in His work. The unenlightened mind cannot see God nor understand His ways, like the dying and philosophic agnostic professor, who confessed, " My researches have revealed to me a soulless universe, looked down upon by a godless heaven." On the other hand the Spirit-illuminated man can say, as Adolphe Monod declared, " All in Christ, by the Holy Spirit, for the glory of God, all else is nothing."

XI. Oil in, and on, the Meal-Offering.

Some of the meal-offerings had oil mingled with the flour and also had oil poured upon them (Leviticus ii. 4, &c.) The fine flour is typical of Christ's perfect humanity, the oil mingled with it is typical of Christ being born of the Spirit (Luke i. 35), and the oil being poured upon the offering is typical of Christ being empowered by the Spirit for His life's work (Luke iii. 22 ; iv. 1, 14, 18). The above have their correspondence in the life of the believer in Christ. The new life is the product of the Spirit, and that new life is holy (John iii. 5), and yet we need in addition the Spirit as the Spirit of power to qualify for service, that all may be done by Him to God's glory. Dr. Kellogg, in his book on Leviticus, has reminded us of the possibility of being actively engaged in God's work, and yet not being occupied with the Lord Himself and doing all to Him—" It is sadly possible to call Christ ' Lord,' and, labouring in His field, do in His name many wonderful works, yet not really unto Him. A Christian worker may sow continually the undoubted seed of God's Word, and the apparent result of his work may be large, and even real, in the conversion of men to God, and a great increase of Christian zeal and activity. And it is quite possible to do this, and still do it for himself, and not for the Lord ; and when success comes, begin to rejoice in his evident skill as a spiritual husbandman, and in the praise of men which this brings him ; and so, while thus rejoicing in the fruit of his labours, neglect to bring of this good corn and wine which he has raised for a daily meal-offering in consecration to the Lord. Most sad is this, and humiliating." Is there a cure for such a state of things ? Verily, yes. It is for the Christian worker to recognise God can do without him, and then to recognise that the Great Worker is the Holy Spirit. He alone can make us shine and serve. Without Him we are like the foolish virgins, lacking the essential thing.

XII. OIL FROM THE OLIVE.

The kind of oil is specially mentioned, it was to be " Pure oil olive beaten for the light " (Exodus xxvii. 20 ; Leviticus xxiv. 2, R.V.) The process by which this beaten oil was obtained is described by Dr. Cunningham Geikie. He says, " In ancient times the gathered olives were either pressed, or trodden by the feet, in an olive-vat. The finest oil, however, was that which flowed from the berries when they were merely beaten, not from those that were pressed, and hence it was expressly required for religious services." It is also the " fresh oil " of which David speaks (Psalm xcii. 10). This pure, fresh oil was only obtained by the bruising of the olive berries. In describing a further process the same author says, " The mills used in obtaining the oil are of two kinds ; the one worked by hand, consisting simply of a heavy stone wheel, which is rolled over the berries thrown into a stone basin. When crushed, they are taken out as pulp, and put into straw baskets, which are then placed in a screw-press and squeezed. The oil thus obtained is of excellent quality, though inferior to the ' beaten ' ; but a third quality is obtained by subjecting the already pressed pulp to a second squeezing. The other mill is a hollow cylinder, with iron rods projecting at its lower end. It stands upright, and turns on a round framework of stone, the iron rods beating the olives to pulp as they are thrown in. After this maceration they are put under a beam heavily weighted at the end, and thus, one would think, the last possible yield of oil is obtained. But there is still a little left, and a second pressing, after the already sorely squeezed pulp has been heated, secures this final portion."

The oil of the Spirit's consecrating grace comes to us because of the Saviour's atoning sacrifice. As we see the oil beaten out of the berry, or pressed out of it by the mill, we are reminded of Him Who was pressed by awful sorrow in Gethsemane, beaten by wicked hands in Gabbatha, and crushed by Divine wrath on Golgotha. The place of Christ's agony was fitly named Gethsemane, which means olive press, as Hart says :—

> " Gethsemane, the olive press!
> (And why so named, let Christians guess.)
> Fit name, fit place, where vengeance strove,
> And gripped and grappled hard with love."

We are reminded that the oil of blessing often comes by means of the beating of affliction, the rod of chastisement, and the fire of trial. "In what university were you educated?" was asked of a coloured man. He replied " The 'Varsity where I was educated was in the School of Adversity."

> " When storms of sorrow round us sweep,
> And scenes of anguish make us weep ;
> To sad Gethsemane
> We'll look, and see the Saviour there,
> And humbly bow, like Him, in prayer."

And as we do so we shall find the angel of the Spirit's ministry coming to us, to our comfort and triumph.

"What you need is more oil in your vessel," said one Christian to another, as they were talking to each other about their Christian experience. "May-be," the other replied, " but I do not believe in being too particular, I like to serve God in a general way." There are too many who believe in generalities, but the Spirit is always definite and particular. Mark how this is brought out in the epistles, where in nearly everyone of them the Spirit points His finger on the sore place. Let Him search and save, wound and heal, strip and clothe, humble and exalt, empty and fill, and all shall be well.

Syllabus of
The Fire as an Emblem of the Holy Spirit

Fire associated with seven things—Legend of Prometheus—I. *Fire consumes*—Bon-fire at Ephesus—Spurgeon and the hot iron—II. *Fire purifies* (Isaiah vi. 7)—Prophet's lips touched—Unchristian tongues—" Cleanse her tongue, Lord "—III. *Fire breaks*—Samson's withs—Bacillus of fear—Man in Toronto rushing past the saloon—IV. *Fire softens*—The melting mountain—The monk who would not die—Verses which tell a story—V. *Fire hardens*—" Everlasting burnings "—Fixing the colours—Jonathan Edwards' note in diary—VI. *Fire inflames*—Eating the sin-offering—The Nun's disgrace and substitute—VII. *Fire warms*—" Aha! I am warm "—The Lord's fire—Two secrets of George Whitfield's life and labour—The Word an inspiration to prayer—George Müller's saying—VIII. *Fire cheers*—Why is a fire cheerful? Seven lamps of fire—Collier boy and the light which made him sing—" Good cheer "—IX. *Fire fuses*—What made their hearts, " heart " ?—Iron ore and the furnace—The woman who could not love her daughter-in-law—X. *Fire assimilates*—" Cherubim "—" Blue eyes "—" Let it be done exactly "—I want to be clean " within "—John the Baptist a burning lamp—XI. *Fire tests*—" Eyes of fire "—" Tried by fire "—Testing of faith—XII. *Fire illuminates*—Secret source of things—Why she saw differently—XIII. *Fire moves*—" Tongues of fire and hearts of love "—The schemes to make the factory's machinery move—XIV. *Fire ascends*—" Ano "—Michael Angelo's upward look.

THE FIRE

WE often find that one symbol may represent two or more things. Lion, for instance, is used as a metaphor of Christ and Satan, and yet with a difference, for while it is used to express the boldness and achievements of our Lord, it symbolizes the cruelty and ferociousness of Satan (Revelation v. 5 ; I. Peter v. 8). Fire also, is used of several things. It is a symbol of the Lord's presence, hence, Jehovah appeared to Moses " in a flame of fire " (Exodus iii. 2). Fire is a sign of the Lord's approval. Thus in connection with the Tabernacle (Leviticus ix. 24), at the dedication of the temple (II. Chronicles vii. 1), and on Mount Carmel, fire came down from heaven and consumed the sacrifice, as a sign of God's approval and acceptance (I. Kings xviii. 38). Fire is associated with the protection of God's presence, hence, He was as a " pillar of fire " to the children of Israel for illumination and defence (Exodus xiii. 21), and He promises to be a " wall of fire " about His people (Zechariah ii. 5). Fire is a simile of His discipline and testing. When the Lord purifies the sons of Levi, He does it as a refiner purifies gold, by the action of fire (Malachi iii. 3) ; and when Christ searched the seven Churches, His eyes are described as " a flame of fire " (Revelation i. 14) ; and when believers are tried, they are reminded " the trial of your faith " is " much more precious than of gold that perisheth, though it be tried with fire " (I. Peter i. 7) ; and we are also reminded, " Our God is a Consuming Fire " (Hebrews xii. 29). Fire is an emblem of God's Word, igniting and warming. Jehovah's declaration to Jeremiah was, " Behold I will make My words in thy mouth, fire " ; and later, when the prophet resolved not to speak the Word, he had to confess, " Then I said, I will not make mention of Him, nor speak any more in His name. But His Word was in mine heart as a burning fire shut up in my bones

The Fire

".... and I could not stay" (Jeremiah v. 14; xx. 9). Fire speaks of God's judgment. When Aaron's sons brought the strange fire in their self-willed effrontery, "there went out fire from the Lord, and devoured them" (Leviticus x. 2); and fire is also an emblem of the Holy Spirit, for He is compared to "seven lamps of fire burning before the throne" (Revelation iv. 5), and His gifts at Pentecost are compared to "cloven tongues like as of fire" (Acts ii. 3).

There is an old Greek legend of one Prometheus, who is said to have climbed up to heaven and stolen fire from thence. Because of his act Jupiter is said to have chained Prometheus to a rock on Mount Caucasus, where he was tormented by an eagle. Christ is our Prometheus, Who by means of His atoning death has procured for us the fire of the Holy Spirit's presence and power. The Pascal Lamb of Calvary has secured for us the Pentecost of the Comforter. The opened heaven of the Coming Spirit has been secured by the open side of the crucified Saviour. The smitten Rock sends forth the streams of the Spirit's grace.

Directly and indirectly the Spirit's might and ministry may be compared to fire. The zeal of service, the flame of love, the fervour of prayer, the earnestness of testimony, the devotion of consecration, the sacrifice of worship, and the igniting-power of influence are attributable to the Spirit.

> " Every virtue we possess,
> And every victory won,
> And every thought of holiness
> Are His alone."

As we ponder the action of fire, we shall find how the Spirit is represented by this emblem.

I. FIRE CONSUMES.

One of the most searching of the designations applied to God is, "A consuming Fire." As such He has been the Consumer of the enemies of His people (Deuteronomy ix. 3); the Destroyer of those who, like Achan, have dared to touch God's devoted things (Joshua vii. 15-25); and a deterrent to His people to keep them from disobedience (Deut. iv. 24; Hebrews xii. 29). One of the practical outcomes of the ministry of Paul at Ephesus was, " Many of them also which used curious arts brought their books together, and burned them before all " (Acts xix. 19). In other words, the things which were associated with their old life were burned. Well for all God's people if there was a bonfire of all the old things of the Egyptian world and self-life at the commencement of the Christian career, but alas! we often find, as Israel brought some of the dough out of Egypt with them, so the saints often bring some one thing into the new life. " Utterly destroy all," was God's command to King Saul (I. Samuel xv. 3) regarding Amalek, but Saul compromised, and received his death-thrust from an Amalekite in consequence (II. Samuel i. 6-10).

The dross of pride, the rags of self-righteousness, the leaves of an empty profession, the stubble of questioning doubt, the thorns of prickly temper, the filth of unholy desire, the chaff of useless endeavour, the roots of black bitterness, the straw of pretentious unreality, and the refuse of unprofitable talk, need to be consumed. Who can consume these ? " The Spirit of Burning " (Isaiah iv. 4). He can, and He will if we will let Him. Mr. Spurgeon says : " You may write on wax and only make the record fair. Take a hot iron and roll it across the wax, and it is all gone. That seems to be what the Lord did with Paul's heart. It was all written over with blasphemy and rebellion, and He rolled the hot iron of burning over his soul and the evil inscription was all gone. He ceased to blaspheme, and he began to praise." Christ will do the same for all who will let Him.

II. FIRE PURIFIES.

When Isaiah confessed his undoneness and his uncleanness, then the Seraph took a live coal from the altar and placed it to his lips, and said, " Lo, this hath touched thy lips ; and thine iniquity is taken away, and thy sin purged " (Isaiah vi. 7). The sin of which he had been made conscious was undoubtedly some lip-sin. There is no member of the body which sins so readily, and which needs to be purified, as the tongue. There is the thoughtless tongue of hasty speech, like David's, when he said in his haste, " All men were liars "

(Psalm cxvi. 11); there is the self-assertive tongue of self-confidence, like Peter's, when he avowed his fidelity to the Lord and then denied him (Luke xxii. 33); there is the proud tongue of self-inflation, which boasts with Nebuchadnezzar, and says, "Is not this great Babylon, which I built" (Dan. iv. 30); there is the unguarded tongue of hasty conclusion, like Paul's, when he called the high priest "a whited wall" (Acts xxiii. 3); there is the gossiping tongue of unholy exaggeration, like the widows about whom the apostle wrote to Timothy (1. Timothy v. 13); there is the unclean tongue of suggestive allusion, which we are commanded not to allow—"Put off . . . . all filthy communication out of your mouth" (Colossians iii. 8); there is the questioning tongue of crippling doubt, like Gideon's, when he met the Lord with his vocabulary of unbelief (Judges vi. 13); there is the fiery tongue of unbridled temper, like Jonah's, when he was angry at the action of God towards Nineveh (Jonah iv. 1-4); there is the unkind tongue of unjust reflection, like Absalom's, when he stole the hearts of the people from David (II. Samuel xv. 1-9); and there is the dumb tongue of unfaithful reserve, like Isaiah's, for his confession may read, "I have been dumb."

As the Seraph touched the lips of the prophet to his purification, so the Spirit of God can cauterize the tongue of the child of God and thus cleanse away the unholiness and uncleanness of the lips. "I confess I have been guilty of gossiping," wailed a child of God in humble contrition, "and I want the Lord to forgive me." At this, the friend kneeling at her side, said, "Oh! He'll forgive you, He'll forgive you," and then she prayed, "But cleanse her tongue, Lord." That's it, it is not enough to obtain forgiveness, there must be cleansing too, yea, the inner being must be right with the Lord, for a foul tongue has its root of evil in an unclean heart. Let the Spirit purge away the uncleanness, and make the tongue sweet, because sweetened by His presence within.

Don't draw back from the fire of discipline, remember it is a proof of sonship. "Everything that may abide the fire, ye shall make it go through the fire, and it shall be clean" (Numbers xxxi. 23).

> " For the common wooden vessel,
>   'Tis enough it should
> Simply have the water cleansing,
>   It is only wood ;
> But for vessels, costly, golden,
>   Used for service higher,
> They are only made the brighter,
>   Passing through the fire.
> Am I tempted in the furnace
>   From my heart to cry,
> ' Stay Thine hand ! Oh, 'tis enough, Lord !
>   Still the agony.
> Till Thine image is reflected
>   In the burnished gold,
> Lord, I ask that Thou wilt grant me
>   Patience manifold.' "

III. Fire breaks.

When Samson was endued with the Spirit's power, through the locks of his consecration, he was able, when the Philistines bound him, to snap the withs " as a thread of tow is broken when it toucheth the fire " (Judges xvi. 9). During a cholera scare, at a meeting of physicians in Berlin, a practitioner in that city, said that all fear of a cholera epidemic in the German metropolis was groundless, adding : " But we have much to fear from another source. A bacillus has recently been located here which prostrates those whom it attacks, increases with alarming rapidity, enters and works havoc despite cleanliness and rational diet, spreads not only by contact, but is communicated through the mail and public press. No class is exempt and no physician has devised a remedy. I refer to the fear bacillus. It embitters the lives of those whom it attacks, for it marks as poison the things that are the most toothsome, it banishes cigars and beer from the homes of men to whom a smoke and drink are essential, and it converts the ordinary kitchen into a laboratory. Even medical students have been attacked, and it is a sad spectacle to see these fellows drinking milk while they sing ' Gaudeamus igitur.' In its virulent form there is no disease so difficult to conquer."

It goes without the saying we are not prepared to endorse what the physician said, about " cigars and beer," but what he said about the "fear bacillus" is only too true. Many frighten themselves into illnesses. The same is true with some of the Lord's people, they fear they will fail, and they fail because they fear. A Christian man in Toronto, whose weakness had been indulgence in strong drink, was filled with such fear, after his conversion, when passing a drinking-saloon, that he would come out in a sweat and rush past the place as if the devil was after him. He felt it was not becoming to a child of God, that he should have such a haunting fear pursuing him, he therefore prayed that the Holy Spirit would break the yoke of fear, and He did, and the consequence was, as he himself said, "I can now walk past these places with all the dignity of a child of God, and without any fear of entering them."

One feature of the Spirit's enduement at Pentecost was, the boldness or confidence which characterized the saints (Acts iv. 13). Peter, for instance, before the Spirit's delivering grace, was afraid of a servant maid, but afterward no fear is seen. The fire of the Spirit had snapped the withs of fear and he was a free man. The fear of man, the fear of failure, the fear of the world's laughter, the fear of ridicule, the fear of loss, and the fear of not having the good opinion of others, will bind us tighter than ever Samson was bound by the Philistines, and only the Spirit can free us, but He can, to our joy in God and confidence before others. He, who fears God, need fear no one.

IV. FIRE SOFTENS.

The Psalmist says, "As wax melteth before the fire, so let the wicked perish before Elohim" (Psalm lxviii. 2). The prophet also prays, "Oh that Thou wouldest rend the heavens, and come down, that the mountains might flow down at Thy presence, as when the melting fire burneth" (Isaiah lxiv. 1, 2). The wicked that the spiritual mind cries against is the wicked and wilful self. The mountain that needs to be melted by the Spirit's fiery presence is the mountain of our own will. There is a story told of a monk who was disobedient to the law of his superior in the monastry, and was taken out to be buried alive. He was placed standing in the grave, and the earth was filled in so that he could not move his feet. The superior asked him, " Are you dead yet ?" and he said, " No." The earth was then filled in, until it rose to his chest, and it was difficult for him to breathe, and when the question was repeated, he said, " No, I will not die." The earth was then filled in until it was almost impossible for the man to speak, and a few more shovelfuls of earth would have smothered him, and he said, " I will give up. I will die." When we are willing to die to self, then the Lord points to the cross, and says, " See yourself dead in My death, now believe yourself is dead, and henceforth let it be, no longer your self-life, but I Myself, your life.

> " Yes, I was living to myself—was dead ;
> Self, with its hopes and dreams, was all I had ;
> But soon the Lord fulfilled my prayer to know
> The power of HIS CROSS—'twas death below,
> I asked contrition—and He sent me pain ;
> For purity—but anguish came again ;
> I asked I might be meek—He broke my heart ;
> I asked—I knew not what—the better part ;
> I asked to know what death was to the world,
> And quickly all my living hopes were spoiled :
> I asked to be like Him—His image bear—
> He placed me in a furnace, sitting there
> Like one refining silver, till He see
> The reflex of His image bright in me ;
> I asked that I the daily Cross might bear,
> It lacerated me—the wounds I wear ;
> I blindly prayed, not knowing how nor what—
> He took me at my word, it mattered not.
>
>   * * * *
>
> Then I began to shrink from following near,
> And well-nigh prayed Him to depart, through fear ;
> To suffer was not pleasing to the flesh—
> I feared to pray, lest suffering come afresh.
> But I had gone too far—*on I must go*—
> The virtues of His Cross had pierced me through ;
> In me, His promise now fulfilled must be,
> ' I, lifted up, will draw all men to me.'
> Ah ! I had only heard of love, but now
> I feel it—oh ! I feel its living glow.
> He fastened on me *such* a look of love,
> Withering to self, tender all words above—
> Follow I must, whatever may betide ;

THE FIRE

I love the Cross, I shelter in His side—
That riven side, from which the glory beams,
Whence life and healing flow in living streams.

* * * *

Only by *gazing* I become like Him—
His name is all to me—He dwells within ;
My calling is to live with Him alone,
Unlike all others, lacking what they own ;
Content to be by all the world despised,
Knowing that I by HIM am loved and prized ;
Content to be like HIM, and call HIM mine,
In fellowship, ineffable, Divine ;
Happy to lose the brighter portion *here*,
That I may gain the weight of glory *there ;*
Happy that when I well-nigh turned away,
His hand was on me, would not let me stray ;
Happy to know that He does all in love—
To bear the Cross below, the crown above ;
Happy that not *my* will but *His* be done ;
Happy in prospect of the rest of Home."

V. FIRE HARDENS.

The prophet asks very pertinent questions when he says, " Who among us shall dwell with the devouring fire ? Who among us shall dwell with everlasting burnings ?" Then he gives a sixfold description of the man who will be able to dwell in the fire of God's holy presence. (1) He is an upright walker—" He that walketh righteously." (2) He has a clean tongue—" And speaketh uprightly." (3) He is a considerate worker—" He that despiseth the gain of oppressions " (marg., " deceits "). (4) He is an honest dealer—" that shaketh his hands from holding of bribes." (5) He is a holy hearer—" That stoppeth his ears from hearing of blood." (6) He is an upward looker—" And shutteth his eyes from seeing evil." The consequence of these actions, which mark the doer as a man of God, is, " He shall dwell on high : his place of defence shall be the munitions of rocks " (Isaiah xxxiii. 14-16). Being in Christ, our " Munitions of Rocks," we have " a Place of Defence on high," and can in Him dwell with " our God, Who is a Consuming Fire," and as we do so " we can offer service well-pleasing to God " (Hebrews xii. 28, 29, R.V.) And thus dwelling in Him, He makes it a holy habit of life to do what He wishes, and thus we become hardened in this trend of life, and do not receive the impressions of evil. Beautiful colours, rich gold-work, exquisite designs, and artistic skill may be seen on the porcelain vase, but a careless touch may spoil them, there is a needs-be that the vase should be placed in the fire, that the artist's skill may be burnt in, and then the colours become permanent. The Holy Spirit is the Artist and the Fire. He alone can produce the beautiful colours of a holy life and make the character impervious to the attacks of evil. He alone can make us resolve with Jonathan Edwards, who wrote in his diary these words, "*If I believed that it were permitted to one man—and only one—in this generation, to lead a life of complete consecration to God, I would live in every respect as though I believed myself to be that one.*" The Apostle Paul was another one, hence, he made it his ambition to be well-pleasing to his Lord (II. Corinthians v. 9, R.V.) The result was he was hardened by the Spirit's grace, Who fired him with such an ambition. The Spirit-fired-believer is hardened against evil, he is not moved away from the principles of the gospel, he is fixed in his purpose to glorify God, he presses on to gain the prize of the high calling, and stands in the grace of the Spirit and says in the face of all opposition, "None of these things move me, neither count I my life dear unto myself, so that I might finish my course with joy" (Acts xx. 24).

VI. FIRE INFLAMES.

"While I was musing," the Psalmist exclaims, "the fire burned" (Psalm xxxix. 3). The word "burned" is a primary one, meaning to kindle, or to consume by fire or eating. There were some of the offerings which the priests were allowed to eat. For instance, the sin-offering could be eaten, if the blood had not been brought into the holy place (Leviticus vi. 25-30 ; x. 16-20). When the blood was brought into the Tabernacle, then the animal was wholly consumed outside the camp by fire; but when the blood was not brought into the Tabernacle, then the priests could eat it in the holy place. This has a typical significance for us, who know Christ as the One Who was made sin for us. There is

The Fire

nothing which will so inflame our love to Christ and others, as the remembrance of His love for us. The altar of His sacrifice is where the being of our love is kindled. Adelaide Proctor tells the story of a young girl who lived in a convent in France centuries ago. She was sweet and pure, and admired by all who knew her. Wars swept over France, and a wounded soldier was brought to the convent and placed under her care. When he recovered he persuaded her to leave the convent. She went with him, and lost her good name and everything which made life worth living. Years passed, and she came back to die within the sound of the convent bell. She fell fainting upon the steps, and there came to find her, not such an one as she had been, but a pure and noble matron. She picked her up and carried her in and placed her on her bed. All the years the wanderer had been gone, the other had faithfully done her work, and none knew of her disgrace. When the restored one got well, she glided back into her old place, and until the day of her death, none knew of her sin. What a picture this, of all Christ has done for us. We had wandered out into the night of sin, but Christ came and took our place, and suffered for our sin, then in love He took us into His palace of grace, and gave us a better position than we ever had. We may well feed upon Christ our Sin-bearer, and as we do so, we shall find the Spirit igniting a holy flame of ardent passion, moving us to Him in practical love.

VII. FIRE WARMS.

"Aha, I am warm, I have seen the fire" (Isaiah xliv. 16). These words are put, by the prophet, into the mouth of one who has warmed himself at the fire. The first thing which greeted the disciples at the Sea of Tiberias when they landed was, "a fire of coals there, and fish laid thereon, and bread" (John xxi. 9). The Lord knew the disciples were cold and hungry. What that meal was to those hungry men, the Word of the Lord is to the needy soul. It is food to feed us and a fire to warm us. I know of nothing which will move and warm, when we feel dark and cold, like the Word, and I have never known the Spirit fail to meet me when I have come prayerfully to His Word. There are two things which are said to have been the secret of George Whitfield's life and labour—"his unusual prayerfulness and his habit of reading the Bible on his knees. The great evangelist had learned that first lesson in service, his own utter nothingness and helplessness; that he was nothing, and could do nothing without God. He could neither understand the Word for himself, nor translate it into his own life, nor apply it to others with power, unless the Holy Spirit became to him both insight and *unction*."

There is no power which is so potent as the Spirit's ministry through the Word as an inspiration to prayer. We cannot ponder the words of the Spirit without being led by the Word in the words of the Word to pray. One has well said, "When the believer uses the Word of God as the guide to determine both the spirit and the dialect of his prayer, he is inverting the process of Divine revelation and using the channel of God's approach to him as the channel of his approach to God." Let us remember, as George Müller said, "The Word of God is our only standard and the Holy Spirit our only Teacher." Remembering this practically, we shall always find the Spirit is a Coal of Fire to warm us, and that His Word is ever a meal to satisfy us, and we too shall say, "I am warm, I have seen the fire."

VIII. Fire cheers.

Some one has said, "A fire is cheerful because it is a live thing in a dead room." When John saw the glory of heaven, among other things there were "seven lamps burning before the throne," which are said to be "the Seven Spirits of God." The Spirit is represented in His perfection, hence, the spiritual perfect number "seven"; and He is seen in all His aliveness, for the lamps are "*burning*." There is a reference to the sevenfold designation of the Spirit in Isaiah xi. As the "Spirit of Jehovah," He cheers us by His unchanging love; as the "Spirit of Wisdom," He cheers us by His unfailing guidance; as the "Spirit of Understanding," He cheers us by His unmistakeable knowledge; as the "Spirit of Counsel," He cheers us by His uplifting instruction; as the "Spirit of Might," He cheers us by His unctionizing grace; as the "Spirit of Knowledge," He cheers us by His unspeakable secrets; and as the "Spirit of the Fear of Jehovah," He cheers us by crucifying our affections to Himself, for the fear indicated is not the fear of festering dread, but the love of filial delight.

There is a touching story of a collier boy, whose lot it was to sit all day in the dark and to open a trap-door to allow the trains to pass. He told a gentleman one day that he used to beg the candle-ends from the grim colliers as they passed him. "And what do you do then?" He replied, "When I gets a light I sings." As the colliers cheered the boy by the candle-ends, which he lighted, so the Spirit comes to us and cheers us by the words of our Lord. For instance, think of the six "good cheer's" of Christ. The good cheer of sins forgiven banishes all fear about the past; the good cheer of His Word assures of His imparted life; the good cheer of His presence saves us from all sinking into the depths; His good cheer of calling beckons on to follow Him; His good cheer of victory imparts to us His victory; and His good cheer of direction points out the way of His will (Matthew ix. 2; ix. 22, R.V.; xiv. 27; Mark x. 49, R.V.; John xvi. 33; Acts xxiii. 11). And as we know His cheer we are able, as the apostle was, to pass on the cheer to others (Acts xxvii. 22, 25, 36).

IX. FIRE FUSES.

"Did not our heart burn within us, while He talked with us by the way" (Luke xxiv. 32). Mark it does not say, "our *hearts*," but, "*our heart*." They were so completely occupied with Christ that they lost sight of their misery and themselves, and found their hearts fused into one. Who has not seen a heap of iron ore, cold and mixed with the refuse of earth. How can the precious metal be separated from the stony matrix, and be made one glowing mass? Only in one way. Fling the ore into the furnace and let the fire, fanned by a powerful draught, play upon it, till the dross and rubbish are parted from the metal, then let the latter run off a golden and fiery stream, and it will be shaped by the mould into which it is directed. The love of God is a fire to soften the hardness of the heart, to separate the precious from the vile, and to fuse us into a glowing mass. Many are trying to get the metal of love from the stony matrix of their own heart by the hammer and chisel of their own endeavour, and they never succeed. The baptism of love is the fire to melt and fuse into glowing action and loving act. " I cannot love my daughter-in-law," said a saint to me, as I knelt beside her. She was seeking the fulness of the Spirit's power in a Convention at Beulah Park, Ohio. " No," I replied, " you cannot." " I have tried again and again." " Yes, but you cannot, and will not succeed, and I would therefore give it up." " But," she exclaimed, " is it not right to love my daughter-in-law ?" " Yes, but you cannot do it with your love." " What do you mean ?" " I mean, you have tried in your effort and with your love to love your daughter-in-law, and upon your own confession have failed. The only thing you can do is to abandon yourself to the love of God, and let the God of love so fill and flood your heart, that the Spirit Himself will love your daughter, and then it will be His love and not yours." She yielded herself up to that love, and the consequence was the daughter-in-law soon found out the difference in the considerate action, the quiet tongue, and the helpful ministry, and she was attracted to the love in the mother, and the latter found what had been an insurmountable task became a uniting bond. The same is true in Church life and in every walk in life. Where the Spirit dominates, He never divides, but always makes an indivisible outcome.

X. FIRE ASSIMILATES.

The living creatures in the Book of Ezekiel are said to be in " their appearance like burning coals of fire, and like the appearance of lamps : it went up and down among the living creatures ; and the fire was bright, and out of the fire went forth lightning " (Ezekiel i. 13). They were what they were because of the " Spirit " which was " in them " (Ezekiel x. 17), for He is the " IT " which went up and down among them. Matthew Henry says, " Fire makes all it seizes like itself." The Spirit takes hold of what we are and makes us what He is. " Why are your eyes so blue ?" said one to a blue-eyed child. She replied, " I guess it is because I looks up to the blue sky." The blue of heaven was seen in the eyes of earth.

"Whatsoever is commanded by the God of heaven, let it be done exactly" (Ezra vii. 23, R.V.) "Exactly" is the Revised Version, and it expresses more than the "diligently" of the ordinary version. Exactly, that is, a perfect correspondence. Thus when Moses was commanded to make the Tabernacle, he was definitely enjoined—"See thou make all things according to the pattern shewed to thee in the mount" (Hebrews viii. 5). The same principle holds good in the holy life to which we are called, "Like as He Who called you is holy, be ye yourselves also holy in all manner of living; because it is written, Ye shall be holy; for I am holy" (1. Pet. i. 15, 16, R.V.) Because we are holy in Christ, we are expected to be holy in all manner of conversation, and this is possible as the unction of the Holy One rests upon us. "I want to be clean within," cried a fashionable dressed young woman, as she in soul-agony was endeavouring to get back to the Lord. There was a defiling presence which debarred the presence of the Lord. The heart must be cleansed before there can be "the incoming Spirit in His fulness." A man was diligently rubbing at a window-pane, and being short-sighted, did not see that the dirt was on the inside, till someone shouted to him, "The window is dirty inside." When the inside—the heart—is cleansed, then the light streams into the room, and makes it luminous. John the Baptist was a bright and shining lamp—"He was the lamp that burneth and shineth" (John v. 35, R.V.) The cause of his brightness and burning is found in the Holy Spirit, for he was filled with Him from his birth (Luke i. 15). Would that it could be said, that from the spiritual birth of every child of God he is filled with the Spirit. He alone can make us like Himself, and He will if we will let Him.

XI. FIRE TESTS.

When the Lord appeared to the seven Churches His searching eyes are said to be "a flame of fire" (Revelation i. 14); when believers are made manifest at the judgment seat of Christ, their works will go through a baptism of fire, to test their quality (1. Corinthians iii. 13-15); and the Lord tests the faith of His people, that its reliability and strength may be made known (I. Peter i. 7). Work, faith and character are the three things which are tested in the above Scriptures. Let us look at the testing of faith and see how the Spirit puts it under pressure. Every cable which is used for the anchor on board British ships is put under great hydraulic strain, and when it stands the standard gauge, it is stamped by the Board of Trade as being fit for service. The Lord qualifies His servants by the fire of trial. He tests our faith to find out its *genuineness*, whether we are like the children of Ephraim, who " turned back in the day of battle," and why ? Because they " kept not the covenant of God " (Psalm lxxviii. 9, 10). He tests our faith to manifest its *degree*, to see if we have " so great faith " like the Centurion's (Matthew viii. 10), a " great faith " like the Syro-phenician woman's (Matthew xv. 28), or only a " little faith " like Peter's (Matthew xiv. 31). And He tests our faith that we may become more fruitful, and that He may reward in the future.

" Is not the way to heavenly gain through earthly grief and loss ?
Rest must be won by toil and pain. The crown repays the Cross.
As woods when shaken by the breeze, take deeper, firmer root,
As winter's frosts but make the trees abound in summer fruit ;
So every Heaven-sent pang and throe, that Christian firmness tries,
But nerves us for our work below, and forms us for the skies."

XII. Fire illuminates.

" He led them . . . . all the night with a light of fire " (Psalm lxxviii. 14). The luminosity of His presence was their joy and warmth. Very suggestive is the expression " light of fire." We must have the luminosity of the Spirit if we would be luminaries for the Lord. The light of a joyful face comes from the kindling communion of the Lord's presence, as Moses' face demonstrates (Exodus xxxiv. 35) ; the light of an intelligent expression, comes from the fire of the Spirit's illumination as Paul expresses (Eph. i. 17, 18) ; the light of a kindly heart is the outcome of the flame of Christ's love, as Mary of Bethany illustrates (John xii. 3) ; the light of a beaming hope is resultant from an inspiring revelation, as Abraham unfolds (Hebrews xi. 8-10) ; the light of a shining countenance comes from the inward feeder of the Spirit's blessing, as Stephen shows (Acts vi. 15); the light of a burning zeal has its source in the flame of the glowing Word, as Jeremiah declares (Jeremiah xx. 9); and the light of a faithful testimony is ignited at the altar of Christ's consuming sacrifice, as the early Christians manifest (Acts viii. 4, 5).

One of the outcomes of a Spirit-filled life is a new illumination to understand God's Word. A sister in New York tersely put it, when she said, " His Word is a new book now, and what was uninteresting and difficult is easy and soul-absorbing." When He shines within by a new revelation, we have eyesight to see the truth of what is already revealed.

XIII. FIRE MOVES.

" Who maketh .... His ministers a flaming fire " (Psalm civ. 4), or a " kindling " or " blazing flame." The flaming tongue is the product of the kindling Spirit. He gives—

"Tongues of fire and hearts of love,
To preach the reconciling Word."

The following too sadly illustrates what we find in too many Churches. A minister describes his experience in the following allegorical language:—

" A man had a factory!

" He walked round the outside and then walked round the inside. There were the shafts, all properly set, the cogs, all sharp and clean, the great engine all complete. The machinery was all there, but it didn't move a spoke.

" He was looking disgustedly at the factory when a man came up and said, ' Your factory?' ' Yes,' he replied.

" ' What do you make?' ' That's the trouble: I don't make anything.'

" ' Doesn't it run?' ' No.'

" ' What's the matter with it?' ' I don't know.'

" ' Ah,' said the man, ' I'll tell you; you want to get some hook-nosed oil-cans, and some imported oil,' and he employed men to go round and oil the machinery and all the bearings.

" Then he came down again, walked round inside and outside. Nothing moved. A man came up to him and said, ' Your factory?' ' Yes,' he replied.

"'What do you make?' 'Don't make anything.'

"'Don't it run?' 'No.'

"'What's the matter?' 'I don't know.'

"'I'll tell you; you want to fresco it—side walls and ceiling—and I would recommend you to put a couple of barefooted angels with trumpets eternally ready to blow—and do it properly.'

"So he put workmen in and frescoed the factory, putting a couple of angels on the ceiling, with trumpets at their lips ready to blow.

"Then he came down and looked it over again, but still it did not move, and while he was looking a man came up and said, 'Your factory?' 'Yes.'

"'What do you make?' 'Nothing.'

"'Why? Don't it run?' 'No.'

"'What's the matter?' 'I don't know.'

"'Ah,' said he 'I'll tell you. It has no steeple. You want to put up a nice steeple on one of the corners, and I'd advise you to put in a fine pipe-organ, and get a quartette choir at the same time.'

"So he set men to work, got the steeple up, with a chime of bells that was marvellous, put in a pipe-organ with lots of pipes, got a quartette choir that would beat anything you ever heard, specially on the 'Amen.'

"Then the man came down, saw the steeple and the organ, and heard the choir and the chimes. But not a thing moved.

"'This your factory?' said a man who came up. 'Yes.'

"'What do you make?' 'Nothing.'

"'What's the matter?' 'Don't know.'

"'Does it run?' 'No.'

"'Ah,' he said, 'you want a picture of the thing taken. Get a photographer to take a picture, have a lot of big copies made and framed and hung up all round—in the railway stations, in the hotels, in the barbers' shops, and so on, telling all about the time the thing is expected to move. Say it will move at 11 o'clock in the morning and 7 o'clock at night, and the people will come to see it move.'

" So he got a great big picture taken, and had copies hung up at all the places the man told him about.

" Then he came down, walked round inside and out ; but couldn't see a hair moving. He was perfectly disgusted. Not a cog trembled !

" Just then a working man came up, a hard-handed man. He took off his hat—he was very polite—and said, ' Beg pardon, sir, is this your factory ?'

" ' Who told you to ask me that ?' grunted the owner of the factory.

" ' Beg pardon, but is that your factory ?' repeated the man. ' Yes.'

" ' What do you make ?' ' Don't make anything.'

" ' Don't it run ?' ' Run ! No, it don't run at all—except into debt !'

" ' What's the matter, sir ?' ' I don't know. A man told me to get some hook-nosed oil-cans—and there they are. Another man told me to fresco it, and put in a couple of angels. I frescoed it, and if you will come in and have a look you will see two bare-footed angels on the ceiling ready to blow their trumpets.

" ' Another man told me to put on a steeple, to get a pipe-organ, to engage a quartette choir, and I did. Do you hear those chimes ? See that organ ? Listen to that choir chasing that " Amen " up and down ! Another man told me to get a photograph taken and hung up. I have hung it up ! But the machinery don't move a spoke, and I am disgusted with the whole business.'

" ' Well,' said the working man, ' pardon me, sir. I have never been to school, and I don't know anything about those angels ; but I would like to ask you one question : Did you ever put any fire under the boiler ?'

" ' Why, I never thought of that.'

" ' Well,' said the working man, ' it you will take the chances—it will scare the choir, likely—I will put some fire under the boiler.'

"'Oh,' said the man, 'go ahead. Move it somehow. Make something of it, if it's only ashes!'

"So the working man went inside, took off his coat, opened the door of the furnace, put in the wood, threw on the petroleum, put in the coal, lighted a match, got the fire going, set on the draughts, shovelled in some more coal, and pulled back the throttle valves. The steam rushed into the cylinder, hit the end of the piston rod, the great wheel began to tremble, it revolved, and the machinery all over the factory began to move. A little more coal—and more—and more—and more, while faster—and faster—and faster went the machinery. The quartette choir got scared, and went out of the back door. The whole machinery was moving. Something had happened. Praise the Lord!"

Some few years ago I related the above in one of the most fashionable places of worship in Philadelphia. At the close of the service, the Secretary of the Church said to me, "Mr. Marsh, without knowing it, you have described the sad condition of the Church here. We are rich financially, but poor spiritually; as you see we have a palatial building and a fashionable congregation. We have a professional paid quartette and a skilled organist, but none of them are converted. Everything about the church building is elaborate and expensive, but there are no conversions, and the majority don't want them. Your sermon would displease many, but the spiritually-minded would thank God for it. We want the fire of the Holy Spirit to burn up the rubbish, and to move the machinery of the Church. Pray for us."

Not knowing the inner life of the Church I was not in a position to say whether the statements were absolutely correct, although the brother spoke in no fault-finding way, but as one who had a burden on his heart. This one thing we all need to ask ourselves, "Am I right? Is my life adjusted to the Spirit? Is my heart pure? Am I living to God's glory? Am I filled with the Spirit? Does the fire of His love glow in my heart? Does His grace beautify my character? Has His gentleness made me great? Am I moved as I look on the great mass of heathendom? Have I kept back part of the price? Does Christ dwell in my heart?

THE FIRE 133

Do I love my brethren with a pure heart fervently? Am I sweet in temper, righteous in business, and loving in the home? Do I lift up the fallen?"

XIV. FIRE ASCENDS.

The burnt-offering is sometimes called "the ascending offering," because the word "*holah*" means to ascend. There are many words for "burn" in the Old Testament. There are two words found in relation to the sin and burnt-offerings. The word for burn in connection with the sin-offering means to utterly consume as with fiery judgment (Leviticus iv. 12). and is frequently so used (Isaiah i. 7; Genesis xxxviii. 24; Joshua vii. 15); but the word which is connected with the burnt-offering means to burn as incense and then to ascend as fragrance, hence, the word in its several relations is rendered "*burn incense*" (1. Chronicles xxiii. 13), "*perfumed*" (Canticles iii. 6). The word "*burnt-offering*" also might be rendered "*ascending-offering.*" The word is rendered "*ascent*" (1. Kings x. 5), and "*go up*" (Ezekiel xl. 26). The Spirit of God is not only the Spirit of Burning to consume, but He is also the Spirit of worship to make our priestly service well-pleasing to the Lord. The Apostle Paul was attracted by the "prize of the high calling" without, and was fired by the holy impulse of the Spirit within, hence, he was the man he was. "The high calling of God in Christ" might be rendered "the *upward* calling" (Philippians iii. 14). The Greek word "*ano*," rendered "*high*," means upward or that which is on the top. The word is translated "*brim*" in speaking of the water-pots filled to the top (John ii. 7), "*above*" where Christ says, "I am from above" (John viii. 23), and "*up*" when Christ is said to lift "up His eyes" (John xi. 41). Paul also uses the word twice in his letters to the Colossians, when he exhorts the saints to "seek those things which are *above*," and to set their "affection on things *above*" (Colossians iii. 1, 2). This upward life is the result of the ascending grace of the Spirit. He fixes our affection Christward, and causes the mind to have communion with Him. It is said that Michael Angelo, after painting the Sistine ceiling, found the habit of looking upward so natural that he could not read a book or look carefully at a drawing except in the same attitude. We do not want to be star-gazers, but we do need to be Christ-lookers, for where our treasure is there will our heart be also. The upward life of the Spirit is easy if we have the upward heart with Christ.

So let us pray.

"O Thou, Who camest from above,
　The pure celestial fire to impart,
Kindle a flame of sacred love
　On the mean altar of my heart.

"There let it for Thy glory burn
　With inextinguishable blaze,
And trembling to its source return
　In humble prayer and fervent praise."

Syllabus of
The Rain as an Emblem of the Holy Spirit

The three rains of Palestine : winter, latter, and former rains (Hosea vi. 3)—The threefold work of the Spirit—The coloured man's prayer—I. *The rain as a minister of judgment*—The Lord's dealing in chastisement—" Weak " : a sevenfold loss—" Sickly " : sickness often caused by sin—" Sleep " : cases in point—Why the woman thrashed the boy—II. *The rain a bringer of blessing*—A wonderful promise (Leviticus xxvi. 3-12)—A bunch of " I will's "—Rain : a hand which proclaimed its coming—" The vision was upon him "—Rain is timely in its arrival : " in His season " (Deut. xxviii. 12)—" In due time " and " fully come "—Seven alls—Rain is nourishing in its ministry : " the rain doth nourish " (Isaiah xliv. 14)—Use of the word " nourish "—Rain is refreshing in its blessing (Isaiah lv. 10)—Brainerd on a life of fellowship—Rain is plentiful in its supply (Psalm lxviii. 9)—The two women and their different sized jugs.

THE RAIN

"HE shall come unto us as the rain, as the latter and former rain upon the earth " (Hosea vi. 3). Rotherham's translation is, " That He may come upon us like a downpour, like the harvest rain and the seed rain of the land." There is a similar verse in Joel ii. 23 : " He hath given you the former rain moderately, and He will cause to come down for you the rain, the former rain, and the latter rain in the first month." There are three Hebrew words for the rains, as Dr. Geikie remarks, " of different seasons, and these, very strikingly, are all found in one verse in Hosea. He will come unto us as the heavy winter rain (*Geshem*), as the latter rain (*Malkosh*), and the former rain (*Yoreh*) upon the earth—come, that is, in fulness of blessing, like the triple rainfall that covers the earth with corn. In Joel, also, the three occur together. " He will cause to come down for you the heavy winter rain (*Geshem*), the early rain (*Moreh*), and the latter rain (*Malkosh*) as in former times, and the floors shall be full of wheat." The translation of the beautiful description of spring in Canticles ii. 11 is not true to nature, for the flowers appear on the earth, and the time of the singing of birds comes, at least six weeks before the rain is over and gone. It is when the heavy winter rain ceases, and the warm spring weather begins, that the flowers appear, but it is precisely during this time that, at intervals, the latter rain falls. ... The first, or early rain, moistens the land, fitting it for the reception of seed, and is thus the signal for the commencement of ploughing. It generally begins in October or November, falling at intervals till December. The plentiful winter rains which soak the earth, fill the cisterns and pools, and replenish the springs, come, also at intervals, from the middle of December to March. The latter, or spring rain, which fills out the ears of corn, enables it to withstand the drought before harvest, lasts, with light rains between, from the middle of March till the rains finally cease in April or May."

There are four principal words for rain. First, a general one, as found in Deuteronomy xxxii. 2 : " My doctrine shall drop as the rain." Second, " *Yoreh* " and " *Moreh,*" which are used to express the former rain, which is necessary to prepare the ground for ploughing and seed-planting. " *Yoreh* " is rendered " *first rain* " in Deuteronomy xi. 14, and " *former* " in Jeremiah v. 24 ; " *Moreh* " is translated " *the rain* " in Psalm lxxxiv. 6, and " *former rain* " in Joel ii. 23.

" *Geshem* " is the word used of the heavy winter rains, and is rendered " *great rain* " and " *much rain* " in Ezra x. 9, 13, and is used to describe the rain of the flood, and is translated " *shower* " in Ezekiel xiii. 11, 13 ; xxxiv. 26. The word signifies an abundance.

" *Malkosh* " is always rendered " *latter rain* " in all the eight places where it occurs (Deuteronomy xi. 14 ; Job

xxix. 23 ; Proverbs xvi. 15 ; Jeremiah iii. 3 ; v. 24 ; Hosea vi. 3 ; Joel ii. 23 ; Zechariah x. 1).

The three rains are very suggestive in their spiritual application, as we think of them in their natural setting. The former rain finds its correspondence in the Spirit's initial work of conviction. He must prepare the heart for the plough of God's Word to break up the fallow ground of a degenerate condition, and plant within it the life-producing seed of the truth ; then there is the requisite supply of the abundance of the Spirit's mighty power, that every want in the life may be filled up ; and then there is the essential work of the quiet operation of the Spirit in bringing to perfection the full character of a consecrated life in the Spirit, that the full fruit of Himself may be seen.

How many there are who fail to have the latter rain which is productive of a full Christian life, because they have not had the abundant supply of the overflowing shower of the Spirit's inundating grace. Do we not need to pray for the abundant and latter rain ? A coloured man in a prayer meeting, which had been convened to pray for rain, prayed the following prayer : " We pray for rain, Lord, for rain we pray. We don't pray for a drizzling, fizzling rain, but for a regular down-comer, gully-washer, and ground-soaker !" When we are willing for the Lord to fulfil His promise to send the abundant rain of His power, and the fructifying shower of His grace, He always soaks us with His love. There are no half measures with God, because our God is no God of half measures.

In calling attention to rain as an emblem of the Holy Spirit, we shall note its association in God's Word.

I. RAIN IS A MINISTER OF JUDGMENT.

Sometimes the absence of rain is a sign of God's judgment against sin, hence, in the time of Ahab's wicked reign, there was no rain for three and a half years (I. Kings xvii. 1), and Solomon recognized in his prayer that the absence of rain might be " because they have sinned " (I. Kings viii. 35 ; II. Chronicles vi. 26 ; vii. 13). On the other hand a devastating rain causing disaster and dismay was a sign of

God's judgment, as in the case of the Flood, when " the rain (the great rain) was upon the earth forty days and forty nights " (Genesis vii. 12). Of the rain of hail which came down upon Egypt in judgment, it is said, " There was none like it in all the land of Egypt since it became a nation " (Exodus ix. 23, 24, 34). In the days of Samuel the prophet he called for the great rain, which did not usually come in the time of harvest, because of the people's " wickedness," and the consequence was, " the people greatly feared the Lord of Samuel " (1. Samuel xii. 17, 18). Against Israel's great enemy, Gog, in the latter times, the Lord declares, " I will rain upon him, and upon his bands, and upon the many people that are with him, an overflowing rain, and great hailstones, fire, and brimstone " (Ezekiel xxxviii. 22); and of the man who in his self-confidence will not build upon the Rock of Christ and His Word, but in his self-confidence builds upon the sand of his self-sufficiency, we read: " Everyone that heareth these sayings of Mine, and doeth them not, he shall be likened unto a foolish man, who built his house upon the sand: and the rain descended, and the floods came, and the winds blew, and beat upon that house; and it fell: and great was the fall of it " (Matthew vii. 26, 27).

The Holy Spirit often has to deal in judgment with God's children. He does not deal in judgment with us to our condemnation as sinners, but He does deal with us in chastisement to our cleansing as saints. We have an impressive example in His dealing with " many " in the Church at Corinth, of whom we read: " For this cause many are weak and sickly among you, and many sleep. For if we would judge ourselves, we should not be judged. But when we are judged, we are chastened of the Lord, that we should not be condemned with the world " (1. Corinthians xi. 30-32). Mark the three words which describe the condition of the disciplined saints—" weak," " sickly," " sleep."

" *Weak* " denotes loss of power, spiritual weakness. There is always a cause for spiritual weakness. There are many kinds of power which may be lost. The *power of consecration* will be lost by compromise, as Abram found when he went down to Egypt, instead of staying with God in Bethel (Gen.

xii. 10 ; xiii. 1-4) ; the *power of testimony* will be lost by worldly association, as Lot discovered in Sodom, when he was rebuked by the Sodomites (Genesis xix. 9, 14) ; the *power of a clear conscience* will be lost by self-scheming, as Jacob found, when he was haunted by his wrong against his brother Esau (Genesis xxxii. 6-8) ; the *power of victory* will be lost by fleshly indulgence, as Samson experienced when he lost his locks of power, through lying in the lap of Delilah (Judges xvi. 16-21) ; the *power of faith* will be lost by trusting in the human instead of the Divine, as Jehoshaphat illustrates when he joined affinity with Ahab (II. Chronicles xviii.) ; how different was the case when he trusted the Lord and got the victory over Ammon and Moab (II. Chronicles xx.) ; the *power of joy* will be lost by sin, as David discovered when he lost the joy of God's salvation through his wrong doing with Bathsheba (Psalm li. 12. See title of Psalm) ; and the *power of unity* will leak out, as is demonstrated in the case of the Church at Corinth, by their sectional action, their party spirit, the big head of pride, allowance of evil, quarrelsome contentions, and carnality of disposition (I. Cor. i. 11-13 ; ii. 1-4 ; v. 6 ; vi. 1-7).

The many at Corinth were not only " weak " in spiritual power, but some were " *sickly.*" The sickness was undoubtedly bodily sickness. Sickness may arise from constitutional causes, from contact with infection or contagion, but in many instances with God's children, I do not say *all*, the cause may be permissable in discipline. There are many promises of protection from sickness and disease to God's children, such as the 91st Psalm ; and He promised Israel none of the diseases of Egypt should come upon them if they obeyed Him, which implied on the other hand, they would come upon them if they failed to obey Him (Exodus xv. 26). It may be said believers in Christ are not under law, but under grace ; but we are under the Lord, and therefore have greater responsibility, because we have greater privileges. There are two things we are not to do with His judicial act in chastisement, we are not to despise it by self-assertiveness and non-recognition, and we are not to faint under it through discouragement and fear, but to remember the end in view, namely, to prevent the cause and to yield the peaceable fruits of righteousness (Hebrews xii. 5-11).

Yet another act in the discipline is stated in the case of the Corinthians, " Many *sleep*." The sleep here is the sleep of death. The earthly life of usefulness was cut short. Parallel cases *may* be those of Ananias and Sapphira, and the brother mentioned in 1. John v. 16. Many a Christian worker has had the candlestick of his testimony removed or put out because of disloyalty to his Lord.

The Lord often seems to deal in a hard manner with His children, while He leaves the worldling to his sin and folly. Two boys on one occasion were splashing themselves with mud, as they jumped up and down in some pools of filthy water. Their clothes were being spoiled, and they made themselves liable to take cold by being wet. Suddenly a woman rushed out of a house near by, and took hold of one of the boys, and commenced to trounce him severely, to his pain and distress. When she finished, and the boy was sobbing off to bed to think over the situation, she was asked, " Why did you not thrash the other boy ?" " Oh ! he is nothing to me. He is not my boy, the other was." The mother's love expressed itself vigorously in the needed personal application, although it made her heart bleed sorely, because the boy was her own. So the Lord in the love of His heart's care, often has to give us the rod's share. It hurts Him to hurt us, but we should be more hurt if we were not hurt. He hurts to heal and not to harm. He sifts to winnow away the chaff, and to conserve the wheat. He frowns to make us smile. He takes away to give us more. He burns to bless. He kills to make alive. He chastens to make us chaste.

II. Rain, a bringer of blessing.

One of the promises of God to Israel, upon their obedience to His Word, was : " If ye walk in My statutes, and keep My commandments, and do them ; then I will give you rain in due season, and the land shall yield her increase, and the trees of the field shall yield their fruit. And your threshing shall reach unto the vintage, and the vintage shall reach unto the sowing time : and ye shall eat your bread to the full, and dwell in your land safely. And I will give peace in the land, and ye shall lie down, and none shall make you afraid : and I will rid evil beasts out of the land, neither shall the sword go through your land. And ye shall chase your enemies, and they shall fall before you by the sword. And five of you shall chase an hundred, and an hundred of you shall put ten thousand to flight : and your enemies shall fall before you by the sword. For I will have respect unto you, and make you fruitful, and multiply you, and establish My covenant with you. And ye shall eat old store, and bring forth the old because of the new. And I will set My tabernacle among you : and My soul shall not abhor you. And I will walk among you, and will be your God, and ye shall be My people " (Leviticus xxvi. 3-12). Here are seven " *I will's* " of precious and pregnant promises, which are fulfilled in the life of obedience.

The " I will " of Abundance—" *I will* give you rain in due season, and the land shall yield her increase." The productiveness of the Spirit is always secured when there is the practice of God's commands. Precepts fulfilled will command the promises to be filled to the full.

The " I will " of Peace—" *I will* give peace in the land." Encircled in the peace of God, and garrisoned by the God of Peace, no disturbing foe can alarm us and no distressing care can harm us, for they must pass Him before they can reach us.

The " I will " of Extermination—" *I will* rid evil beasts out of the land." The evil beasts of pride, impurity and selfishness cannot be allowed to prowl around in the land of the Spirit-possessed heart.

The " I will " of Love—" *I will* have respect unto you."

The " I will " of Presence—" *I will* set My tabernacle among you."

The " I will " of Power—" *I will* walk among you."

The " I will " of Fellowship—" And *will* be a God unto you," &c.

Rain : a hand which proclaimed its coming. " There is the sound of abundance of rain," said the man of faith to the wicked Ahab, when there was no visible sign of it. Then with head bowed between his knees, he prayed in the intensity of earnest supplication (James v. 18) till the answer came. Seven times he told his servant to go and look and see if there were any rain clouds visible. At last he came and said, " There was the sign of a cloud like a man's hand," which was the precursor of the " great rain " which followed (1. Kings xviii. 41-45). The cloud like a man's hand, and the prophetic word of Elijah coupled itself in my mind with a greater blessing and other hands. I refer to the uplifted hands, the pierced hands of Calvary, which were held over His disciples as Christ told them of the coming of the Holy Spirit. Those pierced and raised hands of Calvary's Lord, were the guarantee of the shower of the Spirit's rain of blessing. The Calvary of Christ's atonement brought the Pentecost of the Spirit's bestowment. The pierced hands of Jesus secured for us the powerful hands of the Spirit's equipment.

Ralph Connor describes one of his characters, having a terrible conflict with himself as he pleaded in prayer that he might avenge himself against one who had done his brother a grievous injury, and upon whom he wanted vengeance. " Let me go, O Lord ! Let me go !" He pleaded now in Gaelic and again in English. " Let not this man be escaping his just punishment. Grant me this, O Lord ! Let me smite him but once !" Then after a pause came the words, ' Vengeance is Mine, saith the Lord ! Vengeance is Mine !' Ay, it is the true word ! But, let not this man of Belial, this Papist, escape !" Then again, like a refrain, would come the words, " Vengeance is Mine. Vengeance is Mine " in ever-deeper agony, till throwing himself on his face, he lay a long time.

Suddenly he arose to his knees and so remained, looking steadfastly before him into the woods. The wind came sighing through the pines with a wail and a sob. Macdonald fell on his face again. The Vision was upon him. " Ah, Lord, it is the bloody hands and feet I see. It is enough. . . . It is not for me. The Lord will do His own work."

As the Lord Jesus ever reminded His own of the **necessity**

The Rain

of His death to secure the Spirit's blessing (John iii. 14, 15; vii. 37-39); so the Spirit ever leads us back to that death for inspiration and incentive, for that death is not only the killer of all hate, as illustrated in Macdonald Bhain, it is the securer of all blessing, the igniter of all holiness, the essence of all love, the soul of all sacrifice, and the bliss of all joy.

Rain is timely in its arrival. " The Lord shall open unto thee His good treasure, the heaven to give the rain unto thy land in His season, and to bless all the work of thy hand " (Deuteronomy xxviii. 12; Leviticus xxvi. 4; Deuteronomy xi. 14). " In his season," or as in other places, " in due season," that is, at the appointed time. The Lord's blessings are always on time and timely. This is true in nature, for He gives to all " their meat in due season " (Psalm civ. 27); at the appointed time Christ, as the provision of God's grace, died to atone for sin, for we read, " In due time Christ died for the ungodly " (Romans v. 6); and of the day of Pentecost we read, " When ' it ' was fully come " (Acts ii. 1), the disciples were " all filled with the Holy Ghost." We do not need now to wait for a Pentecost, for Pentecost is waiting on us. The Spirit is ready with His grace to bless, waiting with His power to equip, efficient in His strength to overcome, and standing to supply every need. One of the most remarkable passages of God's Word is II. Corinthians ix. 8, 11 (verses 9 and 10 are a parenthesis) : " It is the passages of the seven alls." It might be paraphrased as follows :—" God is able to make—-

" *All* grace to abound towards you, that ye having at
all times,
all-sufficiency, in
all emergencies, may abound in
all good work. Being enriched in
all things to
all bountifulness."

Rain is nourishing in its ministry. " He planteth an ash and the rain doth nourish it " (Isaiah xliv. 14). The ministry of heaven's rain maketh the trees of earth to grow by its nourishment. The Hebrew word " *nourish* " means to become great. It is rendered "*make great*" in Genesis xii. 2; "*magnified*" in 1. Chronicles xxix. 25, and Psalm lxix. 30; "*grow*" in Numbers vi. 5; "*advanced*" in Esther x. 2; "*excellent*" in Isaiah xxviii. 29, and "*increased*" in Isaiah ix. 3. The Spirit alone, by means of His Word, is the One Who can make us great in spiritual things. He can " make us great " in faith as He did Abraham; He can cause us to be " magnified " by a consecrated life, as He magnified Solomon with " royal majesty," for there is no royalty to be compared to a holy character; He can develop the graces of His grace, which shall make us powerful in influence, even as the locks of the Nazarite's hair were allowed to " grow " to his empowerment; He will surely enable us to advance to the higher ground of a waiting prayer-life, even as King Ahasuerus " advanced " Mordecai to the place of nearness to himself; He will by His working lead us to the place of Christian perfection, and thus bring our character into the " excellent " description of His own ideal, which is correspondence to the truth; and He will minister to us His joy, so that we shall be " increased " with the gladness of His ennobling joy.

Rain is refreshing in its coming. " In the light of the King's countenance is life; and his favour is as a cloud of the latter rain " (Proverbs xvi. 15). The word " favour " means to delight in, and to be well-pleased with. God loves all men with the love of compassion, but He only loves His obedient children with the love of complacency. The rain of the Spirit's favour can only make us answer to the desire of God's heart. One of His desires is to see the clean face of a holy life, and hear the true voice of believing prayer. He says: " Let me see Thy countenance, let me hear Thy voice; for sweet is Thy voice, and Thy countenance is comely " (Song of Solomon ii. 14). Brainerd knew what this life of fellowship was. He writes in his diary: " Feeling somewhat of the sweetness of communion with God, and the constraining force of His love, and how admirably it captivates the soul and makes all the desires and affections to centre in God, I set apart this day for secret fasting and prayer, to entreat God to direct and bless me with regard to the great work

The Rain

which I have in view of preaching the Gospel. I had little life and power in the forenoon. Near the middle of the afternoon God enabled me to wrestle ardently in intercession for my absent friends, but just at night the Lord visited marvellously in prayer. I think my soul was never in such an agony before. *I felt no restraint for the treasures of Divine grace were opened to me.*" Mark the words I have put in italics, for they give the clue to soul refreshment. When the Spirit unctionizes with His grace, we are supple in His hands, and suppliants to purpose at His throne.

Rain is plentiful in its supply. The Psalmist says: "Thou, O God, didst send a plentiful rain, whereby Thou didst confirm Thine inheritance, when it was weary" (Psalm lxviii. 9). The word "*plentiful*" means copious, and is rendered "*willing offering*" in Exodus xxxv. 29, "*voluntary*" in Leviticus vii. 16, and "*freely*" in Hosea xiv. 4. The Lord is ever ready to give us His blessing freely. If we were as willing to be blessed as the Lord is willing to bless us we should be blessed indeed. We often grieve the Lord by the meanness of our thought about Him, and the consequence is there is leanness in our experience. If we judge Him according to our conceptions, instead of believing the promises of His Word, we shall have an empty larder instead of a full cupboard. Two women in the East End of London, during a time of great distress, were told to bring jugs to receive some nourishing soup. One took a small jug and the other a large one. The woman with a small jug said to the woman with a large jug, "You don't expect to get that jug filled, do you?"

"Yes," was the reply, "we were told to bring a jug, the size was not mentioned."

The women met outside of the soup kitchen and both of the jugs were filled. Whereupon the woman with the small jug exclaimed, "Well, well, to think you should have got that big jug filled, if I had known it I would have brought a big jug too!"

"Ah!" replied the other, "you have to suffer, you see, because of your unbelief."

He Who loves us freely (Hosea xiv. 4), and Who has forgiven us frankly (Luke vii. 42), and Who has justified us freely (Romans iii. 24), bids us take the Water of Life freely (Revelation xxi. 6); therefore let us take freely, for then we shall have much to give, for as He says, " Freely ye have received," therefore " freely give " (Matthew x. 8). Let us not doubt His willingness to give, but let us ever remember the language of faith. " He that spared not His own Son, but delivered Him up for us all, how shall He not with Him freely give us all things ?" (Romans viii. 32).

" Oh ! Spirit of God, Whose voice I hear,
Sweeter than sweetest music, appealing
In tones of tenderness and love ;
Whose comforts delight my soul, and
Fills the temple of my heart with joy beyond compare.
I need Thee day by day, and each moment, LORD.
I sigh for greater likeness
To Him Who loved me unto death, and loves me still.
'Tis Thine to lead me to Him ; 'tis Thine to ope the eye,
To manifest His royal glories to my longing heart ;
'Tis Thine the slumbering saint to waken
And discipline this blood-touched ear
To hearken to my Heavenly Lover's voice,
And quickly speed His summons to obey.
Oh ! Spirit of the mighty God, uplift my faith
Till Heaven's precious light shall flood my soul,
And the shining of my face declare
That I have seen the face of God."

Syllabus of
The Atmosphere as an Emblem of the Holy Spirit

"In the Spirit"—I. *The Atmosphere sustains*—The water spider—Dr. Moffat's question to the African—II. *The Atmosphere presses*—The three times the Spirit is said to "fall upon"—Pressing in and pressing out—Question put to Christian in House Beautiful—III. *The Atmosphere protects*—The meteor—Works of the flesh and fruit of the Spirit—What the monks did with the endangered organ—IV. *The atmosphere transmits*—Blessing transmitted—Saint who lost her peace—Prayers transmitted—Bunyan on prayer—Gospel transmitted—How the Spirit performs His work—V. *The atmosphere reflects*—"He shall show"—VI. *The atmosphere reveals*—Seven things the Spirit reveals—How F. R. Havergal saw what was needed—Simeon's, Stephen's and John's experiences—Boy trying to read sundial by the light of a lantern—VII. *The atmosphere revives*—Three important tenses—Dr. Moule on Ephesians v. 18—Why the supply of water ceased.

THE ATMOSPHERE

WHAT is the highest form of expression which covers all the work of the Holy Spirit? It is the sentence "IN THE SPIRIT."

The Holy Spirit as the Spirit of Adoption is in every believer, but it is not every believer who is in the Spirit. Paul said of the saints at Ephesus, that in Christ they were sealed with the Holy Spirit (Ephesians i. 13), and yet he urges them to be "filled with the Spirit," or more correctly, "be, being filled in the Spirit." The Spirit is here viewed, not as filling to the full, as the water from the jug fills the glass, but as an element in which the saints were to move, as the fish in the sea, or as the bird in the air. As the air fills the lungs because we are in the air, so the Holy Spirit, as we are environed by Him, not only fills the lungs of our spiritual being, but He environs to our protection. The atmosphere which surrounds our earth is a beautiful and suggestive emblem of the Spirit's protection and grace. Let us think of what the atmosphere is and does as portraying the person and work of the Spirit.

I. THE ATMOSPHERE SUSTAINS.

The atmosphere is absolutely essential for the sustenance of natural life. The breathing of the air yields us three-quarters of our nourishment, while the other quarter is supplied by the food, solid and liquid. The atmosphere is the great fund and storehouse of life to plants and animals : its carbonic acid is the food of the former and its oxygen is the nourishment of the latter. Without the carbonic acid the whole vegetable kingdom would wither and die, and without the oxygen the blood of the animals would only be serum and water.

What the atmosphere is in the natural world, the Spirit is in the spiritual realm of grace. In the highest sense of the word, " In Him we live and move and have our being." The water spider makes its nest in the water, but it cannot live in the water and yet it does. The spider comes to the surface of the pond, and with a quick movement captures a globule of air, and then puts it in his nest and lives in the air, which is in the nest, which is in the water. The child of God, while he is in the world, lives in the inner circle of the Spirit.

There is an incident in the life of the African missionary, Dr. Moffat, which illustrates how the saint lives in the Spirit. The natives had refused food to Moffat, but in the evening a Christian native brought him food, and he asked her why she did it. The native replied, " I love Him, Whom missionary serve." Dr. Moffat asked this Christian how she sustained the life of God in her spirit, amid such uncongenial surroundings. She pulled out from her dress a Dutch Testament, and replied, " This is the fountain from which I drink, this is the oil which makes my lamp burn, and the food which sustains my life." The word of the Spirit is the saints' food. As we walk in the truth of the Spirit, we walk in the Spirit of Truth. The Word of God is God-breathed (the word " inspired of God " as descriptive of the nature of inspiration means God-breathed, 1. Timothy iii. 16), that is, it is the breath of God. So if we want the breath of God, all we have to do is to believingly receive the Word of God.

II. THE ATMOSPHERE PRESSES.

If it were not for the pressure of the atmosphere we should not be able to keep our position on the earth. The weight of the atmosphere is about one millionth part of the entire weight of the earth, and extends about fifty miles above the earth's surface, and it presses upon the earth with a force proportionate to its height and density. It is estimated that the atmosphere presses with a weight of 15 lbs. to every square inch of the earth's surface ; therefore its pressure upon the body of a middle-sized man is about 32,000 pounds, or 14 tons : a pressure which would be intolerable and even fatal were it not equal in every part and counterbalanced by the spring of the air within. The pressure on the surface of the earth of the whole atmosphere, is computed to be equivalent to a globe of lead sixty miles in diameter, or about five thousand millions of millions of tons.

There is one expression which only occurs three times in connection with the Holy Spirit, which suggests the pressure of His prevailing presence, and that is, where He is said to fall upon individuals. Of the Samaritan believers it is said the Spirit had not "*fallen upon*" them before the apostles went down to Samaria (Acts viii. 16) ; of the household of Cornelius, while Peter was preaching the Word, " the Holy Ghost *fell on* them " (Acts x. 44) ; and Peter, in recommending what God had done to the household of Cornelius, says : " The Holy Ghost *fell on* them, as on us at the beginning " (Acts xi. 15). The word rendered " *fell on* " is translated in Mark iii. 10, " *pressed upon,*" where the multitude is said to have " *pressed upon* " Christ to touch Him.

Studying the context of the above three Scriptures it will be noticed, the Holy Spirit came upon those who believed in Samaria, but in the case of the household of Cornelius it was before they believed. With the disciples at Pentecost, they definitely tarried for the enduement of power, but with the others there was no such specific waiting. While Peter spake the word He fell upon the household of Cornelius, while the apostles prayed for the Samaritans they were baptized with the Spirit, and while the disciples tarried, He came upon them (Acts viii. 15 ; xi. 15). This goes to show the Spirit is an absolute Sovereign, and that we cannot command Him as we will, but He will command us as He desires. When we submit to the sovereignty of His grace, we get the grace of His sovereignty. When He determines upon the terms of His visitation, it is well for us that we have no terms to dictate.

> " He gives the very best to those
> Who leave the choice with Him."

When the Spirit presses upon us in the grace of His power, then self is pressed out of the way and Christ is enthroned in the heart ; He presses upon us with the compassion of His love, and loves others through us to God ; He presses us into the realm of His truth, and conforms us to the make of its life ; He presses us with a holy ambition to please God, and makes us careless about the pleasing of men ; He presses us towards the mark of the high calling and fires us with a holy determination to obtain its prize ; He presses upon us the privilege of prayer, and causes us to travail in birth for souls ; and He presses us close up to the heart of Christ, and makes us satisfied with naught but His complacent love.

One of the questions which was put to Christian in House Beautiful, as represented in Bunyan's *Pilgrim's Progress*, was, " Can you tell me by what means your annoyances vanished ?" Christian replied, " When I think of what I saw at the cross, that will do it ; when I look upon my broidered coat, that will do it ; when I look upon the roll I carry in my hand, that will do it ; and when my thoughts wax warm about whither I am going, that will do it." 'Tis the office of the Spirit, as Bunyan suggests, to remind us what we owe to the Christ of Calvary, for all our blessings are blood-purchased and blood-hued ; He brings to our remembrance what God has done for us, in clothing us with the perfection of Christ ; He stimulates us by the promises of His Word ; and He attracts to the coming of Christ, and makes us long to see Him Whom we love.

III. THE ATMOSPHERE PROTECTS.

The meteor as it flashes across the sky, leaving its trail of light behind, might fill the ignorant with dismay, but to those who know, its flash of light is a signal of safety. The meteoric-stone as it falls towards the earth comes in contact with the atmosphere, the consequence is, there is friction set up by the resistance of the atmosphere, and the meteor instead of falling to the earth in its compact form, is frittered away into dust, which is intimated by the flash of light.

As the inhabitants of the earth are protected from the meteors by the atmosphere, so " walking in the Spirit we shall not fulfil the lusts of the flesh." It is with Divine intention that the works of the flesh and the fruit of the Spirit are found in vivid contrast in Galatians v. 19-23. There is the trinity of hell's unholy alliance, and the Spirit's three-fold unique production. Let us briefly note the contrast :—

WORKS OF THE FLESH.

1. *Sins against God and His commandments.*

"*Adultery.*" Defilement of the marriage bed and unholy intention (Matthew v. 28).

"*Fornication.*" Sins of uncleanness committed by persons in the single state.

"*Uncleanness.*" General name for everything that is unchaste in thought, word, or deed : such as the unclean heart, self-abuse, sodomy, and filthy literature.

"*Lasciviousness.*" Wantonness, impure words, suggestive gestures, and unholy sights.

"*Idolatry.*" The worship of anything or anyone other than the true God.

"*Witchcraft.*" Prying into the unseen, enquiring from the dead, spiritism, theosophy, and any real or pretended league with the devil.

FRUIT OF THE SPIRIT.

1. *Fruit of the Spirit in its Godward application.*

"*Love.*" True love has its source, sphere and end in God Himself. Love is Heaven-born, Christ-centralized and Spirit-produced.

"*Joy.*" Joy is a plant which grows in the soil of holiness, and is planted by the best of gardeners, the Spirit.

"*Peace.*" Peace is the calm of God stilling the spirit of man to its rest and refreshment.

All these are the product of the Spirit, and find their life and nourishment in the Lord Himself.

2. *Sins against others, as expressed in malice and social disorder.*

"*Hatred.*" A smouldering fire of bitterness against another.

"*Variance.*" Contentions, factions, and parties.

"*Emulations.*" Jealousies. Seeking to get what another has got for one's self.

"*Wrath.*" Bursts of passion. Unholy anger.

"*Strife.*" Perpetual contradictions and cavillings.

"*Seditions.*" Plots against others to their damage and hurt.

"*Heresies.*" Bad principles, error, opposing the truth, and seeking to undermine it.

"*Envyings.*" Grieving at the good of others. A sour spirit.

"*Murders.*" The intent or act of taking another's life.

3. *Sins of personal excess.*

"*Excesses.*" All extremes, especially drunkenness. The exciting of the passions.

"*Revellings.*" Lascivious songs. Sinful boisterousness. The madness of pleasure and its sinful associations.

2. *Fruit of the Spirit, in its outworking towards others.*

"*Longsuffering.*" Suffering long without retaliation or recrimination. Enduring under provocation and loss.

"*Gentleness.*" A right and true spirit, which is unruffled by opposition and keeps sweet in all circumstances. Like Him, Who is meek and lowly in heart.

"*Goodness.*" Doing good and helping others for Love's sake. Finding in other's need the opportunity to meet it.

3. *Fruit of the Spirit as identified with the individual believer in his relation to the Lord.*

"*Faith.*" The heart's confidence and rest in God, as expressed in obedience to Him.

"*Meekness.*" A spirit which is satisfied with whatever comes and does not complain.

"*Temperance.*" A spirit under control, which is sober in all things.

The way to keep from the works of the flesh is to be away from the flesh which works, by living in the circle of the Holy Spirit. There is a legend which speaks of a golden organ in a monastery which was in danger of being stolen, so the monks cast the organ into a deep river, where it is said it still poured out its sweet music. When the organ of our spirit-nature is in the river of the Spirit's environment, we are kept from the ruthless hands of the flesh, and the music of the Spirit's life is heard to the pleasure of our Lord.

Living in the Spirit there is no vain and self-effort to overcome the flesh and to keep from its works, the flesh cannot touch us any more than the sea-gull can get at the deep-sea fish. It is also an easy matter to love others as the Lord wishes. I remember a brother who always irritated me by his idiosyncrasies when I looked at him apart from the Lord, but when I saw him in the Spirit then the things which irritated me as I looked at the man were lost as I saw the man in the Spirit. Being in the Divine, we shall be able to divine the Divine in our brethren.

IV. THE ATMOSPHERE TRANSMITS.

The atmosphere is the transmitter of all sound. It is essential and indispensable for all the practical purposes of life. If by some miraculous intervention it would be possible to live without air, it would be useless and vain. Without the air the choir could not be heard, sang the voices ever so sweetly; and the preacher could not communicate his thoughts in language, no matter how eloquently he might speak.

How true this is in the spiritual realm! It was when John was "in the Spirit" that he "heard a voice" speaking to him (Revelation i. 10). The voice of the Lord is heard by His sheep as they are in the Spirit. One of the most wonderful of modern discoveries is the wireless telegraphy, but there are two things which are absolutely essential to it, and these are, a transmitter and a receiver.

Being in the Spirit, the Lord can transmit His blessing to us. "I have lost my peace," said an aged child of God to me, as she was feeling the infirmities of old age. I replied, "Have you lost your Saviour?" "No," was her quick response. In the moment of her doubt, as she relied on the sense of feeling, the ear of her receiver had got out of communication with the transmitter of God's Word. But as soon as she adjusted her spirit to the Lord Himself, the interrupted communication was restored, and peace filled her heart.

Being in the Spirit we can transmit our prayers to God. "Praying in the Holy Ghost" is the injunction of the Word. All other prayer is useless, but thus praying we know experimentally the truth of Bunyan's words, "Prayer is a shield to the soul, a sacrifice to God, and a scourge to Satan." There is no power so great as prayer in the Spirit, for the Spirit-environed and the Spirit-inspired prayer, for this kind of prayer opens the larder of Heaven to our supply, it admits the fresh air of God's love to our spiritual health, it plants in the soil of God's Word to our growth in grace ; it puts us in communication with God's dynamo to our strengthening ; it leads beside the Shepherd of the green pastures, His promises and the still waters of His peace ; it sharpens the senses of the new man, to his consciousness and discernment of Divine things ; and it enables him to rest in the Lord with humble contentment and joy.

Being in the Spirit we can transmit spiritual blessings to others if they are receptive. Christ undoubtedly intimates this in His teaching about the Holy Spirit and His disciples. The Spirit is to convince the world of sin, of righteousness and judgment, not apart from believers but by means of them. For instance, by our faith in Christ we are to convict the world of its sin of unbelief ; by our evidencing that Christ is alive in His living in us and operating through us in practical righteousness of life, we are to convict the world of its wrong in refusing to be saved and sanctified by Him ; and by our victory over the powers of evil we are to show to the world that the evil one has already been judged, and his power overthrown in the death of Christ.

V. The Atmosphere Reflects.

The atmosphere is a reflector of light, hence its mysterious and beautiful blue, which contrasts and yet harmonizes so well with the green mantle of the earth. Were the atmosphere deprived of its reflective powers, the sun would appear in one part of the sky with dazzling brightness, while all around would be dark as midnight and the stars would be seen at noonday.

As we are in the Spirit we shall know experimentally the meaning of Christ's word, " He shall receive of Mine and show it unto you." The word " *show* " which Christ uses three times in John xvi. 14, 15, is " *anangello*." It is a compound word. " *Ana*," as a prefix, signifies repetition and intensity, and "*angelos*" signifies an angel, a messenger, a bringer of good tidings. Thus "*anangello*" means to announce in detail, to rehearse. It is rendered "*rehearsed*" in Acts xi. 4. It is the office of the Holy Spirit to rehearse to us the things of Christ and to unfold to us in detail their wondrous glory. The Spirit delights to rehearse the truth respecting the person and glory of our Lord. Take any one of the epistles by way of illustration; for instance, in the Epistle of Christian Experience, the Epistle to the Philippians, the Spirit unfolds in wonderful harmony and diversity, the pathway and glory of the Man Jesus in the sevenfold progress of His downward course from the glory to the death of the cross, and then the corresponding steps from the cross to the height of majestic glory (Philippians ii. 5-8). Another form of truth the Spirit rehearses in the Epistle to the Philippians is the reference to the Lordship of Christ, found in relation to the expression " in the Lord." To be " in the Lord " is to be fearless of the hate of man (i. 14), to act in the consciousness of His presence (ii. 24), to fulfil our obligations to our brethren (ii. 29), to have a secret feeder of joy (iii. 1), to be kept steady amid things which would otherwise disturb (iv. 1), to be independent of our surroundings (iv. 4), and to be content with whatever comes (iv. 10-12). There is no truth so necessary to emphasize as Christ's Lordship, for when we rightly enthrone Him in the heart of our affection, He will equip us with the might of His presence.

VI. THE ATMOSPHERE REVEALS.

By means of the atmosphere we can see. But the seeing eye is essential to appreciate the beautiful light. Being " in the Spirit " aged Simeon was able to see and recognize the Lord's Christ, hence he exclaimed, " Mine eyes have seen Thy salvation " (Luke ii. 27-29). Stephen, being " full of the Holy Ghost," said, " I see .... the Son of Man standing on the right hand of God " (Acts vii. 55, 56); and of John at Patmos we read, being " in the Spirit " he " saw " Christ in the midst of the seven lampstands (Revelation i. 10-20). Man cannot see and understand the things of God any more than a lad could tell the time by looking at a sundial with a lighted lantern at night. Men are trying to understand the things of God by the aid of the lantern of their own reason, whereas they can only be apprehended by means of the Holy Spirit. We are explicitly told, " Eye hath not seen, nor ear heard, neither have entered into the heart of man, the things which God hath prepared for them that love Him, but God hath revealed them unto us in the Spirit " (1. Cornithians ii. 9, 10).

The Holy Spirit is called " The *Spirit of Wisdom and Revelation " (Ephesians i. 17), and as such enlightens the understanding so that it can discern spiritual things. We find all three persons at this work of revelation, the Son reveals the Father (Matthew xi. 27), the Father reveals the Son (Matthew xvi. 17 ; Galatians i. 16), and the Spirit reveals God in the person of the Son, hence the Spirit of Revelation is to give the "knowledge of Him." Again and again we find spiritual things are made known by the Spirit. There are at least seven things He makes known. By the Spirit through Christ " the thoughts of many hearts are *revealed* " (Luke ii. 35), even as the light in a dark cave will reveal creeping things ; the Spirit in the Gospel has "*revealed*" the righteousness of God (Romans i. 17), even as the light in the holy place revealed the glory of the veil ; the Spirit "hath *revealed*" the secret of God's grace in this dispensation, in making all who believe in Christ one in Him (Ephesians iii. 5), even as Abraham rejoiced to see the day of Jesus and was glad ; the Spirit hath "*revealed*" by means of the Scriptures the sum total of revelation, namely, Christ's sufferings and glory (1. Peter i. 12), even as the flaming coal makes known the heat of the sun received long ago ; the Spirit reveals Christ in us, as Paul confessed, when he said, it pleased God to " *reveal* His Son in me," that he might make Him known to others, even as the moon reveals and reflects the light of the sun (Galatians i. 16) ; the "*revelation*" of Jesus Christ is given to us, that we may understand, being in the Spirit, the things which are to come to pass in the future (Rev. i. 1.); and the Spirit is the Teacher given to the Church to com-

---

* There is no article, as the Revised Version indicates, but as with " *Theos* " (God) and " *Kurios* " (Lord) the article is often omitted, so with " *Pneuma* " (Spirit).

municate the spiritual things of God's grace and glory (1. Cor. xiv. 6, 26, 30).

Frances Ridley Havergal illustrates how the Spirit makes known His requirements in the spiritual life. She says in her diary, " It was Advent Sunday, December, 1873, that I first saw clearly the blessedness of true consecration. I saw it as a flash of electric light ; and what you see, you cannot unsee. There must be full surrender before there can be true blessedness. God admits you by the one into the other. He Himself showed me this. First, I was shown the blood of Jesus Christ, His Son, cleanseth from all sin ; and then it was made plain to me that He Who had cleansed me, had power to keep clean ; so I utterly yielded myself to Him, and utterly trusted Him to keep me."

VII. THE ATMOSPHERE REVIVES.

By the heat of the sun an immense quantity of water in the form of vapour is daily carried up from earth, rivers and seas. If there were no atmosphere this circulation could not exist. There would be no rain nor dew. The air causes the fire to burn brightly when it is stirred. The Holy Spirit is the great Reviver to keep the fire of love continually burning ; the Oil to cause the light of holiness always to shine ; the Dew to refresh and keep the grass of humility ever green ; the Spring to cause the heart to be perennially answering to the Lord ; and the Element to keep us ever fresh in the truth.

The grammar regarding the Holy Spirit is full of grace. The tenses which are used in relation to the Spirit are expressive of His definite and continuous work. First, there is *the aorist tense,* which denotes a past and definite act, this is used of the disciples on the Day of Pentecost, who " were all filled with the Holy Spirit " (Acts ii. 4) ; second, there is *the present tense,* which is generally expressed by the sentence, " full of the Holy Spirit," as in the cases of Jesus, Stephen and Barnabas (Luke iv. 1 ; Acts vii. 55 ; xi. 24) ; and, third, there is *the imperfect tense,* hence, " the disciples were being filled with the Holy Ghost " (Newberry, Acts. xiii. 52), and

---

* The words " *Apokalupto* " and " *Apokalupsis,*" rendered " *reveal* " and " *revelation,*" mean to take off the cover, hence, a disclosure.

the same again in Eph. v. 18, which should read, "Being filled in the Spirit." Dr. Moule says on this last sentence, "Be filled with a fulness, habitual, normal, always supplied and always received, in the Spirit. Let that Holy One, your Sealer and Sanctifier, so surround and possess you that you shall be as vessels immersed in this pure flood."

A question is often asked, is the filling of the Holy Spirit once for all? There is a *crisis* in the experience of the believer which corresponds to the disciples being filled on the Day of Pentecost. This crisis should lead to the *process* of being continually filled that we may know the meaning of being " full of the Spirit," so that we may have the " full corn in the ear " of a developed Christian character (Mark iv. 28), that we may be full of faith, grace and power as Stephen was (Acts vi. 5, 8, R.V.), that we may be " full of good works " as Dorcas was (Acts ix. 36), that we may make full proof of our ministry as Timothy was enjoined to do (II. Tim. iv. 5), that we may have the full assurance of understanding in Divine things (Colossians ii. 2), that we may have the full assurance of faith and never doubt (Hebrews x. 22), that we may have the full assurance of hope in expecting Christ's return (Hebrews vi. 11), that our joy may be full through abiding in Christ and Christ abiding in us (John xv. 11), and that God may " fulfil," or fill to the full, " all the good pleasure of His goodness and the work of faith with power " (II. Thess. i. 11). But in addition to this crisis and process, there may be additional epochs as the occasion demands, hence we find in the experience of Peter, Peter was filled on the day of Pentecost, but yet on two subsequent occasions Peter was " filled with the Spirit " (Acts iv. 8, 31). The same holds good in the experience of Paul : in Acts ix. 17 he is told to " be filled with the Holy Ghost," and yet when a fresh emergency arose he is said again to be " filled with the Holy Ghost " (Acts xiii. 9). I am inclined to think, as impressed by the Word, that the crisis leads to the process, but that there may be many a crisis for special need and service. The wrong teaching is, that the process leads to the crisis, whereas the crisis leads to the process. The *crisis* is the definite reception of the Spirit as Lord, Power, and Sanctifier ; the *process* is the

The Atmosphere

continual ministry of the Spirit, so that we may answer to the normal condition of "full"; but should that supply be intercepted, or special service demand, there is another crisis. Some few years ago, when living on Nyack Heights on the River Hudson, the water supply was found to be cut off. There were two theories as to the cause of the cessation of the supply of water. One was, that the supply in the well was insufficient; and another theory was there was something choking the pipes. It was found there was a plentiful supply, then some of the pipes were taken up, still nothing wrong could be found. I knew there was a stop-valve between the supply and the house, and suggested that perhaps it had been turned, shutting off the supply. The man assured me it was not so. None the less when he was not about I went and got the long key, for the valve was some distance in the ground, and amused myself by turning the tap round and round. When all of a sudden my wife called from the house, "The water is coming in!" What had been the matter? Doubtless some mischievous person had turned the tap and shut off the supply. As there was a crisis when the water was turned into the cistern of the house, and then a process by the continual supply so that the vessels in the house were supplied, and yet there was another crisis when the supply was cut off; so the Spirit comes definitely to the child of God as he surrenders to Him, and continues to minister as the believer abides in Christ, and yet should anything intercept His working another crisis of surrender and blessing occurs. There is no third party who can turn off the supply of the Spirit from us. The only danger is lest we should keep back the supply by coldness and prayerlessness, and thus run dry. The reviving of the Spirit shall ever be ours if we continually live in the sphere of the atmosphere of His presence and power.

> "My bark is wafted to the strand, by Breath Divine;
> And on the helm there rests a hand, other than mine.
> One Who has known in storms to sail I have on board;
> Above the raging of the gale I hear my Lord.
> Safe to the land—safe to the land, the end is this;
> And then with Him go hand in hand, far into bliss."

Syllabus of
The Wind as an Emblem of the Holy Spirit

Wind emblematic of the Spirit's activities—I. *Wind, invisible in its essence*—" *Ruach* " and " *Pneuma* " : Hebrew and Greek words for wind—Unseen colours of the Spectrum—Hidden bar in Tabernacle—What the world cannot see and know, and what the saint knows—Feeling a pain—II. *Wind is confined in its operations*—We know whence and whither and how the wind goes, so John iii. 8 cannot refer to wind as such—Quotation from Dr. Archibald *re* wind—The Spirit's special service and encircling presence—III. *Wind is mysterious in action*—Exegesis of John iii. 8—" *How* " ? A Fool's Question—Those who hear the bell the angel rings—IV. *Wind is powerful in its movements*—What a hurricane did in London in 1703—" *Wind* " (" *Pnoe* ") to breathe—The three persons breathing, namely, at Creation, Resurrection and Pentecost—" *Mighty* " : vital activity—" *Rushing* " : carrying or bearing—Acts i. 8 illustrated in Acts ii.—What the Spirit did in New York—V. *Wind is cleansing in its service*—Three words rendered "*pure*" in N.T.—" Nothing but Almighty God to trust in "—El-Shaddai—VI. *Wind is withering in its work*—What the Spirit disperses—Seven things humility is—Bunyan on the Valley of Humiliation—Fénelon on false and true humility—" Thine own meek Self to me impart "—VII. *Wind is varied in its direction*—The east wind of devastation—The lady who wanted patience but not trial—The west wind of deliverance—The boy and the bed-quilt *versus* the Comforter—The north wind of clearing—Words found in Horace Bushnell's Bible—The south wind of pleasantness—The odours which delight our Beloved.

THE WIND

THE wind as an emblem of the Spirit suggests His active operations. He is the Begetter of the new life, He is the Sustainer of the life He begets, He is the Purifier of the heart, He is the Active Opponent of the flesh, He is the Sanctifier of the saint, He is the Worker in service, He is the Leader in worship, and the Producer of the fruit of love and the fruits of Righteousness.

I. WIND IS INVISIBLE IN ITS ESSENCE.

The invisibility of any given thing does not do away with its actuality. Men may deny its substantiality, but the effects of the wind are none the less substantial. It is easy to say that wind is " air in activity," and that " the principal component parts of air are oxygen and nitrogen," but what is the essence of these gases? Our questions only lead us into agnosticism, whereas faith in God's revelation leads us to rest in Him Who knows. The Hebrew and Greek words which are used of the Spirit, namely, "*Ruach*" and "*Pneuma*," in their crude meaning, signify wind. In the New Testament, as used by us, "*Pneuma*" occurs 385 times. Two hundred and eighty-six times the word is rendered "*spirit*" alone, ninety-three times the word is associated with the adjective "*holy*" (four times with "*spirit*" and eighty-nine times with "*ghost*"), twice the word is rendered "*ghost*," once "*life*," once "*wind*," once "*spiritual*," and once "*spiritually*." Wind cannot express all the Spirit is, for before there was any wind we read, "The Spirit of God moved upon the waters." Although the Spirit cannot be diagnosed or seen, He is none the less real. The fact is, as in Nature, so in Grace, the unseen forces, such as electricity and life, are the vitalities. These are undefinable and unseen, but they are none the less real. The Spectrum, which is formed by the sun passing through a triangular glass prism and falling on a screen, is the phenomenon of the seven rainbow colours. The red colour is at one end and the violet at the other. Photography has demonstrated that there is an invisible spectrum below the red and one above the violet. Thus as there are many things in Nature which cannot be seen, the wind among them, so the Holy Spirit is the Unseen Worker, but none the less the Potential One. As the unseen bar went through the boards of the Tabernacle and kept them steady on the foundation, so the Spirit is the One Who unites believers to Christ and makes them to partake of His fulness, for in One Spirit have all been baptized into one body (1. Corinthians xii. 13).

Christ tells us "the world cannot receive" the Holy Spirit as the Spirit of Truth, "because it seeth Him not, neither knoweth Him"; but contrast this with what He says to His own, "But ye know Him" (John xiv. 17). The word "know" signifies a true and personal relation between the person knowing and the person known, hence, it is more than knowing *about*, it is a personal acquaintance with. When the Spirit is received, He is perceived. To know Him is to be swayed by His truth, inspired in His love, kept by His grace, led by His hand, sustained by His presence, cheered by His promises, and used in His service.

Although we cannot see the Spirit, believers know His working in them. A man once said to a Christian that he did not believe there was a Holy Spirit, simply because he had never seen Him. He did not believe in anything he had not seen; and he put the following questions to the Christian: "Have you ever seen the Holy Spirit?"—"No." "Have you ever tasted the Holy Spirit?"—"No." "Have you ever smelt the Holy Spirit?"—"No." "Have you ever felt the Holy Spirit?"—"Yes." "Now," said the Christian, "let me ask you a question or two. Have you ever seen a pain?"—"No." "Have you ever tasted a pain?"—"No." "Have you ever smelt a pain?"—"No." "Have you ever felt a pain?"—"Yes." "So," said the Christian, "I have felt the power of the Holy Spirit."

THE WIND

II. WIND IS CONFINED IN ITS OPERATIONS.

The wind is governed in its movements. The passage in John iii. 8, where Christ says of the wind, " We know not whence it cometh, nor whither it goeth," is not a correct reading, as we shall see later, for we know where the wind goeth and from whence it comes. In Ecclesiastes i. 6 we are told, " The wind goeth toward the south, and turneth about unto the north ; it whirleth about continually, and the wind returneth again according to his circuits." Job i. 19 states that the wind which smote the house came " from the wilderness " ; and Ecclesiastes tells us that observations may be taken of the wind. Science can tell us why the wind comes, where the trade winds operate, what causes the monsoon, the hurricane and the cyclone, and how winds generally work ; it has even a general definition of wind, for it speaks of it " as a sensible current in the atmosphere." The Inspired Word says, " The wind returneth again according to his circuits." This is confirmed by the observations of those who have studied the subject. In a popular volume on the Atmosphere, by D. Archibald, he says : " We know that there exists an independent dominating scheme of general circulation between the poles and the equator." Mark, he speaks of a " general circulation," and further says : " In general, if a mass of air initially tends to move on a rotating sphere towards a certain point, impelled in the first instance by a difference of density or pressure, it tends to move continually to the right when looked at from a point above the N. pole of rotation, and unless prevented from doing so by any extra force resisting such motion, would continue to deviate until it had turned through a complete circle."

The statement of Ecclesiastes i. 6 is a play upon a word. The root word is rendered " *turneth about* " and " *whirleth about,*" and the derived word is rendered " *circuits.*" Rotherham translates the verse : " Going unto the south, and circling unto the north, circling continually is the wind, and over its own circuits returneth the wind." Whether it be verb, adverb or noun, there is the thought of revolution. The words are used of jewels set in gold (Exodus xxviii. 11), of a prison enclosing a person (Jonah ii. 5), of dogs surrounding an individual (Psalm xxii. 16), of a person walking round a city (Psalm xlviii. 12), of the hem of a garment (Exodus xxviii. 33), of the walls surrounding a house (1. Kings vi. 5), and of the turning round of the cart wheel (Isaiah xxviii. 27).

The Holy Spirit has a special circuit of service in relation to the redeemed. Christ implies this when He says of Him, " He shall be with you and in you." With us and in us as a special privilege and prerogative, in contrast to the world who do not receive Him, nor see, nor know Him. There is no need that He cannot meet and no service too hard for His accomplishment. He encloses us in His love, encircles us by His presence, encompasses us about with His power, and environs us through His Word. Something of the circuit of His encompassing protectorate may be gathered from the use of the words, given above, and associated with the action of the wind. In the following Scriptures the words are rendered " compassed," " on every side," " round about."

On " *every side* " we are protected by the " hedge " of His care (Job i. 10) ; we are " *compassed* " with the eyelid of His protection (Deuteronomy xxxii. 10, margin) ; we are surrounded by the encampment of His skill, for He is " *round about* " us as a vigilant army (Psalm xxxiv. 7) ; we are environed by the mountains of His power, even as the mountains are " *round about* " Jerusalem (Psalm cxxv. 2) ; we are encircled with the assurances of His prowess, so that we can say in anticipation of His victories, " Thou shalt *compass* me about with songs of deliverance " (Psalm xxxii. 7) ; we are guided on " *every side* " by the directions of His Word and the skill of His knowledge (II. Chronicles xxxii. 22) ; we have the inness of His calming presence, no matter how fierce the storm, nor how great the stress, for He gives " rest *on every side* " (1. Kings v. 4 ; 1. Chronicles xxii. 18 ; II. Chron. xiv. 7) ; we are confident, amid all the sorrow of life, we shall be able to say, " Thou shalt . . . . comfort me *on every side,*" or " *go about* and comfort me " (Psalm lxxi. 21) ; and we shall find the Lord ever true to His promise—" I will be a Wall of Fire *round about,* and will be the Glory in the midst "

(Zechariah ii. 5). With such a centre of Inspiration and such a circle of Protection, who can touch us?

III. WIND IS MYSTERIOUS IN ACTION.

While there are many things known about the wind, yet like most unseen and yet vital things, it is mysterious in itself. This is specially true of the Holy Spirit. The wise man said long ago, " Thou knowest not the way of the Spirit " (Ecclesiastes xi. 5), and Christ says, " The wind bloweth where it listeth," or, as Rotherham renders John iii. 8, " The Spirit where it pleaseth doth breathe, and the sound thereof thou hearest; but knowest not whence it cometh and whither it goeth, thus is every one born of the Spirit." The Holy Spirit acts in the sovereignty of His grace, hence, Christ says, " He goeth where He listeth." The Greek word for " *listeth* " (" *Thelo* ") would be better rendered " *willeth*," and is frequently used of the Lord in His willing, for instance, " If the Lord *will* " (1. Corinthians iv. 19; James iv. 15), and of the Spirit Who works in the believer " to *will* and to do of His good pleasure " (Philippians ii. 13). The Spirit in His administration in the Church bestows His gifts " severally as He will," and places the members as it " hath pleased Him " (1. Corinthians xii. 11, 18). The sovereignty of the Spirit is not an arbitrary act which rides roughshod over us, but is an exclusive power which alone can bless us.

Nicodemus was puzzled by Christ's declaration about being " born from above," and said, " How can these things be?" He was perplexed with the " How." " *How* " is a fool's question says the apostle. " *How* are the dead raised? And with what body do they come? Thou fool!" (1. Cor. xv. 35, 36). We might ask another puzzler which we find in the Bible, " As thou knowest not what is the way of the spirit, nor how the bones do grow in the womb of her that is with child: even so thou knowest not the works of God Who maketh all " (Ecclesiastes xi. 5). We can no more explain the mystery of the new birth, than we can fathom the process of natural conception, growth and birth. Both are mysteries, but none the less real.

There is a legend of a wonderful bell which rings in heaven, and whose sweet notes can only be heard by those whose hearts are pure and gentle.

> " It is said, somewhere, at twilight
> A great bell softly swings,
> And a man may listen and hearken
> To the wondrous music that rings.
> If he put from his heart's inner chamber
> All the passion, pain and strife,
> Heartache and weary longing,
> That throb in the pulses of life ;
> If he thrusts from his heart all hatred,
> All thoughts of wicked things,
> He can hear in the holy twilight
> How the bell of the angel rings."

This is only another way of saying, only it does not say so much, " Blessed are the pure in heart for they shall see God." What is mysterious to the uninitiated, is plain to those who are initiated. To know God is the key to all knowledge.

IV. WIND IS POWERFUL IN ITS MOVEMENTS.

Many are the incidents which could be related of the violence of the wind in its velocity. One of the most remarkable hurricanes which visited London, was that of November 26th, 1703. Over two thousand stacks of chimneys were blown down, many houses were levelled with the ground, and many persons were killed. In the Thames 400 wherries were lost, and many barges sunk. At sea the destruction was still greater, twelve ships of war, with upwards of 1,800 men on board, were totally lost.

The results of the wind's action, like that described above, only bring devastation and death, but the working of the Spirit in a spiritual sense brings deliverance and life. On the Day of Pentecost He came as a " rushing mighty wind." Each word of the sentence—" rushing mighty wind "—is significant. " *Wind.*" The Greek word " *pnoe* " denotes respiration, or a breeze. It is rendered " *breath* " in Acts xvii. 25, where God is said to give " life and breath " to all. " *Pnoe* " is derived from " *pneo,*" which means to breathe hard and then to blow. It is rendered " *blew* " in Matthew vii. 27 and " *bloweth* " in John iii. 8. Does not this express the act of a living Person ?

God in creation breathed into the former body of man, uniting spirit with body, and he became a living soul. Christ in resurrection breathed upon His disciples the Holy Spirit, commissioning them to be His representatives in the world. And the Spirit breathed upon the gathered and praying company in the upper room, and they received what Christ had promised, namely, " power " (Acts i. 8, margin). When God breathed upon man in creation he became a living soul, capable of fellowship with God ; when Christ breathed upon His disciples they were commissioned as His representatives to proclaim Him in the world ; and when the Spirit breathed upon the waiting saints at Pentecost, they became empowered believers to accomplish His will.

" *Mighty.*" The coming of the Spirit is said to be as a " rushing *mighty* wind." The word " *mighty* " means violence, and suggests vital activity ; and the word " *rushing* " denotes that which carries or bears. Thus there is power suggested in each of the three words, namely, power to breathe, power to move, and power to bring. The coming of the Spirit in power is strikingly demonstrated and suggested in Acts ii. There was *power in utterance,* for they " all began to speak." Cowardice fled before the incoming tide of the Spirit's courage. There was *power of vision,* for the promise contained that the " young men should see visions." The vision of the Eternal enables us to fill the Divine vocation in time. There was *power of conviction,* for the hearers who listened to the Spirit were " pricked in their heart." The consciences of the people were pierced through and through to their awakening and consciousness of the need of salvation. There was *power of addition,* for the Lord " added " many to Himself that day. The additions which are the product of the Spirit's working are always a spiritual increase and a lasting benefit. There was *power of continuance,* for the disciples " continued steadfastly in the apostles' doctrine," which means, the preached Word was a practised commentary. There was *power of love,* for the saints had " all things common." They were true communists. They did not grab what they could not get, but they shared what they had got. There was *power of consecration,* for they parted with their worldly possessions to meet the need of their brethren. Pocket-ology is a practical one. The giving Saviour expects His saints to give. There was *power of unity*, for they " were " not only " together," but of " one accord." The concord of the Spirit always leads to the one accord of the saints. There was *power of contentment*, for they ate " their meat with gladness and singleness of heart." They took what they received from the hand of the Lord, and had a feast with the Lord in consequence. There was *power of worship*, for they were " praising God." The trinity of worship is—praising Him for what He has done, blessing Him for what He gives, and thanksgiving for what He is; and there was the *power of salvation*, for they were not only saved from sin's penalty and pollution, but they were " being saved " to what the Lord wished (Acts ii. 47, R.V.)

The coming of the Spirit is described, not only as a " mighty wind," but a " rushing " one. The word signifies to bear one's self along as the wind, and then to bear everything before it. The ship as it is " *driven* " before the wind is the very illustration which the Spirit uses in speaking of the prophecy which " *came* " to the holy men who were " *moved* " by the Spirit in the giving of the Scriptures (Acts xxvii. 15; II. Peter i. 21). When He comes in the rushing of His power, who can stand before His sway. Saints are melted, consciences are quickened, feelings are stirred, bitternesses are expelled, wrongs are righted, restitutions are made, love is alert, faith is great, hope is buoyant, prayer is real, zeal is fervent, service is willing, humility is patent, temper is sweet, holiness is seen, testimony is effectual, and God is glorified.

A concrete illustration may not be out of place. Some few years ago, when the writer was co-Pastor with Dr. A. B. Simpson, of New York, he asked me one Sunday morning to give account of a very gracious and definite outpouring of the Holy Spirit upon 200 students in the Missionary Institute at Nyack-on-the-Hudson. I began to tell how the Spirit had come in the searching of His Word, in the holiness of His presence, and in the intensity of His humbling power, when suddenly the Spirit gave me such a sight of the condition of the people before me that I fell over the pulpit Bible and began to sob as if my heart would break. When I recovered myself somewhat, I began, like Daniel in the ninth of Daniel, to confess the sins that came before me. Not confessing for the people, but confessing *with* them and as one of them. With brokenness of heart, with quivering voice, and with the tears streaming down my face, I confessed the impurity of heart, the roots of bitterness, the self-complacency of pride, the gossiping about others, the sin of taking the things of God for the glory of self, the prayerlessness of the inner life, the sin of worldliness, the neglect of the Bible, the self-ease in not going out of our way to save the lost, the want of faith, the unholy ambition to get rich quickly at the expense of others, the want of righteousness in not paying others what was their due, and so on. When I finished and opened my eyes I found the whole congregation was in tears, and many sobbing audibly. Then began a scene which cannot be described on cold paper. A young Jewess rose in the gallery and cried out in anguish of soul, " Please pray for me. This is the first time I have been in a Christian place of worship. I have been mistress to a rich Jew, who has surrounded me with every luxury, but who kept me imprisoned in Chinatown, and paid two Chinamen ten dollars a week each to see that I did not escape. Pray for me, I want to be saved. I escaped from my prison this morning, and now I want to be freed from the life I have been living." Then she began to sob and pray that the Lord would have mercy upon her. Then a Church member rose and confessed she had been gossiping about another member and reflecting on her character ; then another asked us to pray that he might have grace to make restitution to a former employer, which he did, although it cost him a hundred and fifty dollars ; then another confessed he had made unjust charges against a Christian worker ; then another confessed to living in secret sin ; then another confessed to unjust criticism of one of the Lord's servants ; and so we went on to nearly midnight, from half-past ten in the morning, with two short breaks for food. And not only so, but for a fortnight, night after night, from three to four hours at a time the Lord worked in a similar way. There was very little set ministry, but there was a mighty concert of prayer and faith. Sometimes we did not know what the Lord was doing. We were on our faces before God, but the Spirit was manifestly working. One brother asked one day if I knew how many were seeking the Lord on one particular night. I replied, " No." He said, " There were forty who came out to the front and sought and found the Lord."

All this came in answer to prayer. For weeks before there had been an agony of prayer. Pentecostal blessing is always preceded by Pentecostal praying. The working of the Spirit in power is in response to the cry of the saints in the one accord of prayer. Sometimes He comes in the still small voice in the closet of personal character, sometimes He comes in the earthquake of the heart-quake of convulsive feeling, sometimes He comes in the fire of His consuming holiness, and at other times He comes in the winnowing and withering wind of His effective power, convincing sinners of their need of the Saviour and saints of their need to be wholly consecrated to Him.

V. Wind is cleansing in its service.

Elihu said to Job, " And now men see not the bright light which is in the clouds ; but the wind passeth, and cleanseth them " (Job xxxvii. 21). There is a golden glory which is obscured by the clouds, but when the wind dispels them, then the glory is seen. Does not the above verse remind us of one in the New Testament, namely, " Blessed are the pure in heart, for they shall see God " ?

There are three* words in the New Testament that are

---

* There are four other words which are synonymous, which are not rendered " pure." " *Hagios,*" which is rendered " *saints* " and " *holy* " (Romans i. 2, 7), and means that which is set apart for a sacred use ; " *Amiantos,*" which is translated " *undefiled* " in the four places where it occurs, and means that which is unstained, unsoiled (Heb. vii. 26 ; xiii. 4 ; James i. 27 ; 1. Peter i. 4) ; " *Hieros,*" which is given " *holy* " in the two places where it is found, means that which is sacred for God (I. Corinthians ix. 13 ; II. Timothy iii. 15) ; and " *Hosios,*" which signifies that which is free from crime or impious deed, and is rendered " *holy* " (Acts ii. 27) and " *mercies* " (Acts xiii. 35).

rendered "*pure.*" (1) *Hagnos* is rendered "*clearing*" (II. Cor. vii. 11), "*chaste*" (II. Corinthians xi. 2), "*pure*" (Philippians iv. 8), and means that which is free from defilement. The word occurs in three practical connections. The command as to the heart-life is, "Keep thyself pure" (I. Timothy v. 22); the injunction regarding the outer-life, not only to the wife in relation to her husband but to all, is, that the world may be won to the Lord by our "*chaste* behaviour" (I. Peter iii. 2, R.V.); and in reference to the model it is to be "even as He is *pure*" (I. John iii. 3). Christ is the standard. (2) "*Eilikrines*" is rendered "*sincere*" (Philip. i. 10), and "*pure*" (II. Peter iii. 1), and means that which has been tested and found to be genuine. (3) "*Katharos*" is translated "*clean*" (John xv. 3), and "*pure*" (Revelation xxi. 18, 21), and signifies that which is clean. The word is frequently used in relation to the inward and outward life of the believer. The "*pure* in heart" are those who see God (Matthew v. 8); the sum total of the Christian life is "love out of a *pure* heart" (I. Timothy i. 5, R.V.); the prerequisite for faithfulness in ministry is to hold "the mystery of the faith in a *pure* conscience" (I. Timothy iii. 9), the cause of a cloudless sky Godward, is to serve Him "in a *pure* conscience" (II. Timothy i. 3, R.V.); the secret of prevailing prayer is to "call on the Lord out of a *pure* heart" (II. Tim. ii. 22); the badge of a "*pure* religion" is a compassionate ministry to the needy and a life free from worldliness (James i. 27); and the garment which Heaven commands is made "*clean* and white" by the "righteous acts of the saints" (Revelation xix. 8).

Who is sufficient for such holiness and purity? Only the Holy One. Only the Pure One. "Now I have nothing but Almighty God to trust in," exclaimed a simple Roman Catholic woman when her crucifix was broken. She did not recognize the broken crucifix was a gain rather than a loss. As long as we have any sufficiency, God is not sufficient; but when we are broken and all we trusted in is smashed, then we are shut up to the Lord Himself. As long as Abram was walking before Sarah and obeying her instructions, the promised seed did not arrive, but when he found Jehovah was

El-Shaddai (which means the many-breasted God, for Shad is the word for a woman's breast, hence God is enough or sufficient), then his hopes were realized, because he walked before Him Who was efficient and sufficient. The Spirit of God can cleanse the heart and keep the life pure. Let Him do it, and let Him keep the heart and life pure.

V. Wind is withering in its work.

"The voice said, Cry. And he said, What shall I cry? All flesh is grass, and all the goodliness thereof is as the flower of the field: The grass withereth ... because the Spirit of the Lord bloweth upon it" (Isaiah xl. 6, 7). "The Spirit bloweth": the word "bloweth" is a primary one and means to disperse. Oh! how many things He disperses when He begins to work. He dispersed the *self-strength* of David and made him cry out, "I am a worm" (Psalm xxii. 6); He dispersed the *self-righteousness* of Paul, and made him exclaim, "I am carnal" (Romans vii. 14); He dispersed the *self-excellency* of Job, and made him confess, "I am vile" (Job xl. 4), or "I am of small account" (R.V.); He dispersed the *self-satisfaction* of Isaiah, and made him own, "I am a man of unclean lips" (Isaiah vi. 5); He dispersed the *self-acting* of Peter, and made him to say, "I am a sinful man" (Luke v. 8); He dispersed the *self-effort* of Jacob, when He put his thigh out of joint, and made him cling in the helplessness of faith (Genesis xxxii. 25, 26); and He dispersed the *self-comeliness* of Daniel, and caused him to say, "My comeliness was turned into corruption and I retained no strength" (Daniel x. 8).

The Spirit blights and withers that He may bless and ennoble us. The withered grass cut up by the cutting wind is an illustration of His stripping work. The goodliness of the creature gives place to the grace of the Creator. The word rendered "*withereth*" means to dry up as a brook is dried up, and is also used of herbage when it is withered up, hence we find the Psalmist saying, "I am *withered* like grass" (Psalm cii. 4, 11), and "my strength is *dried up*" (Psalm xxii. 15). The Spirit dries up our earthly resources and withers our creature strength, that He may give greater and lasting blessing. He humbles that He may exalt. He brings low that He may lift high. God appreciates humility more than any other grace. It is the queen of graces and the home of Deity. Humility is the soul of contentment (Philippians* iv. 12), the secret of service (Acts xx. 19), the livery of heaven (1. Peter v. 5), the spirit of love (Ephesians* iv. 2), the lesson of grace (Matthew* xi. 29), the reflector of Christ (Philippians ii. 8), and the home of God (Isaiah lvii. 15).

Bunyan's description of the Valley of Humiliation is very happy. He describes it, " As the best and most useful piece of ground. . . . It is a fat ground and consisteth much in meadows."

> " He that is down need fear no fall,
> He that is low no pride ;
> He that is humble ever shall
> Have God to be his Guide."

The end of the Spirit's withering work is that He may winnow away the chaff, and lead to the positive grace of humility. He casts down to lift up. He strips to clothe. He breaks up to plant in. He overturns to reconstruct.

Fénelon voices the humility which is heaven-born and contrasts it with the article which is man-made. He says, " He who seeks not his own interest, but solely God's interest in time and eternity, he is humble. . . . Many study exterior humility, but humility which does not flow from love is spurious. The more this exterior humility stoops, the loftier it inwardly feels itself ; but he who is conscious of stooping does not really feel himself to be so low that he can go no further. People who think much of their humility are very proud. . . . Many men seeking to be humble by an effort of their will, and failing in perfect resignation and self-renunciation, sin against the Divine love without which there is no humility. Fuller light would enable them to see that they are exalting themselves by that which they mean for humility ; their supposed setting aside of self is self-seeking ; they are puffed up with the pride of humility, and glory in the humble acts they perform. But the really

---

* The words for " *humble* " and " *humility* " are rendered in these passages " *abased*," " *lowliness*," " *lowly*."

humble man does not do anything of the sort; he lets himself be carried hither and thither; he is satisfied that God should do as He will with him, as the wind with the straw; and there is more real humility in accepting greatness in such a spirit, than thwarting God's plans beneath a pretext of humility. He who chooses abasement rather than elevation is not necessarily humble, though he may wish to be; but he who lets himself go—up or down—heedless whether to be praised or blamed, unmindful of what is said of him, is really humble, whatever men may think, if it be because he waits solely on God's pleasure." For this we pray with Keble—

"Thou, Lord of Meekness, write it there,
Thine own meek Self to me impart."

VII. WIND IS VARIED IN ITS DIRECTION.

There is distinct teaching in relation to the four winds. We might designate them—the east wind of devastation, the west wind of deliverance, the north wind of clearing, and the south wind of pleasantness.

The east wind of devastation. Many are the references to disaster brought and wrought by the east wind.* It was an east wind that blasted the ears of corn in Pharaoh's dream (Genesis xli. 6, 23, 27); it was an east wind that brought the locusts upon the land of Egypt (Exodus x. 13); it is an east wind which, according to Job's prediction, carries the wicked away (Job xxvii. 21); it is by an east wind that the ships of Tarshish are broken (Psalm xlviii. 7); God's withering work of judgment is compared to an east wind withering the fruit trees (Ezek. xvii. 10; xix. 12); the east wind was the

---

* Dr. Geikie in his book *The Holy Land and the Bible* has an interesting account of the east winds. He says, "In the summer they are known as the sirocco, which, when intense, is a veritable calamity. It dries the throat, bringing on catarrh and other bronchial affections; while its lack of ozone makes one unwilling to work with either mind or body: it creates violent headache and oppression of the chest, causes general restlessness and depression of spirits, etc. . . The east wind in winter brings with it a cold so penetrating that the thinly dressed natives sometimes die from its effects. In spring it frequently shrivels up the young vegetation so that the people of Lebanon call it 'The poison wind.'"

cause of Tyre's rowers being broken in the midst of the seas (Ezekiel xxvii. 26); and it was an east wind which discomfited Jonah till he fainted (Jonah iv. 8). The Spirit of God comes sometimes as an east wind, breaking and discomforting, till like Jonah we faint with despair. A Christian woman went to a friend of mine in Pittsburg and said, " Will you pray for me, Mr. Whiteside?" " Yes, my sister," was the reply, " what shall I ask the Lord for?" " I want more patience," was the response. My friend began to pray somewhat as follows, " Lord, send this sister a lot of trial, and persecution and tribulation." " Stop," exclaimed the sister, " I don't want trial and tribulation, I want patience." The servant of God calmly replied, " Tribulation worketh patience, and patience experience." We want the Christ of blessing, but we don't want the John of baptismal judgment. Before Christ got the brooding Dove of the Spirit, He had gone down into the waters of Jordan's death.

The west wind of deliverance. It was a west wind that took the locusts away from Egypt (Exodus x. 19), and Christ tells us it is from the west that the refreshing shower comes (Luke xii. 54). The Spirit of God comes in the effectiveness of His power and drives away the locusts of evil, and in the shower of His grace to refresh the weariness of the saints. A poor woman in New York who could not get out to the church service as she was wont, sent her little boy with the instruction, he was to bring home as much of the sermon as he could. When the boy got home he had forgotten all he had heard. " Do you remember the text," queried the mother. " Yes, God says, ' He is going to send us another bed-quilt.' " An additional bed-quilt was sorely needed, for the only one the mother had was worn and thin, and it was not sufficient to keep them warm. The mother could not remember such a text, so she asked a friend, who was present at the service, what the text was. The friend replied, " I will send you another Comforter." The bed-quilt was called a comforter, and he knew they needed one, so when he heard that God was going to send the Comforter he concluded it was a bed-quilt. Do we not all need, and always need, this additional Comforter? Verily, we do, and when He is received, obeyed and honoured we find Him a Helper indeed, a Comforter to warm and gladden.

The north wind of clearing. Three things are said about the north, " Cold cometh out of the north " (Job xxxvii. 9), but so does " fair weather " (Job xxxvii. 22), for the " north wind driveth away rain " (Proverbs xxv. 23) : a characteristic recognized in its native name, " the heavenly," apparently from the glorious blue sky which marks it. Who is it that can bring us under the sky of hallowed communion and give us to enjoy the fair weather of God's love ? No one but the Spirit. He alone can clear away the cloudy weather and give us the bracing of His invigorating presence. What a difference it makes when we know the cheer and comfort of the Divine. In the Bible of Horace Bushnell, after his death, were found these words pencilled on a sheet of paper, " My mother's loving instinct was from God, and God was in her love to me first—which love was deeper than hers and more protracted. Long years ago she vanished, but God stays by me still, embracing me in my grey hairs as tenderly and carefully as she did in my infancy, and giving to me as my joy and the principal glory of my life, that He lets me know Him, and helps me, with real confidence, to call Him my Father." His love clears our sky and cheers our spirit, and the Spirit Himself comforts us in all the tenderness of His motherhood.

" No word of all the Scripture thrills a sweeter chord than this,
   Stirs a richer retrospection of the soul's experienced bliss,
Than this promise, where the Spirit strengthens weak and timid
   faith,
With assurance of His comfort, ' As a mother comforteth.' "

The south wind of pleasantness. Elihu says, " How thy garments are warm, when He quieteth the earth by the south wind ? " (Job xxxvii. 17) ; and the bride in the Song of Solomon says, " Awake, O north wind ; and come thou south ; blow upon my garden, till the spices thereof may flow out " (Song of Solomon iv. 16). Dr. Geikie says upon this verse, " The north-west or south-west is meant, since it rarely blows directly from the north or the south. This wind is felt at Joppa as early as nine or ten in the morning, but as becomes the east, it travels leisurely, reaching Jerusalem

The Wind

generally about two or three in the afternoon; sometimes indeed not till much later. Subsiding after sunset, it soon rises again, and continues for most of the night, bathing and renewing the parched face of nature with the refreshing vapours it has brought from the ocean, and constitutes 'the dew' of the sacred writings. Should it not reach the hills, as sometimes happens, Jerusalem suffers greatly, but near the sea its moist coolness is a daily visitor."

As the bride appeals to the wind to bring out the aroma of the spices, so the Spirit brings out the implanted graces of His love. There are spices, fragrant odours, which delight the heart of our Beloved, such as the odour of intercession (Revelation v. 8), the frankincense of a consecrated life (Matthew ii. 11), the spikenard of love's devotion (Mark xiv. 3), the incense of grateful worship (II. Chronicles xxix. 11), the fragrance of lowly adoration (Song of Solomon i. 12), the aroma of a holy character (Psalm xlv. 8), the sweet smell of generous help (Philippians iv. 18), the savour of prayer (Psalm cxli. 2), the perfume of a faithful ministry (II. Cor. ii. 14-16), and the redolence of a forgiving and loving spirit (Ephesians iv. 32; v. 1, 2). How pleasant such a redolent life must be to our Lord. Here again, we are cast upon the Spirit, and we pray in the intensity of earnest longing, " Awake, O Spirit, blow upon the garden of my heart and life, till the spices of Thy graces and gifts flow out in adoring praise and agreeable appreciation to God."

> " Lord, let Thy love,
> Fresh from above,
> Soft as the south wind blow;
> Call forth its bloom,
> Wake its perfume,
> And bid its spices flow!"

Syllabus of
Rivers as Emblems of the Holy Spirit

Rivers of the Bible—I. *Source*—Professor's question to student—Ten things "of God"—Four Edenic rivers—Cowper's verse on love—Canon Liddon on "supersensuous"—II. *The course*—Stier's reading on John vii. 37, 38 and paraphrase—Hebrew word for "fountain"—One of the last sayings of Robert Chapman—The inexpressible things—III. *Mission*—Bacteria—Rivers fructify—Hampton Court vine—Rivers pacify—A robin's nest at Nyack—Rivers gladden—Samuel Rutherford's letter—Rivers vivify—Fountain and cistern—Ezekiel's river—Measured waters—Deep waters—Productive waters—Directed waters—Healing waters—Food-providing waters—Sacrificial waters—"*A Cruce salus*"—Rivers satisfy—Spirit-drenched—Rivers magnify—Paul's three "yet not I's"—What George Müller did—Rivers glorify—Legend of Brittany—IV. *The terminal*—"Men! it must be done!"—Puritan on personal pronoun.

RIVERS

THE rivers of the Bible are significantly suggestive in their association and meaning. A stream of connected thought could be profitably followed in tracing their mention and setting in the pages of the Holy Writ. Take seven rivers by way of illustration. The four Edenic rivers are associated with man's primeval state in Paradise (Gen. ii. 10); the River Euphrates is connected with God's promise in grace to Abraham and his seed regarding the land of Palestine as Israel's inheritance (Genesis xv. 18 ; Deut. xi. 24 ; Joshua i. 4 ; Revelation xvi. 12) ; Jordan plays an important part in God's redemptive programme, being identified with the rolling away of the reproach of Egypt from Israel (Joshua iv. and v.), and the coming of Christ as the One Who was plunged beneath the waters of judgment for us (Mark i. 5) ; the river of Egypt is the proclaimer of God's judgment against sin and Israel's deliverance from bondage (Exodus vii. 17-25) ; the River Chebar is the river of Israel's Babylonish captivity, beside which the prophet saw the vision of God's glory (Ezekiel i. 1-3 ; xliii. 3 ; Psa. cxxxvii. 1) ; Ezekiel's river of vision is suggestive of many symbolical blessings (Ezekiel xlvii.) ; and the river of Acts xvi. 13 is the place of fellowship in prayer.

There are four points suggested by a river, namely, source, course, mission, and terminal.

I. SOURCE.

A professor asked a student one day, " How does the Bible begin ?"

" With creation," was the reply.

" Mine does not," was the rejoinder, " it begins with God —' In the beginning GOD.' "

Everything is wrong if we do not begin with God. He is the explanation of creation, the Sustainer of life, the Ruler in providence, the Author of Scripture, the Giver of Christ, the Source of spiritual life, and the Originator of every blessing of the Gospel. Turn where we will in the sacred page, the Spirit emphasizes one great fact, viz., God is the Source of all things. Take Romans i. by way of illustration, where we read of ten things of God. " Gospel of God " (verse 1). " Son of God " (verse 4), " Beloved of God " (verse 7), " Will of God " (verse 10), " Power of God " (verse 16), " Righteousness of God " (verse 17), " Wrath of God " (verse 18), " Glory of the uncorruptible God " (verse 23), " Truth of God " (verse 25), " Judgment of God " (verse 32).

In Genesis ii. 10, 11, we read of a river divided into four heads. This river of Eden in its fourfold flow cannot definitely be identified to-day. The names of the rivers were Pison, Gihon, Hiddekel, and Euphrates. According to Newberry the names mean spreading, stream, swift, and fruitfulness. The meaning given to these names by Farrer is more suggestive. He says, Pison means changing, doubling, extended; Gihon signifies valley of grace, or impetuous; Hiddekel denotes a sharp voice, and Euphrates indicates, That makes fruitful.

Let us take these rivers as illustrating the Spirit's person and work. There are four things God is said to be: "God is Spirit" (John iv. 24); "God is Light" (1. John i. 5); "God is a Consuming Fire" (Hebrews xii. 29); and "God is Love" (1. John iv. 8). All this the Spirit is.

As Pison means changing or doubling, so the Spirit, as the Spirit, is the Source and the Cause of that change, or additional work, called "the new birth." As natural life is the union of the spirit and body by means of the soul, so spiritual life is the union of man with God through Christ by the operation of the Holy Ghost.

As Gihon signifies Valley of Grace, or impetuous, so the Spirit is the One Who causes us to know the light of the knowledge of God's grace as revealed in the face of Jesus Christ. No darkness of hell, sin, or death, can stay before the impetuous sway of God's grace. The Spirit in His ministration of the Gospel accomplishes this.

As Hiddekel denotes a sharp voice, so the Spirit is a Consuming Fire to purify away the dross of sin and make us beautiful with the cleansing of His Word. His Word is a sharp voice and a fire, as is clearly stated in the opening of the Book of the Revelation, where Christ's eyes are said to be as a flame of fire to burn, and the Churches are exhorted to hear what "the Spirit saith."

As Euphrates indicates that which makes fruitful, so the Spirit as Love is the begetter of that which is called "The fruit of the Spirit." That love is expressed in self-forget-fulness and self-sacrifice. Cowper finely puts it when he says:—

> "All selfish souls, what'er they feign, have still a selfish lot;
> They boast of liberty in vain, of love, and have it not;
> He, whose bosom glows with Thee, he, and he alone is free;
>
> Whether we name thee Charity or Love,
> Chief grace below, and all in all above;
> Who seeks to praise Thee, and to make Thee known
> To other hearts, must have Thee in his own.
>
> Love speaks of Him, her Author, Guardian, Friend,
> Whose love knew no beginning, knows no end.
>
> She flies to save some, and feels a pang for all.
> And from a knowledge of her own disease,
> Learns to compassionate the sick she sees.
> She makes excuses, where she might condemn,
> Revil'd by those that hate her, prays for them;
> The worst suggested, she believes the best;
>
> Such was the portrait an Apostle drew;
> The bright original was One he knew;
> Heav'n held his hand, the likeness must be true."

The only One Who can make this likeness true in us is the Spirit Himself. Canon Liddon once said what is true in its profound simplicity. He said: "It may seem a poor and trite thing to say, but real belief in the Holy Ghost implies an habitual sense of the reality of a spiritual and supersensuous world. There is in fallen human nature a constant and profound tendency to sink under the dominion of materialistic habits of thought, that is to say, to surrender ourselves to the fascination and empire of the bodily senses." As the law of life can only overcome the law of gravitation, so the law of the Spirit of Life in Christ Jesus is the only power that can free us from the law of sin and death.

II. THE COURSE.

At the Feast of Tabernacles Christ said, to give Stier's reading, "If any thirst, let him come unto Me; and let him drink who believeth in Me! Even as Scripture (concerning Me) hath said, Rivers out of Him shall flow, of living water" (John vii. 37, 38). The general interpretation of this passage is to make the living water flow out of the believer, but we are inclined to agree with Stier's paraphrasing, for the following reasons :—

1. Nowhere in the Old Testament do we find that men of God are said to be a source of blessing, whereas, the Lord is frequently said to be " the Fountain of living waters " (Jer. ii. 13 ; xvii. 13). The Hebrew word " fountain " in these Scriptures means " a perpetual spring of water." The Lord promises " to pour water upon him that is thirsty " (Isaiah xliv. 3), and also bids those who are thirsty to come to the waters (Isaiah lv. 1), and in the glory, Christ is the One from Whom the river of life proceedeth and from Whom the needy are directed " to take " (Revelation xxii. 17).

2. The preposition " *ek* " rendered " out of " with the genitive signifies out of as from a source—a starting point. " Out of Him shall flow rivers of living water," even as the " river of water of life " is said to be " proceeding out of the throne of God and the Lamb." Stier paraphrases the whole passage as follows :—

" Are there not then among you joyous guests at this feast, any thirsting souls who are not satisfied with all this ceremonial and typical procedure, commemoration of ancient facts and wonders (the true meaning of which prophesied, however, of a great futurity), who long for righteousness, for Spirit and life ? Whosoever feels this true thirst, let him come now—as long as I am with you this is My invitation—unto Me ! With Me alone is the true water of life, soon will I give it. Then shall everyone who has become a believer in Me, drink to his full satisfaction, in a sense very different from your present beholding merely the water poured out. For if the Scripture speaks of streams of living water issuing forth from Jerusalem and the Temple—quite different from our well-meaning though petty drawing water from the valley, by which, however, ye are reminded of the prophetic word—that is spoken of Me and My body, My entire Person, and specially My humanity. In all those passages Messiah was referred to, Who is Myself, and it is as if it were said—The streams will flow out of Him to water the earth and to give the people a drink."

There is another Hebrew word rendered "fountain "* which refers to a spring breaking through the ground. The same word is used of the "eye," and signifies an orifice through which water comes; or a well, like an eye in the ground. The water of life comes from the broken humanity of the Christ of Calvary and the glorified Lord of ascension glory. The waters that satisfied Israel in the wilderness came from the smitten rock of Horeb (Exodus xvii. 6); the waters of Ezekiel's prophetic vision flow " from under the threshold of the house . . . . at the south side of the altar " (Ezekiel xlvii. 1); and with Divine intent the water of the river of life is said not only to proceed from the throne of God, but also from the Lamb. From the glorified Man of Calvary, Who is the Giver of the Spirit because of what He gave Himself to on the cross, comes the streams of the Spirit's floods. Only through Him does the Spirit come. Those who will not come by the channel bed of the cross, will never obtain the floods of the Spirit's power and ministry. They will only find a dry bed of stony discomfort and the reptiles of unbelief. The riven side is the channel from whence comes the water of life.

One of the last sayings of saintly Robert Chapman, of Barnstaple, was, " I often think the thought: the members of Christ will never come to the end of ' It is finished.' We shall be learning from day to day more and more, but what we shall come to will be the unsearchableness of the work." Is not this suggested by " the rivers " ? The word is " floods," and is so rendered in Matthew vii. 25, 27, hence all He has to give is beyond human expression and definition. Think only of the following inexpressible things. His peace " passeth understanding " (Philippians iv. 7); His love is unquenchable (Song of Solomon viii. 7); His ways are untrackable (Romans xi. 33, R.V.); His riches are unsearchable (Ephesians iii. 8); His gift is unspeakable (II. Cor. ix. 15); His joy is inexpressible (I. Peter i. 8); His words are unutterable (II. Corinthians xii. 4); His love is unknowable (Ephesians iii. 19); He is undefinable (Song of Solomon v. 16); and He cannot be numbered (Psalm cxlvii. 5, margin).

---

* Rendered "*fountain*" in Gen. xvi. 7; "*well*" in Gen. xxiv. 13; "*face*" in Num. xiv. 14; "*eyes*" in Ezekiel i. 18.

III. Mission.

Everything in life has its mission. The bacteria which is such a terrible scourge in one direction, by its scavenger work in the decomposition of dead bodies is a benefactor in another direction. There is a blessing in every curse, a bow in every cloud, a sweet in every bitter, and a joy in every sadness. Rivers and floods have been great devastators, but they have also been great benefactors. In the land of Palestine where a river was such a boon, we are not surprised that it is frequently used to illustrate the beneficent work of the Spirit. Let us briefly ponder a few things rivers are said to do.

Rivers Fructify. The Blessed Man is compared to a tree planted by the rivers of water, and who in consequence brings forth fruit in his season (Psalm i. 3). Rootage in the Word and in the Spirit is the secret of fruitage in the life. The reason why the grapes at Hampton Court are so fine is because the roots of the vine find their feeding ground in the bed of the River Thames. The Christian life is not a negation, it is a production; nor is it an attainment merely, it is an obtainment. The attainment of what the Lord desires is only possible as we obtain the Spirit's enduement. When we obtain Him He can obtain His purpose in us. That purpose is love even as He loved. We may have the clanging cymbals of gift and not the consecrated music of love. We may be busy in the Lord's service, and not be beautiful in His life.

Rivers Pacify. The lives of many are like a shallow stream, noisy and restless; but a true life in the Spirit is deep and true. God's chiding to His people long ago has a promise wrapped up in it for us. He said, "Oh that thou hadst hearkened to My commandments! then had thy peace been as a river, and thy righteousness as the waves of the sea" (Isaiah xlviii. 18). Peaceful as a deep river and powerful as the waves of the sea. But the peace and power of the Spirit only come one way, and that is by hearkening to His commandments. Naught can disturb the one who rests in the will of God. A robin had built its nest in a small garden bush at Nyack-on-the-Hudson. Cats were about and pedestrians were continually passing, but the master of the garden knew the bird was there, and he kept a watchful eye on the mother bird and her nestlings. So when we rest in the will of God by our obedience to His Word, the Spirit sees that nothing disturbs, and He makes us sing :

> " Like a river glorious,
> Is God's perfect peace,
> Over all victorious,
> In its bright increase ;
> Perfect yet it floweth,
> Fuller ev'ry day,
> Perfect, yet it groweth
> Deeper all the way."

Rivers Gladden. " There is a river, the streams whereof shall make glad the city of God " (Psalm xlvi. 4). " Glad " is the prominent word here. To be affected to merriment by joy and delight is the meaning. The believer, who is Spirit-filled, has a right to be " merry " with the prodigal, for he is saved in the grace of the Father ; he can shout with Gideon and his three hundred, " The sword of the Lord and of Gideon," and be victorious over his foes ; he can sing with Miriam and her maidens, " The Lord hath triumphed gloriously," as he beholds the achievements of Jehovah ; he can say in the face of trial with Paul as encouraged by the Lord, " None of these things move me " ; he can glory in His infirmities as he is buffeted by Satan, for he knows the power of Christ protects him ; he can sleep calmly with Peter in the face of persecution, for he knows the Lord can deliver him ; and he can have a praise meeting, although his back is smarting, his feet fast in the stocks, and he is in the dark dungeon of an inner prison, even as Paul and Silas did. All this is only possible as we keep in fellowship with Christ and make Him everything, for it is ever the Spirit's mission to keep us occupied with Him. Samuel Rutherford, in his letters, emphasizes this. He says, " I see that in communion with Christ we may make more gods than one," meaning that we may make the enjoyment itself our god. " I would be farther in upon Christ than at His joys . . . . let the Holy

Spirit lead to this Person, and surely his experience will be, none ever came away dry from David's well."

Rivers Vivify. Of Christ it is said, " A man .... shall be as rivers of water in a dry place " (Isaiah xxxii. 2). What a dry place the world is, and how dry we are in ourselves! Yet a consciousness of need makes us appreciate the Saviour. Rutherford aptly says in writing to one who suffered much for conscience sake : " I approve of your going to the Fountain, when your own cistern is dry. A difference there must be betwixt Christ's well and your borrowed water, but ye have need of emptiness and drying up, as well as ye have need of the well ? Want and a hole there must be in our vessel to leave room for Christ's art. His well hath its own need of thirsty drinkers, to commend infinite love which, from eternity, did brew such a cellar of living waters for us."

The constant, vivifying and renewing work of the Spirit may be illustrated by the descriptions given of the river in Ezekiel xlvii. Let us briefly note the details : (1) Measured Waters—" He measured," &c. (verses 3-5). There is nothing haphazard about the Spirit. Everything is exact. He ever keeps to the measure of the truth. (2) Deep Waters. At first the waters were only to the ankles, then to the knees, then to the loins, and then a river to swim in. Four grades of Christian experience may be indicated here. To walk in the Spirit is good, to have a prayer-life in the Spirit is better, to be strengthened in the loins of a Spirit-empowered experience is best, but better than the best is to be lifted off our feet entirely, and rest in God Himself, even as an expert swimmer trusts to the water. (3) Productive Waters. There were trees on either side of the river, and many of them (verse 7). These were the product of the productive waters. The productiveness of the waters is further seen in the increase in the fish. " There shall be a very great multitude of fish, because these waters shall come thither " (verse 9). A Spirit environed life always produces that which is a blessing and a protection to others, and there is also a great multitude saved when the Spirit works in power. After Pentecost it is said, " Believers were the more added unto the Lord, multitudes both of men and women " (Acts v. 14). (4) **Directed Waters.** The course of the river was towards the East and towards the desert (verse 8). The Spirit leads us towards the desert of the world to proclaim God's love to a thirsty world, as He did Philip the Evangelist, to meet the Ethiopian (Acts viii. 26, 27) ; and He also leads us to look out toward the East of Christ's return. (5) Healing Waters. Wherever the river flowed healing followed—" the water shall be healed " (verse 8)... " the waters of the sea shall be healed " (verse 9, R.V.), and, further, the leaves of the fruit trees produced by the waters are " for healing " (verse 12, R.V.) The Spirit makes alive our " death-doomed " body, as well as vivifying the inner life of the spirit. (6) Food-providing Waters. Every kind of fish is caught (verse 10) by the fisherman. Besides the supply from the waters, there is the supply produced by the waters. The fruit from the trees " shall be for meat " (verse 12). So those who are under the Spirit's direction not only have " enough " but to " spare." Enough in the Spirit for one's own need, and abundance for others. (7) Sacrificial Waters. We are not only told the waters came from the " south side of the altar " (verse 1), but we are also told that all the blessing that came was " because the waters thereof issue out of the sanctuary " (verse 12, R.V.) The motto of the Earl of Mayo is " *A Cruce salus* " (salvation by means of the cross). We may say the same of the Spirit. The Spirit by means of the cross. He comes by no other way, and as we keep near the cross we find the vivifying ministry of the Spirit.

Rivers satisfy. " I will open rivers on the bare heights, and fountains in the midst of the valleys : I will make the wilderness a pool of water, and the dry land springs of water " (Isaiah xli. 18). " They shall be abundantly satisfied with the fatness of Thy house ; and Thou shalt make them drink of the river of Thy pleasure " (Psalm xxxvi. 8). The word rendered " abundantly satisfied " means to give satisfaction, to satiate, and is variously used. The word is used of ground " soaked " with blood (Isaiah xxxiv. 7) ; of a mother who feeds to " satisfy " her child with the breast (Proverbs v. 19) ; of the rain which " watereth " the earth (Isaiah lv. 10) ; of God Who is said to have " satiated the weary soul " (Jer. xxxi. 25), and of one made " drunken " (Lam. iii. 15). Thus when the Lord promises to " abundantly satisfy," it means to soak and drench the soul. What a commentary we have upon this in what was said of the early disciples; they said, " These men are filled with new wine." Surely, too, there is some correspondence in the Lord's Word, when He commands and says, " Be not drunk with wine, wherein is excess, but be filled (drunk) with the Spirit." As a man filled with spirits will do things he would never otherwise think of doing, so the Spirit-drenched believer is moved into the supernatural and accomplishes things beyond the human and is wonderfully and enthusiastically satisfied with Christ, so that sin and worldly pleasures have no charm and attraction.

Rivers magnify. " The waters made him great, the deep set him on high with her rivers running about his plants, and sent out her little rivers unto all the trees of the field. Therefore his height was exalted above all the trees of the field, and his boughs were multiplied," &c. (Ezekiel xxxi. 4-9). These words are wonderful in their descriptiveness, explaining the indebtedness of the Assyrian to God's national blessing. Many a city and country have been enriched by noble rivers. America owes a great deal to its lakes and rivers; and the lochs and lakes of Great Britain and Ireland are waterways of history and beauty. There are names which are illustrious in the annals of grace, which would never have been known but for the grace which made them luminous. David felt this when he said, " Thy gentleness hath made me great," and Paul in his three " yet not I's " tells us that the secret of his life was Christ, the cause of his labour was the grace of God, and that the Lord Who spoke in his testimony was the cause of all he said.

Of the late George Müller it is said, " He brought everything to God, and he brought God into everything." No wonder he was the man he was, since he was possessed by the God he had.

Rivers Glorify. " The glorious Lord will be unto us a place of broad rivers and streams " (Isaiah xxxiii. 21), so says Isaiah in anticipation of what the Lord will be to His people in Zion. The glorious Lord will make His people glorious in the days to come. And it seems to me, the moral and spiritual glory which the Spirit hath wrought in us, will then be made manifest through us, when Christ comes to be admired in His saints.

There is a legend of Brittany, which speaks of a fair city called Is, which long was engulfed by the ocean, and vanished out of human ken. The city, according to the lore, still exists, and the people go about its streets, and sometimes the bells are heard pealing from the church turret, with celestial music. So with the submerged life in the Spirit. There comes forth the celestial music of a chastened spirit, of a willing heart, of a Christ-possessed life, and a sympathetic ministry.

IV. The terminal.

" All the rivers run into the sea ; yet the sea is not full ; unto the place from whence the rivers come, thither they return again " (Ecclesiastes i. 7). The sea in Scripture imagery stands for unorganized humanity, hence, the four great world powers are said to come up " from the sea " (Daniel vii. 3), and the last great world-power heading up in the Antichrist is said to " rise up out of the sea " (Revelation xiii. 1). Ezekiel's river is also said to go " into the sea " (Ezekiel xlvii. 8). We also speak of " the sea of nations."

The purpose and end of the Spirit's bestowment is as Christ Himself says—" Ye shall be witnesses unto Me." The hungry, dying world needs the Lord Jesus, and we have orders to give to it the Bread of Life. During the American war, an order was given to plant some heavy guns on the top of a hill. The soldiers dragged the guns to the bottom of the hill and could get them no farther. An officer seeing the situation, cried, " Men ! It must be done ! I have the orders in my pocket." So we have our orders to be witnesses unto Christ. Not witnesses to ourselves, but to Him, and remember what a witness is, he is one who knows experimentally what he tells to others. One of the later Puritans was one day catechising a number of young disciples, when they had answered the question on effectual calling, he said, " Stop, can anyone say this using the personal pronoun all through ?" Then with broken, sobbing breath, a man stood up and said, "Effectual calling is the word of God's own Spirit, whereby convincing me of my sin and misery, enlightening my mind in the knowledge of Christ, and renewing my will, He doth enable me and persuade me to embrace Jesus Christ freely offered me in the Gospel."

When such a personal testimony is given in the Spirit, it will be effective in blessing others. This makes us cry continually.

> " Oh, for a passionate passion for souls !
> Oh, for a pity that yearns !
> Oh, for a love which loves unto death !
> Oh, for a fire that burns !
> Oh, for a prayer-power that prevails !
> That pours itself out for the lost ;
> Victorious prayer in the Conqueror's name,
> Oh, for a Pentecost !"

Syllabus of
The Dew as an Emblem of the Holy Spirit

Dew-drops—Dr. Geikie on the dew of Palestine—I. *Dew is Divine in its Source*—" The Promise "—" Grace be unto God for His unspeakable grace "—II. *Dew is refreshing in its favour*—His delight—Three classes of Christians *re* God's will—III. *Dew is beneficial in its service*—Canon Tristram on the dew of Hermon—Occupied *with* the Lord—Dionysius and Plato—Occupied *for* the Lord—Nelson's advice to Collingwood and Rotherham—Occupied *by* the Lord—Fable of earthen pots—" One Spirit "—IV. *Dew is precious in its benefit*—The beggar and Paganini on London Bridge—V. *Dew is saturating in its contact*—Gideon's action *re* the fleece—" Pressed " and " wringed "—" Tighten your grips "—VI. *Dew is produced according to law*—Quotation as to how dew is produced—Four laws—VII. *Dew is silent in its coming*—" He certainly do recommen' hisself mos' highly "—VIII. *Dew is refreshing in its ministry*—Sarah Smiley on early communings with God—New things ever made new—IX. *Dew is hiding in its enclosure*—" The Gory dew "—X. *Dew is reflective in its mirroring*—" I know mister, he lives in our street "—XI. *Dew is rich in its contents*—What is found in the dew—The road surveyor and his Christianity—XII. *Dew is emblematic of strength*—Pulsford on " The dew of his youth "—The instruments God uses—XIII. *Dew is glorified in its association*—" I will be as the dew "—McCheyne on the dew—" Reproached " and " resteth "—Dr. Henry Wilson's hand on the dynamo—XIV. *Dew is identified with Christ*—Christ out in the cold—Ullysses and the sirens *versus* Orpheus.

THE DEW

MANY have spoken of the glory and beauty of the dew-drops, Milton calls them

> " Stars of morning, dew-drops, which the sun
> Impearls on every leaf and flower."

Tennyson follows in similar strain—" Every dew-drop paints a bow." Coleridge calls them " gems of the morning," and George Eliot declares

> " The dew-bead
> Gem of earth and sky-begotten."

The dew of the east is not the same as in the west. Dr. Geikie says: " There is no dew, properly so-called, in Palestine, for there is no moisture in the hot summer air to be chilled into dewdrops by the coolness of the night, as in a climate like our's. From May to October rain is unknown, the sun shining with unclouded brightness day after day. The heat becomes intense, the ground hard; and vegetation would perish but for the moist west winds that come each night from the sea. The bright skies cause the heat to radiate very quickly into space, so that the nights are as cold as the day is the reverse. To this coldness of the night-air the indispensable watering of all plant life is due. The winds, loaded with moisture, are robbed of it as they pass over the land, the cold air condensing it into drops of water, which fall in a gracious rain of mist on every thirsty blade."

I. Dew is Divine in its source.

A part of Isaac's blessing upon Jacob was, " God give thee of the dew of Heaven" (Genesis xxvii. 28). The dew is here said to be one of the gifts of God. As the dew is one of the good gifts of God's providence, so the Spirit is the perfect gift of His grace.

> " Dews fall apace,
> The dews of grace,
> Upon this soul of sin;
> And Love Divine
> Delights to shine
> Upon the waste within."

One of the sentences which expresses what the Spirit is, is " The Promise of the Father." Someone has said, " There are 31,000 promises in God's Word," but there is only one which is called " *the* promise " (Luke xxiv. 49 ; Acts i. 4 ; ii. 33, 39 ; Galatians iii. 14), and only One Who is " the Holy Spirit of Promise " (Ephesians i. 13). He is " *the* Promise " because He was promised to Christ as the result of His work upon the Cross, and Christ promised Him to us as His ascension gift ; and the Spirit is " the Holy Spirit of Promise " because He promises we shall have the inheritance of which He is the Earnest.

The bestowal of the Spirit is the gift of grace. Yea, He is called " The Spirit of Grace." But for God's giving there would be no having, so we say, " Grace " (" thanks " is the same word as " grace ") " be unto God for His unspeakable grace " (II. Corinthians ix. 15), for the " gift " spoken of is the grace referred to in the context. Unless we bottom our blessings on God's grace, we have no foundation on which to rest. Giving is His glory, giving is His enrichment, for as in the feeding of the 5,000 there was more food to give out after the feeding of the multitude,* so the Lord's enrichment of us is the enrichment of Himself. Let us keep on the ground of grace, for there we are not only on sure ground for ourselves, but we are on pleasing terms with Him. He delights to bestow upon us the dew of His Spirit, and we give Him double delight when we receive the givings of His grace.

II. DEW IS REFRESHING IN ITS FAVOUR.

" The king's favour is as the dew upon the grass " (Prov. xix. 12). The word "*favour*" comes from a root which means to be pleased with, to satisfy. Its use in the Psalms will illustrate its meaning ; it is rendered " acceptable," " will," " good pleasure," " desire " (Psalm xix. 14 ; xl. 8 ; li. 18 ; cxlv. 16). There is no thought so stimulating as the consciousness of the Lord's delight in us. The joy of giving

---

* The " *fragments* " mentioned in John vi. 13 do not mean pieces the people had handled, but broken pieces ready to give. The baskets were market baskets.

Him joy is the joy of joys. God loves all men with the love of compassion, but He loves those who do His will with the love of complacency. God's will is not some hard rule to follow, some tight-rope upon which one has to balance one's self, some tread-mill upon which we fruitlessly tread, it is a garden of delights, a road of safety, and a task of happy result. Some groan under God's will and complain at His dispensations; others bear God's will as an inevitable which cannot be helped; while others delight in God's will and find Him in every circumstance. When we delight in God's will He has a special delight in us. When His pleasure is our pleasure what pleasure we give Him. There are three classes of Christians in reference to God's will. They might be called submitters, committers and admitters. The submitters give in and surrender because they are obliged to; the committers give over themselves to the Lord, but they rather tremble or wonder what the consequences will be; but the admitters ask Him to come in and will in them, to will and to do of His good pleasure. These latter delight His heart and find His favour to their own satisfaction. The better way is to

" Receive Him as the dew in thy heart,
O thirsty one, who long His grace hath sought.
Dew forms in stillness; struggle not nor strive;
What thou dost need to learn is to receive.

" The air surrounding thee is full of God,
With love and life and blessing for thee stored;
Get cool and quiet and the dew will fall—
A little at a time, not once for all."

III. DEW IS BENEFICIAL IN ITS SERVICE.

" Like the dew of Hermon, that cometh down upon the mountains of Zion: for there the Lord commanded the blessing, even life for evermore" (Psalm cxxxiii. 3, R.V.) Again, we need to remind ourselves that the dew in Palestine is different from that in the west. Canon Tristram speaks of the dew of Hermon in recounting his travels. He says: " We had sensible proof at Rasheiya of the copiousness of the dew of Hermon, spoken of in Psalm cxxxiii. 3, where Zion is only another name for the same mountain. Unlike most other mountains, which gradually rise from lofty table lands, and often at a great distance from the sea, Hermon starts at once to the height of nearly ten thousand feet from a platform scarcely above the sea-level. This platform, too—the upper Jordan valley and marshes of Merom—is for the most part an impenetrable swamp of unknown depth, whence the seething vapour, under the rays of an almost tropical sun, is almost constantly ascending into the upper atmosphere during the day. The vapour, coming in contact with the snowy sides of the mountain, is rapidly congealed, and so precipitated in the evening in the form of dew, the most copious we ever experienced. It penetrated everywhere, and saturated everything. The floor of our tent was soaked, the bedding was covered with it, our guns were dripping, and dew-drops hung about everywhere. No wonder that the foot of Hermon is clad with orchards and gardens of such marvellous fertility in this land of drought."

The dwelling together in unity, the Psalmist likened to the precious ointment running down from the head of Aaron to the skirt of his garments, and to the descending dew from Hermon to the lower heights. How is that unity obtained ? By talking about unity ? No, that will only cause differences. There are three simple things to observe : First, *be occupied with the Lord*. Dionysius went down to the Academy to Plato. Plato asked what he came for. " Why," said Dionysius, " I thought that you, Plato, would be talking against me to your students." Plato made answer, " Dost thou think, Dionysius, we are so destitute of matter to converse upon that we talk of thee ?" To be occupied with each other is to accentuate our differences and to create animosities ; but to be taken up with the Lord is to lose sight of our differences and to create oneness of heart. That was what brought Pentecost. The saints had lost sight of each other in contemplating their Lord, and the consequence was they were fused by the fire of His grace into one glowing mass of concord. Second, *be occupied for the Lord*. On the day before the Battle of Trafalgar, Nelson took Collingwood and Rotherham, who were at variance, to a spot where they could see the foe opposed to them. " Yonder," said the Admiral, " are your enemies, shake hands and be friends like good

Englishmen." Concentration of attention upon the enemies of the Lord will mean their routing and our victory. The old fable of the two earthen pots in the sea makes them say, " If we clash we are broken." " The daughter of dissension is dissolution," but the daughter of common effort is unity. Third, *be occupied by the Lord*. To keep the unity of the Spirit does not mean uniformity in the body of Christ, nor unanimity of mind in everything, but oneness of spirit ; and that oneness of spirit is only possible by the unifying Spirit. He is called " One Spirit " because He produces oneness of spirit. There is not uniformity in the strings of a violin, nor unanimity of sound as the player draws his bow across them, but there is unity of spirit in the harmony produced by the skilled musician. So it is when the Spirit fills us and controls us in the authority of His Word.

When we are thus occupied with the Lord, for Him and by Him, we must be a benefit to poor lost, arid humanity, for, like the dew of Hermon, we shall cause, in the Spirit's life, the desert to be a fruitful plain, and the Lord shall command His blessing to be enjoyed by us to the full, and in a new way, " even life evermore."

IV. DEW IS PRECIOUS IN ITS BENEFIT.

One of the benedictions in Isaac's blessing upon Jacob was, " God give thee of the dew of heaven " (Gen. xxvii. 28) ; and Moses pronounced a similar blessing upon the tribe of Joseph—" Blessed of the Lord be his land, for the precious things of heaven, for the dew " (Deuteronomy xxxiii. 13). When the dew of Heaven's blessing comes into the life it makes it heavenly. The discords of earth are attuned by the hand of the skilled musician, the Holy Spirit.

" On London Bridge, on one occasion, there stood alone and sad, eighty years ago, a poor old beggar man. He scraped away wretchedly on his old miserable violin in the attempt to draw a few pennies from the passers-by, but no one seemed to listen or stop, and his poor old heart was down in his toeless boots, and cold. A stranger passed along the Bridge, and suddenly halted beside the poor old fiddler, and listened while the weary, wistful eyes searched his face for

'Charity, for the love of God!' Instead of the hoped-for penny the stranger asked for the fiddle: he would help with a tune. The stiff, numbed fingers were glad to pass the old thing over, and the new hands began to play a low, plaintive melody that made the first passer-by find a tear start from his heart on the way to his eye, and he stopped and threw a penny in the old beggar's tattered hat, but still lingered, for the tune is going on. Then another stopped; another penny, and he lingered too. Then another, another, another, and yet they are coming and stopping. In the red heap of coppers in the old man's hat there are now appearing the white gleam of sixpences and shillings. In a few minutes there is a dense crowd of thousands of people massing more and more on the Bridge, while yonder big policeman, instead of saying, 'Move on!' places himself, with tears in his eyes, within hearing of the wondrous strains. Still, from that decrepit old violin, melody like an echo of the song that the angels sang is floating over their heads, and the decrepit old hat is brim-full of coins. 'It is Paganini! It is Paganini!' passes the whisper along." A master hand mastered the old man's violin, and when the Spirit masters us with the dew of His grace, what melody of love, and patience, and fortitude, and purity, He produces, even as He did in the life of Joseph.

V. DEW IS SATURATING IN ITS CONTACT.

When Gideon wished to put the Lord to the test he asked that the dew might saturate the spread fleece and that the ground might be dry all around. In the early morning he wrung a bowl full of water from the fleece (Judges vi. 37, 38). Is there not something suggestive in Gideon's action before he got the bowl of dew? "He thrust" (R.V., "pressed") "the fleece together, and wringed the dew out." The word "*thrust*" is a primary one, and means to press together; and the word "*wringed*" is also a primary one, and means to suck out, to drain, to squeeze. It is used of the bird offered in sacrifice whose blood was to be wrung out (Leviticus i. 15). Of the draining of a cup (Ezekiel xxiii. 34). Gideon would never have got the dew from the fleece by a passing touch, there had to be the earnest grip and resolute wringing. The same thing applies to the enduing of the Spirit. Christ went down into the waters of death before He got the enduement of the Spirit. He was tried in the wilderness before it is said of Him, " He returned in the power of the Spirit." Christ has taught that those who plead effectually are those who pray with importunity (Luke xi. 5-10; xviii. 5). The disciples tarried in the upper room before they were clothed with the Spirit's power. It was the prayer which was " made earnestly " by the Church that brought Peter out of prison (Acts xii. 5, R.V.) It was because Elijah " prayed earnestly " that the heavens were shut up and opened again, and it is " the effectual fervent of a righteous man which availeth much " (James v. 16, 17). Our earnestness is not the cause of God's giving, but it is the condition which makes us appreciate His bestowments. Listlessness and slackness God abominates. Unbelief is characteristic of both, but faith grips and goes. " Tighten your grips," Rutherford used to say. They who tighten their grips will find they are gripped and will be able to grip the tighter. Those who press the fleece of God's promises will always find the dew of the Spirit's blessing.

VI. Dew is produced according to law.

" Who hath begotten the drops of dew ?" (Job xxxviii. 28), God asked Job long ago. Dew is produced by a given law. " If clouds are necessary to produce rain, sunshine is an essential to the formation of dew. A dewy morning only follows a day whose sun has well warmed up the earth. It is necessary that the heat should readily radiate into the surrounding atmosphere by night. When the surface of the earth thus cools down more rapidly than the incumbent air about it, and when the air is saturated with moisture, then, by the contact of temperatures, the air becomes unable to retain its moisture, and yields its sprays and vapours to be shaped by a natural law, the same which rounded the world out of chaos, and orbed the universe; and then what was invisible becomes visible in drops of settling dew. So, whenever dew is seen to fall there must first have been a flowing down of sunshine in the day, and then a responsive current of warmth uprising in the night towards the region whence it came. The earth receives and yet returns the heat the heavens gave, and as if to reward such gratitude the dew descends to refresh and gladden its beseeching and thankful breast."

As the dew is formed according to the law specified above, so the Spirit is given and operates according to the law of grace. The Father, like the sun to the earth, comes to us in the Divine love of His grace in Christ, and Christ in the warmth of that expressed love is associated with the moist atmosphere of the Spirit's life, and the consequence is the bestowment of the dew of His grace, namely, the adaptability and suitability of the law of the Spirit of Life in Christ Jesus which makes us free from the law of sin and death (Romans viii. 2). In Romans vii. and viii. there are four laws mentioned. The moral law which is holy, just and good, but like the judge with the black cap pronouncing death upon the guilty criminal, only condemns us to death ; there is the law of sin in our members, which operates like a fatal disease in the body ; there is the law of the mind or conscience, which like an accusing witness puts us to shame ; and there is the law of the Spirit, which like the marriage of the warm earth and the cool atmosphere, produces the freeing life of the dew of His blessing, which throws off the habit of sin, even as the ascending sap in the tree throws off the dead oak leaves.

VII. DEW IS SILENT IN ITS COMING.

Hushai in his subtle advice to Absalom, counsels him to get a sufficient number to go against David, and says, " So shall we come upon him . . . . and light upon him as the dew falleth on the ground " (II. Samuel xvii. 12). The visitations of the Spirit are silent and searching, and yet none the less real and stimulating. All the great forces of nature are silent in their working. Life with its energy, spring with its beauty, gravitation with its attraction, the sun in its coming, the moon in its shining, the stars in their courses, and the earth moving on its axis, are all silent and potent. The Spirit comes not with blare of trumpet, and boom of cannon, but like the gentle dew He comes quietly and surely ; and a proof of His infilling is a quiet and gentle life and an unobtrusive manner. Two coloured men came up to the outskirts of a crowd on one occasion, when a United States' Senator was making a campaign speech. After listening to the speech for about ten minutes, one of them turned to his companion and asked:

" Who am dat man, Sambo ?"

" Ah don' know what his name am," Sambo replied, " but he certainly do recommen' hisself mos' highly."

There will be no recommendation of ourselves if we are filled with the Spirit, but we shall recommend Christ. When Stephen was filled with the Spirit he said, " I see Jesus."

VIII. THE DEW IS REFRESHING IN ITS MINISTRY.

Job says, " The dew lay all night upon my branch, my glory was fresh in me, and my bow was renewed in my hand" (Job xxix. 19, 20). Sarah Smiley, in speaking of the preciousness of early communings with God, says : " It is one of the rarest exceptions when no dew falls in my garden, and perhaps it is nourished even more in this way than by the rains. As I go to my morning work among the flowers, the dew rests everywhere, often as heavily as though a shower had fallen—that is, everywhere that there is life to receive it ; for I do not find the dew upon the garden paths, nor on any barren spot. But every leaf is laden and every flower is. fresh from this baptism by the hand of God. And as I lightly stir the soil around my flowers, where it is becoming hard and impervious to air, these heavy dews contribute their small quota of rich refreshing to the soil itself." Then Sarah Smiley applies the spiritual lesson of the early dew, " Oh, blessed dew of the speech of God ! How faithful and constant is thy coming ! How thou visitest us in the still hours and in the hours of shadow ! How dost thou utter thy wisdom almost inaudibly ! we see no cloud, we hear no sound, and yet Thy presence is with us and our souls are rejoicing. Thy love bathes our souls with delight. We bow down beneath its pressure in adoring gratitude. The fragrance of our souls goes forth to Thee as every pore of our being opens at this soft touch. We are alone with Thee, and Thou speakest to our hearts. Thou canst not come to us thus in the broad light of the busy day. We bless Thee for the still hours in which our souls are charged anew with life."

The word "*fresh*" in the quotation from Job means to be "*new*," as the margin gives—" My glory was new in me." The word means to be new in the sense of renewed, it comes from a root which means to rebuild and to renew. The root word is used in speaking of the repairing of a house, as when Joash was "minded to *repair* the house of the Lord" (II. Chronicles xxiv. 4); to confirm a transaction, as when Samuel said of Saul's election as King, " let us go to Gilgal and *renew* the kingdom there " (I. Samuel xi. 14); and the Psalmist uses the same word when he says, " Thy youth is *renewed* like the eagles " (Psalm ciii. 5). The word which Job uses means new and renewed, or continually new. The products of the Spirit are always fresh. The word is generally rendered " new." Some of its uses will illustrate. The new fruits found in the garden of the Spirit's grace (Canticles vii. 13), the new spirit of God-consciousness (Ezekiel xi. 19), the new heart of affectionate loyalty (Ezekiel xxxvi. 26), the new threshing instrument of effective service (Isaiah xli. 15), the new song of adoring worship (Psalm xl. 3), the new song of glorious victory (Psalm xcviii. 1), and the new things of Divine revelation (Isaiah xlviii. 6), are all the gift of the Holy Spirit. It is only these fresh things of His grace that can keep us fresh in our pace. His renewings are ever " fresh as morning dews distilled on flowers."

IX. DEW IS HIDING IN ITS ENCLOSURE.

" The dew lay round about the host; and when the dew that lay was gone up, behold upon the face of the wilderness there lay a small round thing " (Exodus xvi. 13, 14). Thus the disclosure of the manna is mentioned. As long as the dew was on the ground the manna was hidden, but when the dew was exhaled, the manna was revealed. What a type of the hiding of the Spirit and His disclosing of Christ. Mr. Neil tells us " there is a plant called the Gory dew. It consists of little spots upon the ground. Viewed under a microscope, they appear as minute globules. There is a large spot of grass land near Hastings covered with it. While the earth is dry it remains unseen, but when the rain descends the startled passer-by observes that the whole meadow has suddenly become red, like a gory sea. So with men in their natural state. While all is dry and barren they cannot see the blood of Christ. They fail to discern the rich cleansing tide that stains the wood of the accursed tree, and bedews the ground of Golgotha. It is one of the mysteries of grace, that from the carnal eyes our God is a God that hideth Himself. But, oh! how differently it looks when the Spirit of God descends in showers of grace, taking the things of Jesus, and showing them to us. How plainly the precious blood is seen now, the costly blood of atonement, that has made our peace. Every other object seems to fade away as we stand, and wonder, and adore in the presence of the bleeding Lamb of God."

X. Dew is reflective in its mirroring.

"Jacob shall be in the midst of many people, as a dew from the Lord" (Micah v. 7). Being blessed of the Lord, Jacob in turn becomes a power for Him. Longfellow says, "Every dewdrop hath a whole heaven in it."

An open-air preacher was describing the Lord Jesus to a number of children in a street in the slums of a great city. The children listened with rapt attention to the unfolding of the Man of men. He had not mentioned any name, but when the question was asked as to Who the Personage was, a boy immediately replied, "I know him, mister, he lives in our street." The boy knew a humble follower of Christ who was so like Christ that as he listened to the unfolding of the Lord's character, he recognized the Lord Himself. We are exhorted to walk as Christ walked (1. John ii. 6). If we did, what a revelation of the Christ there would be to the world. The world is hungry for Christ, and He Who is the Bread of Life is the only One Who can feed. He says to us, as He said to the disciples long ago, "Give ye them to eat." And surely if the world sees that Christ satisfies us, they will want to be

The Dew

satisfied too. This satisfied and satisfying life is only possible as we live in the Spirit.

> A dewdrop fell from a far cloud height,
> And through long hours of lonely night
> The little orb with its paling light
>   Was lost from view :
> But earth mists soon withdrew apace,
> And the great sun peering into space
> Finds there his own reflected face,
> And draws the dewdrop to its heaven above.
>
> A soul possessed of heavenly birth
> Came down to do its work on earth,—
> What was the end of honest worth
>   Who cared or knew ?
> But when life's hour of night was run,
> The Father, seeing all " well done,"
> Finds His own Image in His son
> And takes him to Himself in fullest love.

XI. Dew is rich in its contents.

We are told, " The dew seems to be the richest present the atmosphere gives to the earth, having, when purified in a vessel, a black sediment like mud at the bottom ; this seems to cause the darkish colour to the upper part of the ground, and the sulphur which is found in the dew may be the chief ingredient of the cement of the earth, sulphur being very glutinous, as nitre is dissolvent. Dew has both these."

Jehovah, in speaking of His Word, says, " My doctrine shall drop as the rain, My speech shall distil as the dew " (Deuteronomy xxxii. 2). God's Word gently drops into the heart and imparts its nature in those who allow it to work. As the glutinous sulphur and the dissolvent nitre are found in the dew, so the Holy Spirit dissolves the hardness of the heart, and causes His grace to be an adhesive quality in our lives. There is no greater proof of His presence than when His character is reproduced.

A road surveyor who was finishing the levelling and paving of a long stretch of street, asked a minister of the gospel, in an enthusiastic tone, if he did not think it was splendid. " You see," he said, " I am trying to put my Christianity into the streets I make." If Christ is in the heart by the Spirit, Christianity will certainly be in the street, yea, in everything. He will be in the home as the Harmonizer, in the market as the Adjuster, in the service as the Worker, in the Church as the Lover, in the world as the Example, in the heart as the Purifier, and in the Lord's work as the Mover, when He dwells within as the Sanctifier.

XII. Dew is emblematic of strength.

Speaking of Christ and His future glory as King and Victor, we read of Him, " Thou hast the dew of Thy youth " (Psalm cx. 3), that is, fulness of power and strength. Pulsford comments on these words, " Jesus has the beauty of eternity's morning upon Him to-day and will retain it for ever. As though He were but now proceeding from the Father, He wears, unchanged, the pledges of His youth. And from the womb of the resurrection morning He ascended, in the clothing of our glorified humanity. Everlasting morning sits upon His brow, and comes forth from Him as the regenerative power of all souls. With Him the fresh, fragrant morning, the rich, dewy morning, standeth still for ever."

The Spirit is the believer's power and strength. Remember the prayer of Paul for the believers at Ephesus, " that they might be strengthened with might by the Spirit in the inner man " (Ephesians iii. 16). That is what we want and may have—the power, the strength of the Spirit working in us mightily. In Him we are strong to be weak and nothing, that Christ may be everything; strong to go forth in willing, loving service; strong to be empty, that He may fill us; and strong to be humble, that He may exalt us. Remember how our Father delights to use weak things, viz., a worm, Jacob, to thresh a mountain; a little David to overcome a Goliath; a stammering Moses to lead God's people; a once-backsliding Peter to preach the Gospel; a young lad to feed a multitude; 300 lapping men to defeat a host of Midianites; and the jawbone of an ass to slay a thousand Philistines. Oh! believers, let Him be your strength, not only in theory, but in living reality.

XIII. DEW IS GLORIFIED IN ITS ASSOCIATION.

One of the most precious promises of God to Israel is, " I will be as the dew unto Israel : he shall grow as the lily, and cast forth his roots like Lebanon " (Hosea xiv. 5). McCheyne in commenting upon this verse as typifying the Spirit, says, " It is peculiarly true of the dew that it moistens everything where it falls ; it leaves not one leaf unvisited ; there is not a tiny blade of grass on which the diamond drops do not descend ; every leaf and stem of the bush is burdened with the precious load. Just so it is peculiarly true of the Spirit, that there is not a faculty, there is not an affection, or power, or passion of the soul on which the Spirit does not descend, working through all, refreshing, reviving, renewing, recreating all." Similar promises of God's favour and blessing are found in Isaiah xviii. 4 ; and xxvi. 19.

The Spirit is also glorified in His association. He glories in glorifying Christ, and He is glorified in the description which Christ gave of Him as recorded in His parting message to His disciples. One of His names is " The Spirit of Glory " (1. Peter iv. 14), and not without significance is the association in which it is found—" If ye be reproached for the name of Christ, happy are ye, for the Spirit of Glory and of God resteth upon you." The reproach to which reference is made is no mere taunt, it means real persecution. The word is rendered " *revile* " (Matthew v. 11), " *cast in teeth* " (Matthew xxvii. 44), " *upbraideth* " (James i. 5), and " *suffer reproach* " (1. Timothy iv. 10). When we are suffering wrongfully for the sake of Christ, then we need the tempering of the Spirit and we have His benediction, for He is said to rest upon us. The word " *resteth* " is a forceful one—" *anapauo.*" It is a compound word. " *Pauo* " means to pause, to stop, and " *ana,*" as a prefix, signifies intensity or repetition, hence, the meaning is to repose, to take rest, to be refreshed. The word is rendered " *rest* " in Matthew xi. 28, " *take ease* " in Luke xii. 19, and " *refreshed* " in 1. Corinthians xvi. 18. The compensation to the sufferer is, the Spirit " *resteth* " upon him to his spirit's repose in God, ease of mind, rest of heart, and refreshment of soul. A dear friend of mine, the late

Dr. Henry Wilson, of New York, when lying ill in Atlanta and suffering much, for one lung was hardened and the other was hardening, looked up in the face of one who was nursing him, and with a sweet smile said, " It is all right when your hand is on the great dynamo." When we rest in Him, and the Spirit rests upon us, all is well, no matter from where the suffering comes.

XIV. Dew is identified with Christ.

" My head is filled with dew " (Song of Solomon v. 2). These are the words of the Bridegroom. The Bride is asleep while the Bridegroom is outside in the cold night air, with the dew upon His head and locks. He wanted to come in and bless her with His presence. Alas! alas! how many Christians there are who are asleep, like the Church at Laodicea, mixing up with the world; asleep as to their privileges and responsibilities, while Christ is outside in the cold. Christ is waiting with fulness of blessing, fulness of power, fulness of peace and joy. Often we hear Christians asking if there is any harm in this or that, referring to doubtful books and questionable places. An old classic story illustrates this. It is supposed that the sirens of the Mediterranean sang so sweetly as to allure the sailors who came within their charms to destruction. One, Ullysses, returning from the Trojan war, was warned of this danger by Circe, who directed that he should stop the ears of his men with wax and then have himself tied to the mast. This was done, but when Ullysses came within hearing of the music he was so enchanted that he made frantic signs to his sailors to unloose him that he might steer for the shore. But, as previously instructed by him, they only bound him all the more. But when the Argonauts came, they needed not to have recourse to any such expedients; and why? Because they had one Orpheus, a sweet singer, on board, and so the sirens had no charm for them. Oh! if we were fully alive to the attractive power, the charm, the beauty of the person of Christ,—if He dwelt in our heart by faith,—we should be so enraptured with Him that everything else but Himself would lose its attractiveness for us, and we should be so full of Christ that we should have no time, but for Him ; no voice, but to speak of Him ; no eyes, but to look to Him ; no hands, but to serve Him ; no feet, but to walk with Him ; no mind, but to think of Him. Thus we should indeed be filled with the Spirit, for the proof that we are filled with the Spirit is as Christ is seen in our life. May He of Whom we have been thinking draw our hearts closer to our Beloved.

" O dewdrop ! O dewdrop !
 I would be a dewdrop too !
 When the fatal glow,
 Sultry, still, and slow,
 Makes the scentless flowers
 Droop in withering bowers,—
 Leaf and shade and bloom
 Touch with early doom,—
We would follow, sweet and bright,
Blending life and love and light,
Making what was parched and dreary
 Glad and lovely, fresh and fair ;
Softly cheering what was weary,
 Sparkling, starlike, everywhere."

Syllabus of
The Water as an Emblem of the Holy Spirit

I. *Propitiatory Pictures*—Atonement a finished work—Water under the ark—Carey and the soldier—Water out of the Rock—The Smitten Rock and the Supplying Stream—Water in the cloven place—" Jaw " or " Lehi " ?—Quotation from Grant—Water over the bird of sacrifice—Lady's gift to wounded soldier—Water and ashes on the individual—Water beside the altar—Augustine on Christ's death—II. *Pentecostal Portraits*—Bathed in water—" *Louo* " and " *Nipto* "—Water in bottle and well—Spring at Lititz—Dyer's sayings—Bottles and wells—Water in Egypt and Canaan—Sixteen particulars—Lapping up the water—" My life is a complete failure," and energized—The water of the upper and nether springs—Walley on " God is able " and his experience—Water in the ditches—Human and Divine—" Give candy to each other "—III. *Pointed Particulars*—" Living water "—" Springing up "—" Holy water "—Methodist class leader's reference—Purifying water—Cleansing of the Levites—IV. *Pertinent Points*—Water is essential—Spiritual water—Begetter and maintainer—Water is growth-producing—Threefold growth—Michael Angelo and work—Water is lifting—How the scows lifted—From what the Lord lifts us—Water is submerging—The Pontoon's work—Love and prayer got her in—Water is cleansing—Pure things which the purity of the Pure Spirit gives—Water is satisfying—Elohim and El—We need Father, Son and Spirit—" Thou art what I want "—Water is reviving—The old tree sprouting—Water is refreshing—Where the surveyor found water in Florida—Sir E. Denny's testimony—V. *Precious Promises*—The Word speaking at Edinburgh Conference.

THE WATER

AS David took five smooth stones out of the brook, so we take five points out of the stream of the Word, as suggested by the references to water, namely, propitiatory pictures, Pentecostal portraits, pointed particulars, pertinent points, and precious promises.

I. PROPITIATORY PICTURES.

We speak of Christ's sacrifice as propitiatory, because the consciousness of sin makes us feel Christ alone can give satisfaction for it. This He has done " once for all." God has met His own requirement in Christ's work. Atonement is not a work continuous in us, it is the completed work apart from us. Christ gave to God for us a perfect sacrifice, which gives perfect satisfaction, bestows a perfect conscience, and provides a perfect salvation.

Water under the ark. Noah and his family are said to be " saved by *water " (1. Peter iii. 20). The waters that overflowed the disobedient to their destruction bore the ark up to Noah's deliverance. There were two factors in his salvation, namely, the water and the ark. So there are two workers in our redemption, the Holy Spirit and Christ. He enabled Christ to offer Himself to God, and He brings us into contact with Christ, and as the ark passed through the judgment, so we have died with Christ in His death (this is the meaning of baptism), as the dying soldier said to Carey, when the latter asked him if he was afraid to die, " Oh, no, sir, I have died already !" He meant that in Christ's death he had died for his sin, and therefore did not fear the falling asleep.

---

* " *Dia,*" with the genitive, means " saved by means of water," and indicates an active agent.

Water out of the rock. " Behold, he smote the Rock, that the waters gushed out, and the streams overflowed " (Psalm lxxviii. 20), thus tersely does the Spirit describe the incident of God's provision to thirsty Israel, and He further adds, " That Rock was Christ " (I. Corinthians x. 4). *The smitten rock.* Before the water came the rock was smitten— " He smote the rock." The word " *smote* " is a primary one, and means to smite, and is often used in a punitive sense, hence, it is rendered " *punish* " (Leviticus xxvi. 24), " *smote* " (Exodus xii. 29), and " *smitten* " in referring to God's judicial acts, and is also the word employed in Zechariah xiii. 7—" *smite* the shepherd." He was smitten by judgment that we might be saved from it. He was punished that we might be pardoned. Our rock was stricken that He might supply all our need. *The supplying stream*— " The waters gushed out." The Hebrew for " *gushed out* " means to flow freely and is used to describe the plenitude of the land of Canaan as a land " *flowing* with milk and honey " (Exodus iii. 8, 17). That the water was abundant is emphasized by the supplementary statements—" The streams overflowed," and that " they ran in the dry places like a river " (Psalm cv. 41). The word " *overflowed* " gives the thought of abundance, for it not only means to gush, but to inundate, and with the added significance of force, hence, to gallop, to cleanse, to conquer. The word is used of " *rinsed* hands " and a " *washed* chariot " (Leviticus xv. 11 ; I. Kings xxii. 38), hence, to cleanse ; of a running brook— " The brook that *ran* " (II. Chronicles xxxii. 4) and of a flood that " *can* . . . . *drown* " (Canticles viii. 7), hence, of force ; and of an " *overflowing* rain " (Ezekiel xxxviii. 22), and of a horse that " *rusheth* into the battle " (Jeremiah viii. 6). From the wounded Saviour, by the Spirit, there comes to the child of God a cleansing which is thorough, a blessing which satisfies, a power which is irresistible, a love which is unquenchable, a life which is abundant, and a supply which is constant.

Water in the cloven hollow place. The Authorized Version says, " God clave a hollow place that was in the jaw " (Judges xv. 19), but the Revised Version says, " That is in Lehi."

The Water

"Lehi" and "jaw" is the same Hebrew word. Rotherham renders the verse, "So then God clave open the hollow that is in Lehi, and there came water therefrom, and he drank and his spirit revived." The water was not found in the jawbone of the dead ass, but in a hollow place that God clave open at Lehi. The word "*clave*" means to rip, to divide, to break; and is used of one who "*cleaveth* wood" (Ecclesiastes x. 9), of David's mighty men who "*brake through*" the host of the Philistines (II. Samuel xxiii. 16), of a bird who lays her eggs to "*hatch*" them (Isaiah xxxiv. 15), and of God's act when He "*divided* the sea" (Psalm lxxviii. 13). Christ was cloven in a place called Calvary, the place of a skull, and from His wounded side there flowed a cleansing stream, and because of it, there comes the Spirit's consecrating power, as Toplady says,—

> "Let the water and the blood,
> From Thy riven side when flowed,
> Be of sin the double cure,
> Cleanse me from its guilt and power."

The "*hollow place*" which was cloven means the "bruising place." The word for "hollow place" only occurs in one place, and there it is given "*mortar*"—"Though thou bray a fool *in a mortar*" (Proverbs xxvii. 22). Grant in his numerical Bible comments, God answers by cleaving the "Bruising place that is in Lehi," so that water comes out of it, and Samson revives. The likeness to the cleft rock in the wilderness can hardly escape us. The cross and its results for us are needed to be held in constant remembrance; and the place of bruising—*machtesh*, the "mortar"—is not likely to make the reference here less plain. The connection with the scene that has just been before us is also evident: so plain that our common version speaks of it as "the hollow place" —"socket" it might mean—"that was in the jaw." That this is not right, the fact of its being "in Lehi unto this day" is sufficient witness. And the bruising-place that is in Lehi reminds us surely of the Philistine defeat. Yet the spring of water is in marked contrast. Not by "bruising," but by *being* "bruised for our iniquity," did the Lord of glory bring forth the living water for our death-faint souls.

Water over the bird of sacrifice. For the cleansing of the leper, two birds had to be taken by the priest, one of which had to be killed over running water, and the other, with the blood of its fellow on its wings, was let loose into the open field. The two birds are a type of the death and resurrection of Christ, and the running water is a type of the Spirit in His association with Christ, for it was by His power that He fulfilled His atoning work. The water was in an earthen, or a vessel of earth, which is representative of Christ's humanity. In that humanity, filled with the Spirit, He had the acquired capacity to die, and by that death the Spirit assures us there is cleansing from the leprosy of sin's defilement. A lady in Italy once put a magnificent bouquet of flowers upon the bed of a wounded soldier. The soldier looked up with his pale face and his eyes full of tears and said, " That is too much kindness !" " No," she replied, " not too much for one drop of Italian blood." The Spirit reminds us that Christ gave all His precious blood for us, and now the least we can do for Him is to consecrate our life to Him.

Water on the individual. The ordinance of the red heifer was for cleansing the person who had come in contact with death. The heifer had to be free from blemish, red in colour, killed and consumed outside the camp, and then its ashes were to be kept in a clean place. When a person was defiled some of the ashes were to be taken and then " running water was to be put thereto " and it was to be sprinkled upon him. The whole ordinance is described in detail in Numbers xix., and its typical meaning is summarized in Hebrews ix. 13, 14. As in the Old Testament the ashes (memorial of death) and the water are associated, so in the New Testament the " blood of Christ " and " the Eternal Spirit " are identified. When the believer comes in contact with the dead things of the world, he needs the application of the death of Christ through the Spirit to restore the fellowship which has been interrupted.

Water beside the altar. Ezekiel's vision of the holy waters describes how they "issued from under the threshold of the house . . . . at the south side of the altar " (Ezekiel xlvii. 1) ; and then a description is given of these waters in their life-giving flow and fruit-producing qualities. It will be noticed the waters are identified with the altar. The blessing of this millennial scene has its source, as all blessing has, in the atoning sacrifice of Christ. God has no blessing to bestow apart from that death. His death is the hub around which all the universe revolves, His death is the sun which blesses all with the warmth of God's love, His death is the mystic key that opens the treasure-trove of His riches, His death is the vital wand that silvers every cave with its benediction, His death is the forerunner to secure the blessing of heaven, His death is the paralyzer of the powers of hell, His death is the harbinger of all the good of grace, and all the grace of glory. We say with Augustine, " Christ's cross is the Christcross of all our happiness ; it delivers us from all blindness of error, and enriches our darkness with light ; it restoreth the troubled soul to rest ; it bringeth strangers to God's acquaintance ; it maketh remote foreigners near neighbours ; it cutteth off discord, concludeth a league of everlasting peace, and is the bounteous author of all good."

II. PENTECOSTAL PORTRAITS.

Incidents abound which might be taken as illustrating the Spirit's work. The Word is luminous with Heavenly light, throbs with the Spirit's life, and thrills with Divine love as it operates in the heart.

Bathed in water. Before Aaron and his sons entered upon their priestly office they were washed* or bathed in water (Exodus xl. 12) ; the leper had to " wash himself " after he had been sprinkled with the blood (Leviticus xiv. 8, 9) ; anyone touching anything unclean and being touched by an unclean person had to " bathe " himself in water (Leviticus xv. 5, 6, 7, 8, 10, 11, 13, 16, 18, 21, 22, 27) ; the high priest on the day of atonement had to " wash " himself before he put on the holy garments (Leviticus xvi. 4), and after the atoning work and before he put on his priestly robes he had to wash (Leviticus xvi. 24), and also those who attended upon him (Leviticus xvi. 26, 28) ; before Naaman was cleansed from his leprosy he had to " wash in Jordan seven times "

---

* The same Hebrew word occurs in each of the Scriptures cited. Rendered " *washed* " and " *bathe.*"

(II. Kings v. 10); and the priests in their attendance upon the tabernacle had first to wash their hands and feet (Exodus xxx. 20, 21). Wherever the whole body of a person was bathed, apart from the contact which made unclean, it seems to typify the work of the Holy Spirit in the new birth, where the hands and feet only were washed it shadows forth the preparation in the Spirit which is essential for acceptable service, and where the bathing was because of uncleanness contracted, it denotes the Spirit's work in applying the blood which alone can cleanse.

When Christ washed His disciples' feet, He referred to a twofold cleansing when He said, "He that has been bathed needeth not save to wash his feet" (R.V., John xiii. 10). Christ uses two words, namely, "*louo*," which means to bathe the whole person, and is used of being "*washed*" in the blood (Revelation i. 5), and symbolically of purity (Hebrews x. 22); and the other word is "*nipto*," which means to cleanse a part of the body, such as the face, hands and feet.* The Spirit of God alone is the one Who can bathe us in the cleansing tide of Calvary whereby we are washed; He alone can put away all the old associations of the former life of sin's habit, even as the water removed the traces of leprosy from the leper; and He alone can give us, by means of the laver of His Word, that personal purity and fitness for service in Divine things.

Water in bottle and well. When Abraham sent Hagar and Ishmael away he gave them bread and a bottle of water. The supply was soon exhausted, and Hagar expected that Ishmael would die, but the Lord opened her eyes to see a well (Genesis xxi. 14-19). What a difference between water in a well and water in a bottle. At the Lititz Springs in the Moravian Settlement at Lititz, Pennsylvania, over the principal spring are the words, "*Gottes Bruennlein hat Wasser die Fuelle*," which means, "The Spring of the Lord is full of water." There is in our Saviour an inexhaustible supply

---

* "*Wash* thy face" (Matthew vi. 17); "they *wash* not their hands" (Matthew xv. 2); and "*washed* the saints' feet" (I. Timothy v. 10).

as good W. Dyer, of the 18th century, said, " He is so excellent that no good can be added to Him ; and so infinite, that no good can be diminished in Him." The bottle of past experience will run dry, but the well of constant supply is unfailing. The bottle of the means of grace will sometimes fail, but the well of grace is perennial in its freshness. The bottle of ordinances may be cracked, but the well of truth is an ever-living source. The bottle of our conceptions of truth may be limited, but the promises of God are constant and ever-availing. The bottle of our service may be meagre, but the livingness of His priesthood is evermore. The bottle of our devotions may give out, but the devotion of His ever-welling love is inseparable. The bottle of our resources will surely fail, so we had better throw it away ; but the well of His all-sufficiency is God Himself, so we had better be supplied from Him, for as Dyer says, " He is a Spring full of the water of life, a Hive of sweetness, a Magazine of riches, a River of pleasures, wherein you may bathe your souls to all eternity."

Water in Egypt and Canaan. " The land, whither thou goest in to possess it, is not as the land of Egypt, from whence ye came out, where thou sowedst thy seed, and wateredst it with thy foot, as a garden of herbs : but the land, whither ye go to possess it, is a land of hills and valleys, and drinketh water of the rain of heaven" (Deuteronomy xi. 10, 11). Egypt is a type of the world (Revelation xi. 8), and its water of earth's resources ; but the land of Canaan and its heaven watered country is typical of the fulness of the Spirit's blessing in Christ. What that land was like and its supplies is given in Deuteronomy viii. 7-9, in sixteen particulars. We can only indicate their spiritual suggestion. The " *brooks* " of the Spirit's power flowing out in testimony (John vii. 38) ; the " *fountains* " of the Spirit's graces springing up to God's praise (John iv. 14) ; the " *depths* " of God's love and grace in His Divine purpose (Romans xi. 33) ; the " *valleys* " of Christ's grace in His humiliation and suffering (II. Corinthians viii. 9) ; the " *hills* " of Christ's ascension and coming glory (Acts i. 12 ; Zechariah xiv. 4) ; the " *wheat* "* of the Spirit's

---

* The wheat harvest began at Pentecost (Leviticus xxiii. 15, 16) and is therefore typical of what the glorified Christ can be to us in the power of the Spirit.

supply in revealing Christ (Ephesians iii. 16, 17); the "*barley*"* of Christ's death to satisfy the need of our hearts (John vi. 51); the "*vine*" of Christ's life-producing fruitfulness (John xv. 1-4); the "*fig-tree*" of the Spirit's earnest of coming blessing (Matthew xxiv. 32; Ephesians i. 13, 14); the "*pomegranate*" of the priestly service of Christ (Exodus xxxix. 24; Hebrews iv. 14, 15); the "*oil olive*" of the Spirit's sanctification and service (1. John ii. 27); the "*honey*" of the Spirit's words of precious promise (Psalm xix. 10); the "*iron*" of the Spirit's enabling power (Deut. xxxiii. 25); the "*brass*" of Christ's enduringness (Revelation i. 15); the "*milk*" of the Spirit's nourishing truth (1. Peter ii. 2); and the rain of the Spirit's abundant supply (Isaiah xliv. 3; 11. Corinthians ix. 8). How foolish that any of us should go to the world of unsatisfaction, or wander in the wilderness of crippling unbelief, when we might feed upon the old corn of the land. How unwise that we should endeavour to water God's gardens with the effort of our own endeavour, when we might have the rain of the Spirit's all-sufficient enduement.

Lapping up the water. Only the lappers in Gideon's army were chosen for Jehovah's special service. They were careless of their comfort and consecrated and courageous for the fray (Judges vii. 4-7). We should be willing to take a dog's place (Matthew xv. 27), and to follow our Lord like a dog follows his master, as †Caleb did (Numbers xiv. 24). "My life is a complete failure," said a wealthy Christian man. Why? Because he had gone in the wrong direction. There is a success which is a failure, and a failure which is a success. Many a Christian worker is energetic, but we need to be energized. The energy which is self-generated, generates to self; but the energy which is God produced, produces for God. When we get low enough to lap as dogs, God can lift us high enough to be deliverers. Paul gives us the secret of his

---

* The barley harvest began to be gathered at the season of the Passover.

† Caleb means a dog. How appropriate when He says, "He followed the Lord fully."

ministry in the expression, "Striving according to His working"* (Colossians i. 29). There is all the difference in the world between a hand-saw used to saw wood, and a circular-saw attached to machinery, cutting through a log. The efforts of our labour are tiresome and trying, but the operations of the Spirit are trenchant and triumphant. Our wisdom is therefore to be attached to the Spirit's might, and be detached from our self-reliance.

The water of the upper and nether springs. When Achsah was asked by her father what he should give her she replied, "Give me springs of water. And Caleb gave her the upper springs and the nether springs" (Joshua xv. 19; Judges i. 15). He gave her a double portion. So our Divine Caleb gives to His own a double blessing of the Spirit. The "nether" blessing of His indwelling presence, and the "upper" spring of His enduring power. We need the Spirit as the Spirit of Adoption crying in our hearts, "Abba, Father"; and we also need the Spirit as the Spirit of Ability accomplishing in our lives. A servant of Christ gave this personal testimony in Chicago at a Convention held there. He said, " Within a week after my conversion, thirty years ago, I passed by the window of a picture store in St. Louis, and I saw hanging in the window an engraving of a painting of Daniel in the den of lions. The prophet with his hands behind him, and the lions circling about him, is looking up and answering the king's question. The one thing that I was in mortal fear of in those days was that I might go back to my sins. I was a drunken lawyer in St. Louis when I was converted, with no power over an appetite for strong drink, and I was so afraid of a bar-room, or a hotel, or a club that when I saw I was coming to one I would cross the street. I was in torment day and night. No one had told me anything about the keeping power of Jesus Christ. I stood before that

---

* See the use of the words rendered "working" in the Epistle to the Ephesians, rendered "working," "worketh," "wrought," and "effectual working" (i. 11, 19, 20; ii. 2; iii. 7, 20; iv. 16).

picture, and a great hope and faith came into my heart, and I said :—

"'Why, these lions are all about me,—my old habits and my old sins, but the God that shut the lions' mouths for Daniel can shut them for me!'

"I learned that my God was able. He had saved me, and He was able to deliver me from the lions. Oh, what a rest it was! It had been proposed to me to go to some railroad men over at East St. Louis, but I refused to go, and I did not give the reason. The reason was that East St. Louis simply bristled with bar-rooms, and I was afraid I should smell that breath of hell coming out of those open places, licensed by a paternal government that needs the money so badly. After I saw that picture I went."

Water in the ditches. "Make this valley full of ditches" was God's command through Elisha to the King of Israel, and "It came to pass in the morning, when the meat offering was offered (R.V., 'The time of offering the oblation'), that, behold .... the country was filled with water" (II. Kings iii. 16-20). These words give us the combination of the human with the Divine, or the human filling the condition of the Divine promise, and the Lord fulfilling His Word as a result. We make the ditches and the Lord fills them with water. When we have the ditch of whole-hearted faith in God's Word, then we may expect the inflow of the Spirit's grace, and know, what George Macdonald calls, "The Eternal thought speaking in your thought." When we make the ditch of intense brotherly affection for each other, then we feel the heart-throb of the love of God. "What is the subject for the next young people's meeting?" I asked the Secretary on one occasion. She did not speak very distinctly. She said, "By love serve one another." I thought she said, "Give candy to each other." "Why that's a sweet subject!" I exclaimed. Love is ever a sweetener and it is certainly toothsome to the Lord. When we make the ditch of holy prayer and intercession, then there is sure to be the manifestation of Divine power. The pleading of prayer ever brings the prevailing of power.

THE WATER

III. POINTED PARTICULARS.

The many adjectives found in association with water illustrate the characteristics of the Spirit's nature and service.

Living water. The adjective "*running*" in connection with water, which is mentioned several times in Leviticus xiv., is the same word as rendered "*living*" in the same chapter, and it is also translated "*alive.*" Christ promised to the woman of Samaria "*living* water" (John iv. 10). The Spirit of Life leads us to the Living Stone to quicken us, to the Living God to shield us, to the Living High Priest to keep us, to the Living Bread to feed us, to the Living Word to assure us, to the Living Way to access us, to the Living Christ to satisfy us, and to the Living Water that He may sway us. Christ said of the Living Water it should be in them "a well of water *springing up.*" The word "*springing up*" is the same as rendered "*leaping*" and "*leaped*" in speaking of the cripples who were made to walk and leap (Acts iii. 8; xiv. 10). How many lame saints there are! The lameness goes when the Spirit comes.

Holy Water. The ordinance for testing a suspected woman's faithfulness is described in Numbers v. 11-31. When the woman drank the water and she was innocent it caused her no harm, but if she was defiled then she came under the curse and judgment of God. The Holy Water is frequently called "bitter water," which is mixed with the dust of the floor. If we are right with the Lord the Holy Spirit will be power and comfort, as He was to the early Church, who walked in the fear of the Lord; but if we are not right with Him then He will be a Spirit of judgment and confusion, as He was to Ananias and Sapphira (Acts v. 1-10; ix. 31). A coloured Methodist class leader said in his class one day, "Brethren, when I was a boy, I took a hatchet and went into de woods. When I found a tree dat was straight, big and solid, I didn't touch dat tree; but when I found one leaning a little and hollow inside, I soon had him down. So when de debbil go after Christians, he don't touch dem dat stand straight and true, but dem dat lean a little and are hollow inside."

Purifying water. At the cleansing of the Levites in fitting them for the tabernacle service, there was sprinkled upon them " water of purifying " or " water of expiation " (R.V., Numbers viii. 7), this seems to be the same as mentioned in Numbers xix. 9, 17, which is there called " water of separation : it is a purification for sin," or a " sin offering " (R.V.) The Hebrew word for " purifying " and " purification " is rendered sin-offering again and again in Leviticus iv. The sin-offering in its Godward aspect was to " make an atonement for sin " (Leviticus iv. 35), but in its manward aspect it was to cleanse from sin (Leviticus xvi. 30). The sprinkling of the memorial (ashes) of the sin-offering with water upon a person, typified the ground upon which the Levites had the qualification to serve the Lord, namely, cleansing by the atoning sacrifice. The Holy Spirit in speaking of priestly service weaves into an exhortation the above thoughts when He says, " Let us draw near with a true heart in full assurance of faith, having our hearts sprinkled from an evil conscience, and our bodies washed with pure water " (Hebrews x. 22). The purity of clean hands, pure hearts, and pure consciences are requisite for true worship and loyal service, and these are the bestowments of the Spirit.

IV. PERTINENT POINTS.

Many are the things which are produced by water. Its essentiality is beyond all question. Its predominence is self-evident. Water forms more than two-thirds of the earth's surface, and it has been estimated that if all the water of the globe could be collected it would form a sphere 900 miles in diameter.

Water is essential. Water is an essential constituent of all animal and vegetable life. The absence of water means death and desert. There are two things which are absolutely essential in spiritual things. The first is life from the Spirit. Christ said, " Except a man be born of water and the Spirit he cannot enter the kingdom of God " (John iii. 5). Many have tried to make the water to mean baptism, but water and spirit stand for the same thing. The sentence comes under the figure of speech called " hendiadys," which means one by means of two, that is, two words are used to express the same thing. We have many illustrations of its use in the Old and New Testaments. Take one illustration from each. In I. Samuel xvii. 40 we read, David put the five smooth stones "in a shepherd's bag, even in a scrip," literally, it is "in his shepherd's leather bag." In Acts iii. 14, "Ye denied the Holy One and the Just." Two persons are not meant, but one. The One denied was the righteous Holy One. Thus John iii. 5 should read, "Except a man be begotten of spiritual water, he cannot enter the kingdom of God. The Spirit is not only essential to implant the spiritual life, but He is essential to maintain it. In Galatians v. 25 we read, "If we live in the Spirit, let us also walk in the Spirit." Surely if we live in the Spirit we walk in Him! The Authorized Version is meaningless. The Revised Version is better—"If we live by the Spirit, by the Spirit let us also walk." The passage might be paraphrased as follows: "Since by the Spirit we are spiritually alive, by that same Spirit we should walk." In other words the Author of the spiritual life is also its Maintainer.

Water is growth-producing. Bildad asked Job the question, "Can the flag grow without water?" (Job viii. 11). We might equally ask, "Can the Christian grow in grace without the Spirit?" There is a threefold growth in the Divine life. First, the *upward growth into Christ* (Ephesians iv. 15). This is obtained by the prevailing of the Word of God in our lives (Acts xix. 20), the feeding upon the Word of God as our food (I. Peter ii. 2), the displacement of self the domination of Christ (John iii. 30), and the personal acquaintance with God (Colossians i. 9, 10). Second, *the downward growth in the truth.* Rootage is essential to foliage. In the soil of God's truth is found life to quicken, grace to grow, love to inspire, truth to sanctify, food to nourish, sun to warm, water to revive, and joy to gladden. Third, *the outward growth in usefulness.* To abound in the work of the Lord, is to have the work of the Lord abound in us. It is said that after the toils of the day Michael Angelo would be so weary sometimes that he would go to bed dressed, and as soon as he was refreshed would be up, and with candle stuck in cap so that its light might fall properly on the figure, he would pursue his loved art. Living in a state of celibacy, he was accustomed to say his art was his wife and his works his children, and when some persons reproached him for living so melancholy a life, he said, " Art is jealous, she requires the whole and entire man." So the work of the Lord requires us all and always. And the Lord the Holy Spirit is the Lord of the work and of the worker.

Water is lifting. The lifting power of water was seen in its lifting the ark upon the mountains of Ararat (Genesis viii. 4). On one occasion a vessel was sunk in the Mississippi River, and the problem was how to raise it. Several attempts were made, but to no purpose. At last an old man undertook to raise the sunken boat. At low tide the hull could be seen. The man made no attempt to raise the vessel by attempting to lift it by an outside power, but he got two large scows,* and got strong chains and lashed them around the sunken vessel and scows. Then he waited and watched for the incoming tide. The tide rose and rose, and soon there was tension and strain on the cables, and at last the sunken vessel was lifted and the scows and it were soon docked. What human effort could not accomplish, God's lifting water did. One of the names by which Jehovah is known is " The Lifter " (Psalm iii. 3). There are many things from which the Lord lifts us. He lifts us from the gates of spiritual death—" Thou that liftest me up from the gates of death " (Psalm ix. 13) ; He lifts us from the realm of our enemies—" Thou liftest me up from those that rise up against me " (Psalm xviii. 48 ; xxvii. 6) ; He lifts beyond the reach of self, for He answers the cry, " Lead me to the Rock that is higher (lifted up above, same word as rendered in the passages above, ' lifted up ') than I " (Psalm lxi. 2) ; He lifts us above the dunghill of the world—" He lifteth the needy out of the dunghill " (Psalm cxiii. 7) ; He lifts from the beggary of spiritual destitution—" He lifted up the beggar " (I. Samuel ii. 7, 8) ; therefore we can say in faith, knowing Him, no

---

* A scow is a boat with a flat bottom and square ends, without sails or motive power.

matter what may arise, " He shall lift me up upon a Rock " (Psalm xxvii. 5, R.V.).

Water is submerging. Jonah in his prayer in the sea-monster said, " Thou didst cast me into the depth, in the heart of the seas, and the flood was round about me ; all Thy waves and Thy billows passed over me " (Jonah ii. 3). There is an experience very similar to this which some of God's servants have to pass through in order to fit them to lift up those who have been called " the submerged tenth." Everyone who has to do with shipping knows how important a pontoon is. A pontoon is a flat barge, which is water-tight. Many a time have I watched the filling of the pontoon on the River Wear, which may be seen at Sunderland. The pontoon is filled with water which makes it sink into the river bed ; then the steamer is placed over the sunken pontoon, the water is pumped out of the pontoon, and as the air fills it, it rises and lifts the steamer, then the steamer's keel can be cleaned and painted. We need to go to where the sinners are, in the mud of the river-bed of sin, in order to lift them out of it. One of the most touching sights I ever saw, was at the close of an evangelistic meeting in Sunderland, when a poor woman of the street, besotted with drink and damned by sin, and just out of prison, was crying for mercy. Twelve sisters got round her and prayed and wept, till, in the sympathy of their loving hearts, they lifted her into the arms of the Saviour. Such contact with sin and dirt was only possible through the love of the Holy Spirit. He makes the impossible possible.

Water is cleansing. Cleanliness was an essential thing in the lives of the children of Israel. Anyone who got defiled by coming into contact with death and defilement had to be washed, and every wooden vessel had to be " rinsed with water " (Leviticus xv. 11, 12). The New Testament words for cleansing and cleanliness are " *katharizo* " and " *katharos*." They indicate the practicality of the Spirit's work. The purity of the Spirit is an eye-cleanser, for it is " the *pure* in heart that see God " (Matthew v. 8) ; purity is a life-washer, for the righteousness of the saints makes their garments " *clean* and white " (Revelation xix. 8, 14) ; purity is a worship-qualifier, for we are to have our bodies "washed with *pure* water" as we draw near (Hebrews x. 22); purity is a truth-holder, for we are to hold the faith "in a *pure* conscience" (I. Timothy iii. 9); purity is a love-yoker, for "love out of a *pure* heart" is the essential thing (I. Timothy I, 5, R.V.); purity is a service-fitter, for, like Paul, we should serve God "in a *pure* conscience" (II. Timothy i. 3); purity is a prayer-prevailer, for when we "call on the Lord out of a *pure* heart" we are sure of His promises being fulfilled (II. Tim. ii. 22); purity is a holiness-precursor, for we are to "*cleanse* ourselves from all filthiness of the flesh and spirit, and then perfect holiness in the fear of the Lord" (II. Cor. vii. 1); and purity is a Christ-recognizer, for He died to "*purify* unto Himself a people for His own possession" (Titus ii. 14, R.V.)

Water is satisfying. "As the hart panteth after the water brooks, so panteth my soul after Thee, O God" (Psalm xlii. 1). "O God, Thou art my God; early will I seek Thee: my soul thirsteth for Thee, my flesh longeth for Thee in a dry and thirsty land, where no water is" (Psalm lxiii. 1). "The river of God is full of water" (Psalm lxv. 9). The names and titles of God are expressive of His nature. There are two names of God in the above verse. "Elohim" is the name used in each except in the second instance of the second verse, where it is "El." "Elohim" is the plural form of "Eloah," and signifies the Godhead in the trinity of their Divine personality, coupled with the thought of ability, hence we read, "God (Elohim) said, Let us make (plural) man in our image" (singular). The plural pronoun and verb are in keeping with the plural noun. When the Psalmist says "O, God (Elohim), Thou art my El" (singular), he expresses the thought of God in trinity with the thought of Divine personality. "El" is singular for God and is generally found with an adjective, hence, "The Almighty God." Here again is a beautiful combination. God is singular, but Almighty* is plural. Only God in all the livingness of His Divine

---

* Shaddai, rendered almighty, means the breasts. Shaddai is derived from Shad, the breast, hence Almighty God means the many-breasted God. The One Who is enough, or All-Sufficient.

sufficiency, and the three persons of the Godhead in their grace and love, can meet the need of man's spirit-nature. When God made man in the likeness of His own indestructible image, it stands to reason, as well as revelation, that only God Himself can meet his need and nature. We need the Father to love us, the Son to lift us, the Spirit to quicken us. We need the Father's gift of the Son to die for us, the Son's work to bring us to God, and the Spirit to quicken us. We need the Father to chasten us, the Son to succour us, and the Spirit to help us. We need the Father's paternity to father us, the Son's propitiation to fit us, and the Spirit's power to furnish us. We need the Father's promises to cheer us, the Son's peace to calm us, and the Spirit's presence to control us. We need the Father's grace to save us, the Son's grace to strengthen us, and the Spirit's grace to sanctify us. We need the Father's grace to beautify us, the Son's atonement to benefit us, and the Spirit's life to beam through us. We need the Father's illumination to teach us, the Son's indwelling to triumph over and through us, and the Spirit's inspiration to throb through our whole being. Our God alone can satisfy, but He is enough. We say with Jean Ingelow—

> " Thou art what I want.
> I am athirst for God, the Living God."

He slakes all thirst and yet He makes us thirst with a thirst which He meets with a constant supply by the Spirit.

Water is reviving. Job says of a tree, " There is hope of a tree, if it be cut down, that it will sprout again, and that the tender branch will not cease. Though the root thereof wax old in the earth, and the stock thereof die in the ground ; yet through the scent of water it will bud, and bring forth boughs like a plant " (Job xiv. 7-9). How truly these words have been illustrated in the lives of many who once knew the Lord and have almost slipped into the hell of despair and eternal death, and yet through the tender mercy of God have had the latent spark of grace revived and become in the latter end of their Christian experience witnesses who have never waned, but plants of vigour in fruitfulness and faithfulness to God. Even the cause of the failure and backsliding may become a blessing, as someone has said, "The besetting sin may become the guardian angel. Let us thank God we can say it! Yes, the sin that has sent me weary-hearted to bed, and desperate in heart to the morning work, can be conquered. I do not say annihilated, but, better than that, conquered, captured and transfigured into a friend ; so that I, at last, shall say, ' My temptation has become my strength ; for in the very fight with it I owe my force.' "

"Noble souls, through dust and heat,
Rise from disaster and defeat
The stronger,
And, conscious still of the Divine
Within them, lie on earth supine
No longer."

Water is refreshing. "He shall come down .... as showers that water the earth" (Psalm lxxii. 6). A writer tells of a surveying party who were resting at noon in Florida, when one of the chainmen exclaimed, "I would give fifty cents a swallow for all the water I could drink." All the men were very thirsty, but there was no spring or stream near. While the men were thus talking, the surveyor saw a crow put his bill into a cluster of broad, long leaves, growing on the side of a tall cypress. The leaves were those of a peculiar air plant. They were green and bulged out at the bottom, forming an inverted bell. The smaller end was held to the tree by roots grappling the bark. Feeding on the air and water that it catches and holds, the air plant becomes a sort of cistern. The surveyor sprang to his feet with a laugh. "Boys," he said, "the old crow is wiser than anyone of us." "How so?" they asked. "Why he knows there are a hundred thousand water-tanks in this forest." "Where?" they demanded in amazement. The surveyor cut an air-plant in two, and drained nearly a pint of pure cold water from it. The men did not want for water after that. Their thirst was slaked and they were refreshed. So as we live in the Spirit we shall find He will refresh by His grace, renew in His strength, gladden us in His joy, sanctify us in His truth, lead us by His direction, revive us in His life, constrain us by

His love, and fascinate us with our Lord Jesus; and we shall say, with Sir E. Denny,—

> "Oh! it is come—the sweet and blessed calm,
> Foreseen and hoped for thro' those darksome years
> Of anguish and of dread? Here, here at last,
> I, a deep vessel in the shoreless sea
> Of Thy own fulness, O eternal God!
> Filled in that fulness, find my prayers, my hopes,
> All, all fulfilled, and nothing more to crave.
> The bright reality, the thing itself,
> Transcends all thought, eclipses every hope:
> Dwelling in God, by God indwelt, I know
> Love in its fulness; life to me is bliss;
> All, all within, beneath, around, above,
> Speak but of Thee, and tell me what I am—
> The happiest of the happy! O Thou peerless One!
> Great God revealed in flesh, the living link
> 'Twixt Godhead and my soul! be Thine the praise,
> The loving worship of a loving heart,
> Rich in Thyself; for, oh! however filled,
> Howe'er exalted, holy, undefiled,
> Whatever wealth of blessedness is mine,
> What am I, Lord? an emptiness, a nothing.
> Thou art my boast, in Whom all fulness dwells
> Of the great Godhead, Thou Whose name I bear,
> Whose life is mine, Whose glory and Whose bliss,
> All, all are mine."

V. PRECIOUS PROMISES.

One of the most profitable seasons at the World's Missionary Conference, held in June, 1910, was the time for devotion in the midst of the morning session. No addresses were given. Appropriate Scriptures were given, and in them we heard the voice of God speaking in the inner recesses of our being, and then they were turned into praise, prayer and intercession. So with the promises associated with water in God's Word. Let them speak for themselves, without any exposition, and let us turn them into prayer, praise and intercession; and also claim them by faith that the Holy Spirit may make them moulders of our lives and streams of blessing to others. Ponder the "*I wills.*"

"I the Lord do keep it; I will water it every moment: lest any hurt it, I will keep it night and day" (Isaiah xxvii. 3).

"A Man shall be as an hiding place from the wind, and a

covert from the tempest ; as rivers of water in a dry place, as the shadow of a great rock in a weary land " (Isaiah xxxii. 2).

" The glorious Lord will be unto us a place of broad rivers and streams " (Isaiah xxxiii. 21).

" In the wilderness shall waters break out, and streams in the desert " (Isaiah xxxv. 6).

" When the poor and needy seek water, and there is none, and their tongue faileth for thirst, I the Lord will hear them. I the God of Israel will not forsake them. I will open rivers in high places, and fountains in the midst of the valleys : I will make the wilderness a pool of water, and the dry land springs of water " (Isaiah xli. 17, 18).

" I give waters in the wilderness, and rivers in the desert, to give drink to My people " (Isaiah xliii. 20).

" I will pour water upon him that is thirsty, and floods upon the dry ground : I will pour My Spirit upon thy seed, and My blessing upon thine offspring " (Isaiah xliv. 3).

" The Lord shall guide thee continually, and satisfy thy soul in dry places, and make strong thy bones : and thou shalt be like a watered garden, and like a spring of water, whose waters fail not " (Isaiah lviii. 11, R.V.)

" I will sprinkle clean water upon you, and ye shall be clean : from all your filthiness and idols I will cleanse you. A new heart also will I give you, and a new spirit will I put within you : and I will take away the stony heart out of your flesh, and will give you a heart of flesh. And I will put My Spirit within you, and cause you to walk in My statutes, and ye shall keep My judgments and do them " (Ezekiel xxxvi. 25-27, R.V.)

" Whosoever drinketh of the water that I shall give him shall never thirst ; but the water that I shall give him shall be in him a well of water springing up into everlasting life " (John iv. 14).

" Jesus stood and cried, saying, If any man thirst, let him come unto Me, and drink. He that believeth on Me, as the Scripture hath said concerning Me, out of Him shall flow rivers of Living Water. But this spake He of the Spirit, which they that believe on Him should receive : for the Holy Ghost was not yet *given :* because that Jesus was not yet glorified " (John vii. 37-39).

Syllabus of
Clothing as an Emblem of the Holy Spirit

Figurative use of clothing—I. *What God puts upon us*—This clothing expensive in its cost—A colloquy—A dress which cost £100,000—This clothing is protective in its covering—How Adam and Eve were clothed—The Best Robe—The flags around the British subject—This clothing is perfect in its texture—Bunyan's experience—Threefold protection—This clothing is imparting in its wear—Hercules—Carlyle on clothes—II. *What the Lord expects us to put on, and what He can put on us*—Joshua clothed, unclothed, and clothed—The Spirit is the Spirit of Equipment—An eightfold putting off and putting on—The Spirit is the Spirit of Reminder—Amasai's words to David—Lincoln's remark—Senses in which we are the Lord's—The Spirit is the Spirit of Faithfulness—Zechariah's faithful testimony—Knox and Queen Mary—The Spirit is the Spirit of Victory—Gideon's experience—The Spirit is the Spirit of Enduement—"*Dunamis*": its derivation, association and meaning—Moody's experience—Quotation from Fenelon.

CLOTHING

" He hath clothed me " (Isaiah lxi. 10).
" Spirit of the Lord clothed Gideon " (Judges vi. 34, margin).
" Clothed with power " (Luke xxiv. 49, R.V.)

THE verb to " clothe " is used in a figurative sense in many different ways. When the flocks cover the pastures they are said to be, " clothed with flocks " (Psalm lxv. 13); when the heavens are concealed by clouds they are said to be, " clothed with blackness " (Isaiah l. 3); the traits of a person's individual bearing are compared to clothing, hence, the Lord is declared to be " clothed with majesty " and " strength " (Psalm xciii. 1; civ. 1); the act of God's grace in beautifying us is compared to the act of clothing, hence, He said to Israel, "I clothed thee with broidered work" (Ezekiel xvi. 10); and to Joshua, the high priest, who was "clothed with filthy garments," Jehovah said, "I will clothe thee with change of raiment" (Zechariah iii. 3-5); and the prophet also says, "He hath clothed me with the garments of salvation, He hath covered me with the garments of salvation" (Isaiah lxi. 10); the habits of a person's life are likened to a garment, hence, Job says, "I put on righteousness, and it clothed me" (Job xxix. 14); and the Psalmist prays that God's priests may be "clothed with righteousness" (Psalm cxxxii. 9); and the power of the Holy Spirit, both in the Old (I. Chronicles xii. 18, margin) and in the New Testament, is compared to the equipment of clothing (Luke xxiv. 49, R.V.)*

There are two centres around which our study revolves, namely, what God puts upon us, and what we are responsible to put on ourselves.

---

* Two very full Bible Readings may be given both from the Old and New Testaments in looking at clothing with a comprehensive view. In the Old Testament the principal Hebrew word for clothing is rendered "*clothed*" (Ezekiel vii. 27), "*put on*" (Jonah iii. 5), "*wear*" (Deuteronomy xxii. 11), "*armed with*" (I. Samuel xvii. 5), "*in their apparel*" (Ezra iii. 10), and "*arrayed in*" (II. Chronicles v. 12). The word is used in the following senses—(1) What the Lord puts on others in His grace (Genesis iii. 21; Psalm cxxxii. 16; Isaiah lxi. 10; Ezekiel xvi. 10; Zechariah iii. 5); (2) of the body as a protection to the spirit (Job x. 11); (3) of the attributes of God (Psalm xciii. 1; civ. 1; Isaiah li. 9); (4) applied to the priestly garments (Leviticus vi. 10, 11; xvi. 4, 23, 24, 32); (5) used in a moral and spiritual sense (Isaiah li. 9; lii. 1; II. Chronicles vi. 41; Job xxvii. 17; xxix. 14; xl. 10; Psalm cxxxii. 9; Haggai i. 6); (6) connected with the shame and judgment of the sinner (Psalm cxxxii. 18); and (7) of the power of the Spirit (Judges vi. 34; I. Chronicles xii. 18; II. Chron. xxiv. 20).

The Greek word "*Enduo*" is of equal interest. It is applied—(1) To ordinary clothing, and is rendered "*put on*" (Matthew vi. 25; xxii. 11; xxvii. 31; Mark vi. 9; xv. 20), "*arrayed*" (Acts xii. 21), and "*clothed*" (Mark i. 6; xv. 17; Revelation i. 13; xv. 6; xix. 14); (2) to grace's provision (Luke xv. 22); (3) to Christ (Romans xiii. 12, 14; Galatians iii. 27); (4) to the Christian's armour (Ephesians vi. 11, 14; I. Thessalonians v. 8); (5) to the Spirit's graces (Ephesians iv. 24; Colossians iii. 10, 12); (6) to the future glory (I. Corinthians xv. 53, 54; II. Corinthians v. 3); and (7) to the Spirit's might (Luke xxiv. 49). "*Enduo*" is rendered "*clothed*," "*endued*," "*put on*," "*having on*," "*on*," and "*arrayed*."

I. WHAT GOD PUTS UPON US.

"He hath made us accepted in the Beloved" (Ephesians i. 6) might be rendered, "He hath graced us in the Beloved." He has made us beautiful in His beauty, comely in His comeliness, righteous in His righteousness, pure in His purity, lovely in His loveliness, holy in His holiness, and graced in His grace.

This clothing is expensive in its cost. Christ's blood is the cost of its procurement. The Robe of Righteousness with which God adorns us was woven on Calvary, as one has said, "It was woven on Calvary for the race of man out of the white ways of Divine mercy, and the blood-red woof of the Redeemer's sacrifice. It is like Christ's own garment, 'without seam, woven from the top throughout.'"

The following ancient colloquy of the soul with Christ touching the Passion gives the inness of the soul's questioning and the directness of the Lord's answer :—

> "*Lord, wherefore didst Thou suffer Thyself to be sold?*
> That I might deliver thee from servitude.
> *Wherefore diddest Thou sweat blood?*
> To wash away the spots of thy sins.
> *Why wouldest Thou be bound?*
> To loose the bands of thy sins.
> *Why wert Thou denied of Peter?*
> To confess thee before My Father.
> *Why wouldest Thou be accused?*
> To absolve thee.
> *Why wouldest Thou be spit upon?*
> To wipe away thy foulness.
> *Why wouldest Thou be whipped?*
> That thou mightest be free from stripes.
> *Why wouldest Thou be lifted up on the cross?*
> That thou mightest be lifted up to heaven.
> *Why were Thine arms stretched out?*
> To embrace thee, O fainting soul.
> *Why was Thy side opened?*
> To receive thee in.
> *Why diddest Thou die amidst two thieves?*
> That thou mightest live in the midst of angels."

and we might add—

> *Why wast Thou stripped to Thy shame?*
> That thou mightest be clothed with glory.

It is said that when one of the daughters of Baron Rothschild was married, that her wedding dress cost one hundred thousand pounds. That was a costly dress, but our robe of righteousness cost our Lord a good deal more. Its expensiveness must be estimated by the stoop of His incarnation, by the peerless worth of His unique personality, by beauty of His perfect life, by the Deity of His Sonship, by the agony and bloody sweat of Gethsemane, by the mockery of Gabbatha, by the forsaking of Golgotha, by the sin He was made and the curse He bore, by the might of His resurrection, the triumph of His ascension, and the gift of the Holy Spirit.

This clothing is protective in its covering. When our first parents were made conscious of their shame by their sin, God graciously "made them coats of skins and clothed them" (Genesis iii. 21). The word "clothed" means to be arrayed, to be wrapped round. Our first parents were wrapped around with that which was obtained by death, for before the skins could be got to clothe them there had to be death to procure the skins for them. When the prodigal came back from the far country to the father's heart and home, the father said, "Bring forth the best robe and put it on him" (Luke xv. 22), or as the sentence might be, "Bring forth the best robe and clothe him." The Greek word rendered "*put on*" ("*euduo*") is rendered "*clothed*" in Revelation i. 13, and "*arrayed*" in Acts xii. 21. It is said that on one occasion a British subject was in danger of being unjustly incarcerated by a foreign power, but that the American and British Representatives wrapped around the man the flags of their several countries, and then dared the authorities to touch the individual. As the man was protected by the named countries, and the other country dared not harm him because he was protected by them, so clothed in the garment of Divine righteousness, even in Christ Himself, who can condemn us? Who indeed, since God has justified us. Justice cannot, for it is satisfied. Law cannot, for it is magnified. Satan cannot, for he is defeated. Since Christ is put to our account, we are made to count in Him.

This clothing is perfect in its texture. There is a threefold perfection in Christ as the Righteous One, namely, His righteous obedience in His life, His righteous sacrifice in His death, and His righteous person in His glory. Man is a sinner in many senses, but he is specially a sinner in three senses,— in his life he missed the mark of perfect obedience to God ; he cannot answer for his sin for he is helpless ; and he is polluted in himself. Provisionally Christ meets man's liability and guilt by His death, for at the Cross where sin abounded as to its climax and culmination, grace did much more abound (Romans v. 20). Practically, Christ in His life of perfect obedience did what we could not do—" As by one man's disobedience many were made sinners, so by the obedience of one shall many be made righteous " (Romans v. 19). Positionally those who believe in Christ are made the righteousness of God in Him (II. Corinthians v. 21). Some tell us we are justified by the righteous life Christ lived, others that we are justified in His atoning death, while others again say we are justified in the Risen Christ. Why divide Christ ? The trinity of His life, death, and glorified Person go to make up what He is, and all are put to our account. As our Head He died for us (that's where we begin), He lived for us and He is for us. Thus we are wrapped in the perfection of His atoning death, His glorious obedience and His holy personality. The whole subject is happily put by Bunyan. He says : " One day as I was passing in the field, and that too with some dashes in my conscience, fearing lest yet all was not right, suddenly this sentence fell upon my soul, ' Thy righteousness is in heaven !' And methought, withal, I saw with the eyes of my soul Jesus Christ at God's right hand. There, I saw, was my righteousness, so that wherever I was or whatever I was doing God could not say of me that He wanted my righteousness, for there it was just before Him. I saw also that it was not my good frame of heart that made my righteousness better, nor my bad frame that made my righteousness worse. For my righteousness was Jesus Christ Himself, the same yesterday, to-day and for ever. 'Twas glorious to me to see His exaltation, and the worth and prevalency of His benefits. And that because I could now look from myself to Him, and should reckon that all those graces of God that were now green on me were yet but like those crack-groats and fourpence-halfpennies that rich men carry in their purses when their gold is in their trunks at home! O, I saw that my gold was all in my trunk at home! Even in Christ my Lord and my Saviour! Now Christ was my all! He was made of God to me all my wisdom, and all my righteousness, and all my sanctification, and all my redemption!"

This clothing is imparting in its wear. When Hercules put on the fabled garment, it poisoned his blood and killed him. There was death in the garment, and it therefore communicated death to its wearer. As the fabled garment communicated what was in it, so when we put on Christ as the Righteousness of God He imparts His nature to us. Carlyle in a sarcastic mood once said of clothes, " Clothes give us individuality, distinctions, social polity; clothes have made men of us; they are threatening to make screens of us. Has not yon red-hanging individual a horsehair wig, squirrel skins, and a plush gown, whereby all mortals know he is a judge. Society, which the more I think of it astonishes me the more, is founded on cloth." Mark the words, " Clothes have made men of us." Yes, but not those which have been made in the looms of earth, but those which have been made in the looms of Bethlehem, Galilee, Calvary, and Olivet. As the glorified Christ made His garments white and glistening, so when He is on us and in us, He shows Himself through us.

> " I want that adorning Divine,
> Thou only, my God, can bestow;
> I want in those beautiful garments to shine
> Which distinguish Thy household below."

The Spirit of God is the One Who makes all the above real to us. It is His business to unfold Christ to us in the Word, to reveal Christ for us in His death, to strengthen the inner man to make Christ real in us, and to empower us with Himself that He may qualify us for His work and be the Qualifier in all things.

II. WHAT THE LORD EXPECTS US TO PUT ON, AND WHAT HE CAN PUT ON US.

One of the most striking pictures of the action of Grace* is found in Zechariah iii. The nation is represented in Joshua the high priest, who is clothed with filthy garments, after it is said to be a brand plucked from the fire, and then the iniquity is made to pass away and Joshua is clothed with a change of raiment, and then a complete change of raiment is given to him, and he is charged to keep the charge committed to him. Then there is this statement, " Behold, the stone that I have laid before Joshua ; upon one stone shall be seven eyes " (Zechariah iii. 9). The stone evidently stands for the temple of God and the " seven eyes " we are distinctly told represent " the seven spirits of God," or the Holy Spirit in the perfection of His grace and government (Revelation v. 6). As in all God's ways the Spirit is the Worker accomplishing His purpose. Let us look at several other Scriptures where we find the Holy Spirit identified with clothing.

The Spirit is the Spirit of Equipment to enable us to " put off " and " put on " what the Lord enjoins. There are quite a number of things we are exhorted to " put off " and " put on." In the former we have the negative aspect of holiness and in the latter the positive aspect. There are two† words embodying the thought of clothing, only the one means casting off

---

* A Bible study can be given on the seven acts of grace. (1) The rebuke of grace—" The Lord rebuke thee." (2) The choice of grace—" The Lord hath chosen." (3) The act of grace—" A brand plucked from the burning." (4) The direction of grace—" Take away the filthy garments." (5) The assurance of grace—" I have caused thine iniquity to pass from thee." (6) The adornment of grace—" I will clothe thee with change of raiment." (7) The crown of grace—" Set a fair mitre on his head."

"† *Apotithemi* " is a compound word, made of " *apo*," which means off or away, and " *tithemi*," which means down, so that the compound word signifies to take off a garment and then to cast it on one side. The word is rendered " *laid down* " in speaking of the men who took off their clothes and cast them on one side before they stoned Stephen (Acts vii. 58, 59). The other word for putting on, " *Euduo*," is also a compound one. " *En* " meaning in, and " *duo* " down, hence its meaning is to sink into a garment, that is, to be invested with it.

as a garment, and the other the being clothed or invested upon with power. Let us notice an eightfold parallelism.

"Put of"

"*Cast off* (apotithemi) the works of darkness" (Romans xiii. 12). Darkness stands for ignorance, unbelief and sin.

"*Put away* (apotithemi), as concerning your former manner of life, the old man" (Ephesians iv. 25, R.V.) The old man is the man of the former manner of life.

"*Putting away* (apotithemi) falsehood" (Ephesians iv. 25). The glib tongue of untruthfulness is to cast away.

"*Put off* (apotithemi) all these anger, wrath, malice, blasphemy, filthy communication out of your mouth" (Colossians iii. 8). These garments are filthy indeed, and belong to that old rag merchant, the devil.

"*Put off*" (apotithemi) the old man with his deeds" (Col. iii. 9). Deeds and doer have been dealt with at the cross. Faith leaves both there.

"*Lay aside* (apotithemi) every weight and the sin" (Hebrews xii. 1). The sin is the sin in good standing, namely, unbelief; and the weights are doubtful things.

"*Lay apart* (apotithemi) all filthiness and superfluity of naughtiness" (James i. 21). Uncleanness and wickedness are corroding and contagious.

"*Putting away* (apotithemi) wickedness, and all guile, and hypocrisies, and envies, and all evil speakings" (1. Pet. ii. 1, R.V.) These are all the spawn of hell, and **progenitors of evil**.

"Put on."

"*Put on* (euduo) the armour of light" (Romans xiii. 12). Light represents knowledge, faith, and holiness.

"*Put on* (euduo) the new man," who expresses himself in righteousness and holiness (Eph. iv. 24).

"*Having on* (euduo) the breastplate of righteousness" (Eph. vi. 14). Right action is ever a protection.

"*Put on* (euduo) . . . bowels of mercies, kindness, humbleness of mind, meekness, longsuffering" (Colossians iii. 12). These garments are pure and beautiful, shining with the lustre of grace.

"*Put on* (euduo) the new man" (Col. iii. 10). Spiritual likeness to the Divine Spirit is proof of His unique work.

"*Putting on* (euduo) the breastplate of faith and love" (1. Thess. v. 8). Faith in the Lord will counteract unbelief, and love to the Lord will make us gladly abandon doubtful things.

"*Clothed* (euduo) in fine linen, white and pure." We are told what this represents—" The fine linen is the righteous acts of the saints" (Revelation xix. 8, 14, R.V.)

"*Put on* (euduo) the Lord Jesus Christ" (Romans xiii. 14). "*Put on* (euduo) the whole armour of God" (Eph. vi. 11). Christ answers to every part of the armour.

The clue to being able to put off the above evil, and to put on the opposite good is found in what precedes the exhortation to put on the armour of God, namely, " Be strong in the Lord and in the power of His might " (Ephesians vi. 10). The expression, " the power of His might," only occurs in one other place, and that is in Ephesians i. 19, margin. The power of God's might was manifested in the resurrection of Christ, and that power was the operation of the Spirit (Rom. viii. 11). It is only as we are energized in His energy that we can effectually obey His Word, and He alone can do it.

The Spirit is the Spirit of Reminder to remind us to Whom we belong. We read of one of David's mighty men, when he came to David, " Then the Spirit clothed (margin) Amasai, who was chief of the captains, and he said, Thine are we, David, and on thy side " (I. Chronicles xii. 18). The same principle will be recognized if we are Spirit-dominated. We shall recognize the proprietary rights of the Lord to us and over us, and we shall say to Him, " Thine are we, Lord Jesus, and on Thy side." During the American Civil War, someone expressed to Lincoln the hope that the Lord was on their side. The reply of Lincoln was apt, he said, " I am not concerned about the Lord being on our side, but as to our being on the side of the Lord." " He always wins," as Faber says, " who sides with God."

In many ways we are the Lord's. We are His by *purpose*, for in His love-heart He has called us to Himself and made us His own (Ephesians i. 4, 5) ; we are His by *purchase*, for in His life-blood He has redeemed us to Himself (I. Peter i. 18, 19) ; we are His by *presence*, for in His Spirit-habitation He makes us His temple (I. Corinthians iii. 16) ; we are His by *life*, for in His life-implanted grace we are made partakers of His nature (II. Peter i. 3, R.V., margin) ; we are His by *preservation*, for in His power-keeping we are kept for Himself (I. Pet. i. 5) ; we are His by *promise*, for by the assuring-word He tells we are His own possession (Titus ii. 14, R.V.) ; and we are His by *self-surrender*, for by consecration we have committed ourselves to Him (II. Timothy i. 12).

The Spirit is the Spirit of Faithfulness to embolden us to bear a faithful testimony. " The Spirit of God came upon ('clothed,' margin) Zechariah the son of Jehoiada the priest, which stood above the people, and said unto them, Thus saith God, why transgress ye the commandments of the Lord, that ye cannot prosper? because ye have forsaken the Lord, He hath also forsaken you (II. Chronicles xxiv. 20). The consequence of Zechariah's faithful word was, they stoned him to death. He was not the first, nor the last, who met a premature death because of the message of God delivered. Consequences do not enter into the concern of the man of God, the one thing about which he is concerned is, fidelity to his Lord. The Spirit-filled man fears not the face and fear of man. He will tell the truth like John Knox did to Queen Mary, and not be moved by threats or tears, and will say as he did to her, "Madam, in God's presence I speak: I never delighted in the weeping of God's creatures, but seeing I have but spoken the truth as my vocation craves of me, I must sustain your Majesty's tears rather than hurt my conscience." The Spirit-filled servant of God will, like Moses before Pharaoh, deliver God's message; like Nathan did David, tell the sinner of his sin; like Elijah did Ahab, rebuke the rebel for his iniquity; like Daniel did Belshazzar, point out where the life is wanting; like Jeremiah told Zedekiah of the judgment that was coming; like John the Baptist rebuked Herod, although he lost his head for doing it; and like Paul, when he charged Agrippa with his sin, as he reasoned before him of righteousness and a judgment to come.

The Spirit is the Spirit of Victory in conflict. "The Spirit of the Lord clothed himself with Gideon" (Judges vi. 34, R.V., margin). Thus Gideon was nothing but clothes. He used him to clothe himself. Gideon's experience up to the time of his enduement was very like that of many of God's people to-day. He was full of complaints and of the vocabulary of unbelief (see the "oh!" "if," "why," "where," of Judges vi. 13). The Lord instead of arguing the situation with him said, "Go in this thy might." What was that might? "The Lord" as "the mighty man of valour" (Septuagint Version of Judges vi. 12). That might be had when the Spirit came upon him, and the consequence was he had the victory over the Midianites. When we too are strong in the Lord and in the power of His might, we shall have the victory over our enemies. The Lord has made no provision for His people to be defeated, but He has made ample provision for them to overcome. The displacement of sin and the effacement of self, are essentials to the enthronement of Christ and the dynamic of the Spirit. But with the dynamite of the Spirit He can bring down any foe, and in touch with that Dynamo He can move us to any service.

The Spirit is the Spirit of Enduement to qualify us for service. Christ's promise to His disciples was, " Tarry until ye be endued with power from on high " (Luke xxiv. 49); and " Ye shall receive power " (Acts i. 8). The word for " *power* " in both these sentences is " *dunamis.*" The derivation and association of this Greek word is of interest and importance. " *Dunamis* " is derived from " *dunamai.*" " *Dunamia* " signifies ability, the power to accomplish anything, hence is frequently translated " *is able* " (Matthew iii. 9 ; Acts xx. 32 ; Hebrews ii. 18); and " *can do* " (II. Cor. xiii. 8). Another word, which is derived from " *dunamis,*" is " *dunamoo.*" " *Dunamoo* " means to be made strong, and is rendered " *strengthened* " in Colossians i. 11. When " *dunamoo* " has the prefix " *en* " it means to be " *inpowered,*" or as we should say, " *empowered.*" This compound word occurs eight times in the New Testament, and is suggestive of a consecutive line of empowerment in the spiritual life. The word is rendered " *increased in strength* " in Acts ix. 22, in referring to Paul's power in testimony ; " *was strong* " in Romans iv. 20, in stating the character of Abraham's faith ; " *be strong* " in Ephesians vi. 10, in calling attention to the necessary power required to put on the whole armour of God ; " *which strengthened* " in Philippians iv. 13, where Paul bears testimony to the sphere—" in Christ "— which enabled him to do " all things " ; " *who hath enabled* " in I. Timothy i. 12, where he bears a like testimony to Timothy ; " *strengthened* " in II. Timothy iv. 17, where again he sounds the same triumphant note ; " *be strong* " in II. Tim. ii. 1, where Timothy is exhorted " *be strong* " in the grace which is in Christ Jesus ; and " *made strong* " in Hebrews

xi. 34, in calling attention to those who were enabled to go through persecution, trial and even death.

Remembering that "*dunamis*" is derived from "*dunamai*," which latter word means the possibility to do a thing; and that "*dunamis*" means inherent ability as the latent power is resident in the dynamite, and that is the power with which we are to be empowered; and calling to mind that "*euduo*" (endued, or clothed) means to sink into, as when a man gets into his clothes; we can see at once we are to be clad with the Spirit, that He may effectually operate through us. Some few years ago it was my privilege to meet at Beulah Park, on Lake Erie, near Cleveland, Ohio, one of the saintly women who prayed for Moody that he might be filled with the Spirit and thus empowered for service. Moody refers to his experience—" When I was preaching in Farwell Hall, I never worked harder to prepare my sermons than I did then. I preached and preached, but it was beating the air. A good woman used to say, ' Mr. Moody, you don't seem to have power in your preaching.' I requested this woman and a few other friends to come and pray with me every Friday, at 4 o'clock. Oh! how piteously I prayed that God would fill the empty vessel. After the Chicago fire I was in New York, and going into a bank in Wall Street, it seemed as if I felt a strange and mighty power coming over me. I went to the hotel, and there in my room I wept before God and cried, ' Oh, my God, stay Thy hand!' He gave me such a fulness that it seemed more than I could contain. May God forgive me if I should seem to speak in a boastful way, but I do not know that I have preached a sermon since but God has given me some soul. I seem a wonder to you, but I am a greater wonder to myself. The sermons I preach to you are the same I preached in Chicago. They are not new sermons, it is not a new gospel, but the old gospel with the power of the Holy Ghost."

The condition for this is well expressed by Fenelon. He says : " Warmth of imagination, ardour of feeling, acuteness of reasoning, and fluency of expression can do but little. The true agent is a perfect abandonment before God, in which we do everything by the light which He gives, and are content with the success which He bestows. This continual death is a blessed life known to few. A single word, uttered from this rest, will do more, even in outward affairs, than all our most eager and officious care. It is the Spirit of God that then speaks the Word, and it loses none of its force and authority, but enlightens, persuades, moves, and edifies. We have accomplished everything, and have scarce said anything."

Syllabus of

The Earnest as an Emblem of the Holy Spirit

The Spirit's Assurance—The Spirit in Ephesians—I. *Who is the Giver of The Earnest?*—Four great givings—" Back of the loaf "—II. *Who is the Purchaser of the inheritance?*—Seven things declared by Christ's resurrection—III. *Who is The Earnest?*—Recognize, not realize—What the man found in the farm—IV. *Where is The Earnest?*—Persons, place and position—V. *Of what is the Spirit The Earnest?*—The Spirit is the Earnest of our inheritance—Points to ponder—Earnest that God's purpose will be fulfilled—" Death cannot sever the ties that bind "—Earnest of our identity of place with Christ—First-fruits—" My soul lies in a coffin "—" With Him "—Earnest we shall be like Christ—" Conformed ones of the Image "—Earnest of an eternity of bliss—Seven Eternal things—Unending and unalloyed things—Earnest of immortality of being—Incorruption displaces corruption—Glory displaces dishonour—Power displaces weakness—Spiritual displaces natural—Heavenly displaces earthly—Immortality displaces mortality—Something displaces flesh and blood—Earnest of coming glory—Dyer on glory—VI. *What is implied by the Earnest?*—Use and derivation of the word earnest—Pledge—Evidence of a contract between two parties—Part of the thing promised—" We know in part."

THE EARNEST

THE Spirit, as the Earnest, assures believers in Christ of what is theirs in Him and the glory that awaits them. " All things are ours," not as to actual or full enjoyment, but as to possession or security ; just as a child who is heir to property left to him, and is allowed a certain part of it until he becomes of age, when he may enter into and enjoy the whole, is assured the property is none the less his, although he has not come into full possession.

The Earnest

The Epistle to the Ephesians is one of the most precious portions of God's Word, and one of the veins of truth we find running through the epistle is the way the Holy Spirit is mentioned. He reveals the purpose of God in Christ (i. 19; iii. 5-7); He quickens dead sinners, and makes them believers in Christ, and unites them to Christ (ii. 5, 6); He is the power of access into the Father's presence (ii. 18); He is God in us (ii. 22); He reveals the mystery that was hid to the Old Testament saints (iii. 5), namely, " Christ and the Church" (v. 32); He is the power to strengthen us, that Christ may dwell in our hearts, and that we may be able to comprehend with all saints Christ and His love (iii. 16-18); He is the power and the source of fruit-bearing (v. 9); He is the author of true prayer (vi. 18); He makes the Word of God effectual against our enemies (vi. 17); He also reminds us of our responsibility to Him, that we do not grieve Him by looseness in walk (iv. 30), but see to it that we are filled with Himself (v. 18), and as the Holy Spirit of Promise He is the Earnest, or Pledge, of the inheritance and glory that awaits every believer. There are six questions which we shall ponder. Who is the Giver of the Earnest? Who is the Purchaser of the inheritance? Who is the Earnest? Where is the Earnest? Of what is the Spirit the Earnest? What is implied by an Earnest?

I. Who is the Giver of the Earnest?

Paul, in speaking of what God would do at the coming of Christ—namely, clothe the believer with the resurrection body—says, " He that hath wrought us for the selfsame thing is God, Who also hath given unto us the earnest of the Spirit " (II. Corinthians v. 5). There are four great givings mentioned in the New Testament. God gave His Son, in love, to make provision for the world's salvation (John iii. 16); the Father has given believers to Christ, as the reward of His soul-travail (John x. 29; xvii. 6); the Spirit gives His several gifts to the members of the Body of Christ, " severally as He will " (I. Corinthians xii. 11); and there is the gift of the Holy Spirit, which is the joint-bestowment of Father and Son (John xiv. 16, 26; Acts ii. 33). The Father is especially the Giver of the Spirit, as Christ Himself says, " Whom the Father will send in My name," and " Whom I will send unto you from the Father." It is the Father's love-gift to the children. To trace our blessings up to the heart of God is to find what is in His heart for us. Let us ever remember—

> " Back of the loaf is the snowy flour,
> And back of the flour the mill,
> And back of the mill is the wheat and the shower
> And the sun and the Father's will."

II. WHO IS THE PURCHASER OF THE INHERITANCE ?

The Purchaser is Christ, the Son of the Living God ; and the purchase price was His priceless blood. As the kinsman under the law had the right, so as Son of Man He had the title to purchase the inheritance we had by sin lost (Lev. xxv. 25 ; Psalm lxix. 4) ; and as the Son of God He had the ability. The ground of the gift of the Spirit is the resurrection of Christ. If Christ is not risen we are yet in our sins, still under condemnation, still exposed to the righteous judgment of God against sin, and the Spirit having quickened us and indwelling us is a myth ; but, blessed be God, we know different. The death of Christ tells us of the love of God, and the resurrection of Christ tells of the power of God, and of the following seven facts :—That God is satisfied and glorified (Romans viii. 33, 34) ; that our sins are gone (I. Corinthians xv. 17-20) ; that we are accepted in Christ (Ephesians i. 6) ; that we are united to Christ (Colossians ii. 12 ; iii. 1) ; that every foe is vanquished (Colossians ii. 15) ; that we shall for ever live with Him (John xiv. 19) ; and that the Spirit is given to the Church (John vii. 39). And a good deal more ; but let us ever remember that the ground of everything that we, as believers in Christ, enjoy, is the death and resurrection of Christ.

III. WHO IS THE EARNEST ?

The Holy Spirit. We do not wish for a moment to sit in judgment upon others, but we beg to differ from those who say that the graces or the gifts of the Spirit are the earnest. We say no, but the Spirit Himself ; not our feelings, not our experiences, but the abiding presence of the Holy Spirit in us. What we have to do is to recognize and remember that He is in us, and not try to realize His presence. Take an illustration: Two gentlemen are walking along a street, deeply engrossed in each other's company and conversation. A friend of these two gentlemen passes by; one of them recognizes him—he realizes the power of his presence; the other one did not recognize the friend passing by. The one who did says to his friend, " Did you see So-and-so ?" " No," said the other, " I did not." If he had he would have realized the power of his presence as well as the other. So we need not to try to feel that we have the Spirit in us, but to open our hearts and receive Him, and then to recognize His presence; and we shall realize the power of His presence as He brings to our remembrance the precious promises of God, which are ours in Christ, and thus we shall be cheered thereby.

How many believers there are who do not recognize in the Word what God says is theirs in Christ, hence, they fail to realize what they have in Him. It is said that five men in succession owned a farm in the United States of America. Each of them in turn had to mortgage the farm, and all of them failed to make it pay. When the sixth man got possession he was not content to farm the farm, he began to bore into the ground and ultimately found a seam of coal; then he dug deeper and found natural gas; then he dug again and found oil. And in a very short time he was worth $600,000. These were all on the farm for the others, but they did not know it. The last man searched into his inheritance and was enriched thereby. So believers, if they will bore into the Word of God the Spirit will tell them what is theirs now, and what will be theirs in the future.

IV. WHERE IS THE EARNEST?

" In our hearts " (II. Corinthians i. 22). There are three things suggested by these three words, " in our hearts." 1. The persons who have the Earnest—" in *our* hearts." We ever need to remember that these epistles were written to believers. The Holy Spirit is not an earnest of the salvation of the soul; we do not need an earnest of that, for we have got Him Who is the Salvation now (Isaiah xii. 3). But He is the Earnest of our inheritance, namely, those who have been quickened by the Spirit are born again, and thus made "children of God, and if children, then heirs ; heirs of God, and joint heirs with Christ." 2. The place where the Earnest is—" in our *hearts*." Not in our head, but in our heart, as if to remind us that our whole affection should be taken up with the glory of Christ which we are to share, and the inheritance which He is. 3. The position of the Earnest—"*in* our hearts." In us as a Light to illuminate ; in us as a Friend to counsel ; in us as Water to refresh ; in us as a Comforter to cheer ; in us as a Teacher to teach ; in us as a Guide to direct ; in us as Oil to make us shine ; in us as a Fire to purge ; in us as a Dove to sympathize ; in us as the Seal to secure ; in us as the Witness to confirm ; in us as the Strength to keep ; in us as the Power to pray ; in us as the Source of fruit-bearing ; in us as Sap to make us grow ; in us as the Remembrancer to remind us that all the precious promises of God are yea and amen in Christ ; and in us as the Earnest of the coming glory.

V. OF WHAT IS THE SPIRIT THE EARNEST ?

As the grapes, pomegranates and figs, which the spies brought from the land of Canaan, were the earnest of the fruit to be found in that land (Numbers xiii. 23) ; and as the jewels which Eleazer gave Rebekah were an earnest of the riches of Isaac (Genesis xxiv. 53) ; so the Spirit is God's assurance of many blessings in the future.

The Spirit is the Earnest of our* inheritance. We can only indicate the largeness of the many-sidedness of the inheritance. God Himself is the Substance of the inheritance, for we are "heirs of God." To possess all He is, all He has, is to be rich indeed. Christ is the joint-heir of the inheritance, for we are "joint-heirs with Christ" (Romans viii. 17). The sons share with the Son and as the Son. The new birth is the basis

---

* God has an inheritance in His saints as well as the saints having an inheritance in Him. "The riches of the glory of His inheritance in His saints" is a remarkable statement in Ephesians i. 18. Eph. i. 11 gives the same thought, for the better reading is, not "we have obtained an inheritance," but "we have been taken as an inheritance."

of the inheritance, for to this we are "begotten" (I. Peter i. 3). Being in the family, we have family rights as God's children—"if children then heirs." The Kingdom is the reward of those who are rich in faith and who love Him (Jas. ii. 5). Eternal life is His gift, but place in His Kingdom is only given to the faithful. Salvation in its fullest sense is the end of the inheritance, for we are said to be "heirs of salvation" (Hebrews i. 14). Salvation in its end is not salvation from what we deserve as sinners (this is past—" we have been saved"), but salvation to what He has promised in the full fruition of His purpose. The character of the inheritance is incorruptible in its substance, undefiled in its nature, unfading in its duration, and untouchable in its reservation (I. Peter i. 4). The overcomer has a peculiar inheritance, for he is promised that he shall "inherit all things" (Rev. xxi. 7). The Spirit Himself is God's Pledge that all this shall surely come to pass (II. Corinthians i. 22 ; v. 5 ; Ephesians i. 14).

The Spirit is the Earnest that God's purpose in grace will be carried through. "Whom He did predestinate, them He also called : and whom He called, them He also justified : and whom He justified, them He also glorified" (Romans viii. 30). "He which hath begun a good work in you will perform it unto the day of Jesus Christ" (Philippians i. 6). "Those whom Thou hast given Me . . . I will that they also . . . be with Me where I am" (John xvii. 11, 24). In each of these passages of Scripture there is a continuity of thought and purpose. We need not be disturbed or distressed by the reference to God's foreknowledge, for all it means is, as He seems to say, "Thou dost adhere by faith to Him Whom I gave thee as thy Saviour ; He will, therefore, belong to thee wholly, and I shall not leave thee till I have rendered thee perfectly like Him."

We cannot explain the subtle difference between God's selection of the believer and the believer's surrender to God, the preservation of the saints and their perseverance. All we know is, they go together. The saints make their election sure by adding to their faith the graces of the Spirit, and the

Lord makes their election secure by His keeping power, for no power can sever the saved from the Saviour.

> "Death cannot sever
> The ties that bind our souls through mortal years—
> They last for ever."

The law of continuity is, nothing passes from one state to another without passing through all the intermediate stages. The state of glory will only be entered by those who are justified, the justified are the called ones, and the called ones are the predestinated ones. With God's secret purpose we have nothing to do. Have we responded to God's call? If so, are we justified by His grace; and we are assured the justified will be glorified. The seed of a plant will furnish us with an illustration. The seed has in it all the plant will be. The seed of God's purpose has in it the stem of His call, the foliage of His justification, and the fruit of His glory.

The Spirit is the Earnest of our identity of place with Christ in the glory. Among the similes which are used to illustrate Christ's worth and work is that of the firstfruits. "Christ, the firstfruits," so says the Holy Spirit in speaking of the coming of the Lord Jesus in resurrection power and glory. A question has been raised as to whether the *Church is included* in the reference to the firstfruits. In other words, does it refer to Christ absolutely in His personality; or does it refer to Christ mystically—that is, to Christ and His people as Head and members of His body? I think the latter. Believers are always said to be "in Christ," and, therefore, are never seen apart from Him. What is true of *Him* is true of *them;* hence, they are already raised *in Him*, as we are distinctly told in Ephesians ii. It is not without meaning that "Christ the firstfruits" is given, and not "Christ the first*fruit.*" The plural, instead of the singular. The same word is used again by the Apostle Paul in his second Epistle to the Thessalonians. The word is rendered "from the beginning," instead of "a firstfruits."* The verses should read:

---

* The Greek word "*arche*" is generally rendered "*beginning*." It means that which is first, such as, "In the *beginning* was the Word." The word rendered "*firstfruits*" is *aparche*, that is, the prefix "*apo*" is added to "*arche*"; hence it is given, "from the beginning."

"But we are bound to give thanks to God alway for you, brethren beloved of the Lord, because God has chosen you a firstfruits to salvation through sanctification of the Spirit and belief of the truth : whereunto He called you by our Gospel, to the obtaining of the glory of our Lord Jesus Christ" (II. Thessalonians ii. 13, 14).

Eugénie de Guérin was so one with her idolized brother, she had become so identified with him by mutual love and common suffering, that when he died, all joy went out of her life. Her lament over her brother's coffin is most touching : "My soul lives in a coffin. Oh, yes, buried, interred with thee, my brother, just as I used to live in thy life ; I am dead in thy death, dead to all happiness, all hope below."

We may use the words of the lamenting sister, and apply them to our Divine Lord in a holier, higher and happier sense, and say to Him, "Lord Jesus, we are not only dead with Thee, risen with Thee, but we are seated with Thee in all the glory of Thine acceptance, at the right hand of God ; and when Thou dost come again we shall be manifested in Thine own splendour, and be admired in the glory Thou hast put upon us."

This is no picture coloured by fevered imagination. If anyone doubts our identity, let him look at the seven "*with Him's*" in Colossians. Let us look at them in the order of Christ's experience and ours.

"Dead* with Christ" (ii. 20).
"Quickened together* with Him" (ii. 13).
"Buried with Him" (ii. 12).
"Risen with Him" (ii. 12 ; iii. 1).
"Life hid* with Christ in God" (iii. 3).
"Appear* with Him in glory" (iii. 4).

---

* The preposition *sun* is used seven times in Colossians. It signifies, to be united to anything, as the "old man *with* his deeds" ; a being together with another, as "quickened together *with* Him" ; something in common to both, as Tychicus was with Onesimus in ministry (iv. 9). The seven places where the word occurs are : ii. 5, 13, 20 ; iii. 3, 4, 9 ; iv. 9.

Five of the " with Him's " are true for us in Christ *now* and the other waits, as Christ waits, till the time of His manifestation. Mark the "*when*" and the "*then*." When he is manifested in glory, then we shall be manifested with Him. Christ was manifested in humble garb when He came to suffer; but when He comes again; He will be revealed in splendour, and we shall be with Him. One feature of the glorified Church is, as is said of the New Jerusalem, " the Lamb is the Light," and she has " the glory of God " (Rev. xxi. 23, 11). Then shall the saints reflect the splendour of the Lord, and *He* will be admired in *them* (ii. Thessalonians ii. 10); for He is glorified in the saints, just as the saints are glorified in and with Him. What a wondrous identity!

The Spirit is the Earnest that we shall be like Christ. The purpose of God is, we are to be " conformed to the image of His Son," and " as we have borne the image of the earthy, we shall also bear the image of the heavenly " (Romans viii. 29; i. Corinthians xv. 49). This must be so, for when we see Him we shall be like Him, and we shall be presented " faultless before the presence of His glory with exceeding joy " (i. John iii. 2; Jude 24). The references in these verses do not directly refer to the moral likeness which believers bear to Christ, but to the actual glory which they shall possess when He returns. We cannot comprehend all that conformity means, but whatever Christ is we shall be, for as Bishop Moule points out, the " likeness is not by accident, but of essence. The Greek literally is, ' Conformed ones of the image,' &c.; as if their similitude made them part of what they resembled." This thought is borne out by the meaning of the word " conformed." It is rendered in Philippians iii. 21, " *fashioned like unto*," where we are told our glorified bodies will be fashioned like unto His glorious body. The word means *jointly formed*, so that there shall be such a similarity that there will be no difference.

The Spirit is the Earnest of an eternity of bliss.

" 'Tis the Divinity stirs within us;
'Tis heaven itself that points out an hereafter,
And intimates eternity."

Yes! but there is more than a mere intimation of eternity to the child of God. The adjective, "eternal," is associated with certain words which proclaim unending felicity; and, more than this, every one of the sentences proclaims an opposite.

"*Eternal life*" speaks of an abiding union with Christ, but it also stands out in unmistakeable contrast to eternal death. "He that believeth on the Son hath eternal life; but He that obeyeth not the Son shall not see life" (John iii. 36, R.V.) The bright bow of grace stands out in vivid contrast to the black cloud of doom. The safety of Noah *in* the ark is in contrast to those who perished in the flood *outside* of it.

"*Eternal salvation*" proclaims the glad and perpetual safety of the believer in Christ, for Christ is the "Author of eternal salvation" (Hebrews v. 9); but it also suggests the lost estate of those who "suffer punishment, even eternal destruction from the face of the Lord" (II. Thessalonians i. 9, R.V.) The salvation of Israel at the Red Sea stands out in contrast to the overthrow of the Egyptians in it.

"*Eternal redemption*" unfolds the hallowed liberty into which the Lord Jesus has brought His own by means of His death upon the cross (Hebrews ix. 12); but it also speaks of those who will be wrapped in the bondage of "everlasting fire" (Matthew xxv. 41). The deliverance of Israel, by the blood of the paschal lamb, stands out in contrast to the doom of the firstborn of the Egyptians.

"*Eternal inheritance*" reminds us of the estate of incorruptibility for which the ransomed are kept (Hebrews ix. 15); but it also brings to our remembrance the "eternal damnation" from which they have escaped (Mark iii. 29).

"*Eternal glory*" impresses us with its vista of coming splendour, shared with, and because of, our Beloved (II. Tim. ii. 10; I. Peter v. 10); but it also points to the "everlasting punishment" which will be the portion of the unbeliever. The bliss of Lazarus in Abraham's bosom in contrast with the torment of Dives in hell.

"*Eternal weight of glory*," and the house which is "eternal in the heavens" (II. Corinthians iv. 17; v. 1), are seen in contrast to the "sufferings of this present time." The Gethsemane of suffering leads to the ascension of glory.

"*Eternal kingdom*" of Christ's rule and glory, which the faithful shall share with Christ, stands out in contrast to the shifting scenes of earth and the impotency of man's rule, for we receive a kingdom which cannot be moved (II. Peter i. 11).

Does not the blackness of the contrast make the brightness the more vivid? It is a solemn fact that God says more about the doom of the wicked to His children than He does to the wicked themselves. "Shall I hide from Abraham that thing which I do?" (Genesis xviii. 17), said God to Himself as He thought of the doom coming upon the cities of the plain. He did not, He told him what He was about to do. The Lord does not hide from us the wrath coming upon the unbeliever. Why? Because He would have us know *from* what we have been saved. But He also desires us to know *to* what we are saved. What it all means we cannot tell, but there will be—

> Love without passion, for we shall be "like Him."
> Service without weariness, for "His servants shall serve Him."
> Holiness without alloy, for "His name shall be on our foreheads."
> Blessing without curse, for there shall be "no more curse."
> Life without death, for there shall be "no more death."
> Joy without sorrow, for all tears will be wiped away.
> Light without darkness, for there shall be no night there.
> Glory without suffering, for there shall be no more pain.
> Singing without crying, for there shall be no more crying.
> Satisfaction without want, for hunger and thirst shall cease.
> Rule without end, for we shall reign for ever.
> Beauty without infirmity, for we shall be "without wrinkle."
> Living without sin, for we shall be faultless.
> Company without absence, for we shall be for ever with the Lord.

The Spirit is the Earnest of immortality of being. In that wonderful resurrection chapter, I. Corinthians xv., we have a sevenfold description given to us, as to what the glorified body of the believer will be in contrast to what it is (see verses 42, 43, 44, 49, 50, 53).

Incorruption is to displace corruption. " It is sown in corruption, it is raised in incorruption." Corruption is decay. Here beauty fades, the sight grows dim, the limbs grow weary, the hand loses its grip, the legs their elasticity, and the mind its veracity ; but there shall be no fading, no dimness, no loss of grip, and no want of agility. Then we shall have perfect beauty, unfailing sight, unweariness of limb, and perpetual youth.

Glory displaces dishonour. " Sown in dishonour, it is raised in glory." The body has been dishonoured by sin. Its members have yielded to the servitude of iniquity. Passion has torn the body, anger has distorted it, lust has debased it, blasphemy has desecrated it, uncleanness has polluted it, sin has marred it, and Satan has ridden in the vehicles of it ; but, in the glorified state, these shall no more have their sway.

Power displaces weakness. " Sown in weakness, it is raised in power." Here weakness cripples our efforts, defeats our purpose, mars our plans, breaks our powers, hinders our progress, crushes our ideals, and paralyses our hopes ; but, in the glorified state, fatigue shall not weary us, exhaustion shall not stop us, for we shall run continuously and not be weary, and walk and not faint. We shall have power to perform our plans and carry out our purposes.

Spiritual displaces natural. " It is sown a natural body, it is raised a spiritual body." The natural body is " physical," that is, soulish, and is adapted for the soul. The spiritual is " pneumatical," and is adapted to the redeemed spirit. The bodies will be identical so as to be recognizable ; but they will be different, for they will move in another sphere. We shall have senses then adapted to the Spirit-world, just as we have senses now suitable for this earthly state.

Heavenly displaces earthly. " As we have borne the image of the earthly, we shall also bear the image of the heavenly." What the heavenly body will be like we do not know, but it will be independent of fire, as is seen in the angel who appeared to Manoah ascending in the flame ; it will not be kept back by walls, as is patent by Christ coming into the

Upper Room, the doors being locked; and it will not be controlled by the law of gravitation, for Christ ascended. The heavenly body will be seen, as the Son of Man was seen in Nebuchadnezzar's furnace; it will be able to take food, as is demonstrated by the angels who came to Abraham; it can be touched, as we may gather from Thomas touching the body of Christ; and it will be identical with the earthly body, for Moses and Elijah are known as such, when they appear with Christ in glory.

Immortality displaces mortality. "This mortal shall put on immortality." "Death cannot reach that body; floods cannot drown it; fire cannot burn it; the sword cannot pierce it"; dynamite cannot touch it; and no destruction can overtake it. Deathless, undecaying, it is. Yea, the glorified are in a state of holiness and bliss, from which it is impossible to fall, for immortality is a changeless, unending state.

Something displaces flesh and blood. What that something is we cannot say, for the Bible is silent. Flesh and blood it will not be, for flesh is a tainted thing, and blood is a decaying thing. We have a picture of the glorified state in Christ's transfiguration, but we have no explanation. Of this we are sure, whatever Christ is, we shall be. "His name shall be in their foreheads," says the Spirit, of the redeemed—which seems to me, as one once said, that as Christ looks upon us, He shall see the reflection of His own glory.

The Spirit is the Earnest of the Coming glory. I do not write in detail about the glory (who can ?), as I have already made some suggestions about it in my little book, *What is Heaven ?**

There are two things which impress me in thinking of the coming glory of Christ and His people, and these are, first, the almost entire absence of the theme in present religious literature; and, second, the frequency of the reference to it in the pages of Holy Writ. In contrast to present literature, we

---

* *What is Heaven ?* 9d. Marshall Bros., Keswick House, London. 25 cents in U.S.A. The Gospel Publishing Company, 54, West 22nd Street, New York.

find constant reference to the glory in the old writers. I picked up Dyer's *Christ's Famous Titles* recently, when my attention was immediately arrested by the following: " O, sirs, meditate upon heaven, for meditation of heaven will make us heavenly. Heaven is not only a possession promised, but a possession purchased; when our contemplations and consecration are in heaven, then we enjoy heaven on earth; to be in Christ is heaven below, and to be with Him is heaven above; there cannot be a better being for us, than for us to be with the best of beings. ' For to me to live is Christ, and to die is gain' (Philippians i. 21). Paul was contented to stay a while out of heaven, that he might bring other souls into heaven; his life to them was most useful, but his death to them was most gainful. Let our condition be never so great, it is hell without Christ; and let our condition be never so bad, it is heaven with Him; ' I had rather be in hell with Christ, than in heaven without Him,' said Luther. Indeed, hell itself would be heaven if God were in it, and heaven would be hell if God were from it. That which makes heaven so full of joy is, that it is above all fear, and that which makes hell so full of horror is, that it is below all hope. The vessels of grace shall swim in the oceans of glory; here all the earth is not enough for one man, but there one heaven is enough for all men."

VI. WHAT IS IMPLIED BY THE EARNEST?

An earnest is a pledge, a part of anything given in advance as security for the rest. "Our old English word ' earnest ' goes back to the old Scottish word ' arles.' And our old Scottish word arles goes back first to a Latin root, and then to a Greek root, and then to a Hebrew root. And in all these five languages both the words earnest and arles mean exactly the same thing. An earnest and an arles in all these five languages mean an instalment: that is to say, a small part of something given now in sure pledge of future full possession. In old days the men of business who made arrangements for the sale and the transfer of an estate were wont to take the buyer to the property for sale, where they dug a spadeful of the best soil, and gave it to him: or they plucked a head of the best corn and gave it to him : or they gathered a handful of the best fruit and gave it to him : they always gave him a little of something to take home that grew on the estate ; something of the same kind as the estate that he was afterwards to possess. And that ceremony, so the lawyers said, gave the buyer an incontestable right and an indisputable title to the whole promised property."

The Old Testament word is rendered " *pledge* " in Genesis xxxviii. 17, 18, 20. Judah promised to send the gift of a kid to Tamar, but she was not satisfied with a mere promise, she wanted " a *pledge*," so he gave her his signet, bracelets and staff, which she afterwards produced to his shame. The Spirit as the Earnest is God's Pledge that He will keep to all He has promised.

An earnest is given as evidence of a contract between two parties. The Hebrew word " *pledge* " in the above reference is derived from a root which means to braid or intermix, to traffic or to barter, hence it is rendered " *mortgaged* " in Nehemiah v. 3. We all know what a mortgage is, it is an undertaking between two parties, whereby they pledge themselves in a mutual contract, the one to lend a sum of money at a stipulated interest, and the other agrees to pay the same. There was a contract, a covenant, between God and Christ. Christ undertook to finish the work the Father gave Him to do, and He having glorified Him by so doing, the Father undertook to glorify Christ by raising Him from the dead and to seat Him at His own right hand ; and then the Spirit was to be sent down to glorify Christ, and the Spirit now indwells every believer as the earnest or pledge that they shall receive the full benefits of the work of Christ.

An earnest is part of the thing promised. As in some parts of the country farmers go to fairs to hire their servants, and upon hiring them give a few shillings as an earnest of their first month's wages, so the Spirit is the Earnest of the glory to come.

Perhaps some will say, " You seem to write very confidently, and seem to be very positive that the believer will be preserved to the end and share the glory that Christ will yet be manifested in "; and the world might say, " You can live as you like "; but, as an old Christian once said when someone said that to him, " How can we who are dead to sin live any longer therein ?" and we add, " If we look for such things, what manner of persons ought we to be in all holy conversation or manner of living ?" Let us ever remember that while the Spirit is the Earnest of our sharing the full benefits of the work of Christ, we are also responsible to be always and entirely subject to Him.

" We know in part : a little of the glory
    Is present with us now ;
The earnest of the resurrection triumph
    E'en now is in our heart ;
But never yet was soul so fair
That all the radiance it could bear.

" We know in part : the Father's full adoption
    Is ours by faith to-day ;
And Jesus' blood for ever, and for ever,
    Has washed our sins away.
We know in part, but what remains to know—
Ah ! this, nor mortal tongue nor pen can show.

" We know in part our Saviour's deep compassion ;
    We know in part His grace ;
A thousand ties our ransomed hearts acknowledge,
    Bending before His face ;
But when we stand around the throne,
Then shall we know as we are known.

" We know in part : the Holy Spirit teacheth
    We are not orphans here ;
The gracious promises of God He bringeth,
    Our drooping hearts to cheer ;
But darkly through a glass we see
Till death unveils eternity.

" O Trinity Divine ! O Three in One !
    We lift our hearts in praise
For all the tender light that gilds
    The darkness of our days ;
But, Lord, we praise Thee even more,
That Thou dost keep the best in store."